ROUTLEDGE LIBRARY EDITIONS:
MANAGEMENT

Volume 7

A STANDARDIZATION OF SELECTED MANAGEMENT CONCEPTS

A STANDARDIZATION OF SELECTED MANAGEMENT CONCEPTS

ARTHUR G. BEDEIAN

Routledge
Taylor & Francis Group

LONDON AND NEW YORK

First published in 1986 by Garland Publishing, Inc.

This edition first published in 2018
by Routledge
2 Park Square, Milton Park, Abingdon, Oxon OX14 4RN

and by Routledge
711 Third Avenue, New York, NY 10017

Routledge is an imprint of the Taylor & Francis Group, an informa business

British Library Cataloguing in Publication Data
A catalogue record for this book is available from the British Library

ISBN: 978-1-138-55938-7 (Set)
ISBN: 978-1-351-05538-3 (Set) (ebk)
ISBN: 978-0-8153-5653-0 (Volume 7) (hbk)
ISBN: 978-1-351-12794-3 (Volume 7) (ebk)

Publisher's Note
The publisher has gone to great lengths to ensure the quality of this reprint but points out that some imperfections in the original copies may be apparent.

Disclaimer
The publisher has made every effort to trace copyright holders and would welcome correspondence from those they have been unable to trace.

A STANDARDIZATION OF
SELECTED MANAGEMENT CONCEPTS

Arthur G. Bedeian

Garland Publishing, Inc.
New York & London ★ 1986

Library of Congress Cataloging-in-Publication Data

Bedeian, Arthur G.
   A standardization of selected management concepts.

   (American business history)
   Thesis (D.B.A.)—Mississippi State University, 1973.
   Bibliography: p.
   1. Management—Terminology—History—20th century.
2. Management—History—20th century.   I. Title.
II. Series
HD30.17.B43   1986   658   86-18318
ISBN 0-8240-8351-2

All volumes in this series are printed on acid-free,
250-year-life paper:

Printed in the United States of America

ACKNOWLEDGEMENTS

The candidate wishes to recognize his indebtedness to Professors Giovanni B. Giglioni, Dennis F. Ray and Billy J. Eatherly. Professor Giglioni supervised the dissertation from its inception, having originally recommended its topic to the candidate. In his position as major professor, he offered innumerable suggestions for improving the final manuscript. Professor Ray and Professor Eatherly provided much valuable guidance and advice for the proper presentation of the material analyzed. Professor Henry W. Nash and Professor Thomas E. Pritchard read the entire manuscript and served on the candidate's dissertation defense committee. Lyndall F. Urwick read parts of the manuscript in its initial stages and made helpful comments on its content and style.

The candidate is grateful to Mrs. Martha Irby and Mrs. Mildred B. Sanders of Mississippi State University and Georgia Southern College respectively for their tireless aid in obtaining materials through the Interlibrary Loan Service.

The candidate also wishes to express his appreciation to his parents for their many years of concern and especially for their financial support during his years of study at the University of Iowa. The contributions of the candidate's wife to this study are immeasurable. She typed numerous drafts of the dissertation and aided in its research

and editing. She not only made the dissertation possible, but also
worthwhile.

A. G. B.

Mississippi State, Mississippi
February 1973

TABLE OF CONTENTS

TABLE OF CONTENTS--Continued

TABLE OF CONTENTS--Continued

LIST OF TABLES

CHAPTER I

INTRODUCTION

Since "modern" management's beginning at the turn of this
century there have been pleas from management practitioners and
academicians alike to solidify the underlying foundation upon which it
is based. However, until the field of management can boast of an all
inclusive and unified body of management theory, it will continue to
remain without such a needed and desired framework. As Dalton E.
McFarland, a past president of the Academy of Management, has noted:

> Management appears to be a discipline of broad scope compre-
> hending wide-ranging research interests, but its aims and
> directions are uncertain. Its identity is vague, its bound-
> aries undefined. Worst of all, conceptual clarity is
> seriously lacking.

During the past half century of management development,
researchers have employed differing methods of experimentation, observation, and theorization to overcome the myriad of problems that
prevent the development of a universal theory of management. Yet,
despite such efforts, it must be realized that a general theory of
management still does not exist.

_____

[1]Dalton E. McFarland, ed., Current Issues and Emerging Concepts in Management, Vol. II (Boston: Houghton Mifflin Company, 1966),
p. 4. (Italics mine.)

In answering the important question of what this means to
management, Frederick comments:

It means there is no general agreement about what management
is. It means further, there is no coherent and consistent
body of scientific principles which can constitute the basis
for a management science. It means also there are no clear-
cut grounds for declaring management to be a profession as
is true of doctors, lawyers, and others. Finally, it means
there are only the sketchiest guide lines for collegiate
business schools in educating for management and for company
training directors in encouraging executive development.
After a half century of management science this seems disappointing and frustrating. But it is, unfortunately, true.[2]

Statement of the Problem

Confusion, controversy, and disagreement are traditionally
characteristic of a new and growing field of study. The field of
management is no exception.[3] The past two decades have found scholars
from a host of disciplines entering into the debate surrounding the
development of a basic management theory. In retrospect their efforts
have produced disappointing results. At times it has seemed almost
impossible to locate two theoreticians who hold the same general
views. In the words of one writer, "disagreement and controversy have

---

[2]William C. Frederick, "The Next Development in Management
Science: A General Theory," Journal of the Academy of Management, VI
(September, 1963), 212.

[3]For a further discussion of this position, see: Harald
Scheuplein, "Towards the Unification of Management Theory," Management
International Review, IIX (November-December, 1968), 95; James D.
Thompson, "On Building an Administrative Science," Administrative
Science Quarterly, I (June, 1956), 109; E. F. L. Brech, The Nature and
Significance of Management (London: Sir Isaac Pitman & Sons, Ltd.,
1946), p. 35.

almost reached the point where any theoretical light that has been generated has been overwhelmed by emotional heat."[4]

A large extent of the basic controversy and confusion associated with management thought can be attributed to disagreement over concepts and terminology.[5] This absence of agreement and the resulting lack of standardization associated with it are the problems addressed by this dissertation. In an early attempt at the development of a general theory of administrative action, Litchfield commented on this point by remarking that "our confusion of terminology makes it difficult to speak accurately to one another within any one field, let alone across fields and cultures."[6] While there are many reasons for

---

[4]Waino W. Suojanen, "Management Theory: Functional and Evolutionary," Journal of the Academy of Management, VI (March, 1963), 1.

[5]"A concept is a generic mental image abstracted from precepts and generally relies on an originally inductive process rooted in objective reality." Frank E. X. Dance, "The 'Concept' of Communication," The Journal of Communication, XX (June, 1970), 202. Associated with every concept is a "term" which serves as a label or name for the purpose of identification. Paul H. Rigby, Conceptual Foundations of Business Research (New York: John Wiley & Sons, Inc., 1965), p. 131. It is through the definition of these associated terms that concepts are given general meaning. Definitions are descriptions of concepts. Thus, concepts, terminology and definitions are generally dealt with simultaneously. May Brodbeck, ed., Readings in the Philosophy of the Social Sciences (New York: Macmillan Company, 1968), pp. 3-6. See also: Donald J. Willower, "Concept Development and Research," in Educational Research: New Perspectives, ed. by Jack A. Culbertson and Stephen P. Hencley (Danville, Ill.: Interstate Printers & Publishers, Inc., 1963), pp. 101-11.

[6]Edward H. Litchfield, "Notes on a General Theory of Administration," Administrative Science Quarterly, I (June, 1956), 6. For a commentary on this article, see: Edward J. Green and Gomer H. Redmond, "Comments on a General Theory of Administration," Administrative Science Quarterly, II (September, 1957), 235-43.

this confusion, Koontz has noted the following major causes: "The Semantics Jungle. . . . Differences in Definition of Management as a Body of Knowledge. . . . The Misunderstanding of Principles. . . . The Inability or Unwillingness of Management Theorists to Understand Each Other."[7]

An ancient Chinese proverb states that "the beginning of wisdom is calling things by their correct name." The field of management has not yet reached this stage in its evolutionary development. Managerial terms are frequently used to mean different things and, consequently, semantic difficulties exist. An even greater awareness of this problem must be forthcoming. The development of an agreed upon management vocabulary with agreed upon meanings is a requirement for communication as well as for the development of management as a discipline.[8]

Need for the Study

Presently there is a movement in the management field which strongly favors the development and clarification of the basic concepts and terminology that are vital to the continued advancement of

---

[7]Harold D. Koontz, "The Management Theory Jungle," Journal of the Academy of Management, IV (December, 1961), 182-85.

[8]Philip W. Shay, "The Emerging Discipline of Management," in Handbook of Business Administration, ed. by Harold B. Maynard (New York: McGraw-Hill Book Co., Inc., 1967), pp. 1-38, 1-39.

management thought.[9] Certainly one of the most basic issues in all
fields is the definition of content. There are numerous reasons for
the desired establishment of a solid base upon which management may
rest. Three of these are most compelling.

First, it is difficult for management knowledge to exist, be
discussed, and be transferred in the form of learning without some
generally acknowledged and accepted meaning for the terminology it
employs. Definitions are vital to the initiation of this understanding
and learning process. The semantics of management are in serious
confusion. Inasmuch as the practice of management is inseparable from
the language of its users, anything which improves the understanding
of management terminology is a positive advantage.

Second, standardized and agreed upon definitions and terminology are needed to incorporate individual research efforts into organized and understandable wholes. Those seeking to contribute to
management knowledge must realize the fundamental necessity of clear
definitions as a prerequisite to further study. Mutual understanding
and reciprocal interaction depend upon conventional definitions. A
terminology that is vague and without explicit meaning is not conducive
to the advancement of common knowledge.

---

[9]For example, see: Lyndall F. Urwick, "The Problem of Manage-
ment Semantics," California Management Review, II (Spring, 1960), 77-83;
Kurt Junckerstorff, "Management--an International Science," Management
International Review, I (November-December, 1961), 150; J. In't Veld,
"Towards a General Theory of Administration," Management International
Review, I (January-February, 1962), 39; Louis A. Allen, The Management
Profession (New York: McGraw-Hill Book Co., Inc., 1964), p. 90;
A. J. Alton, "Comparative Management Theory," Management International
Review, IX (January-February, 1969), 5.

Finally, it seems probable that greater progress could be made toward the development of a universal theory of management if a conceptual framework of management language were developed. "By more sharply defining concepts, by clarifying semantic difficulties, by testing functional propositions--in short, by following the precepts of science--management may become much more of a science than many now think possible."[10]

The need for a clear concept of management, especially in the form of related principles, has been recognized for sometime. Only through a thorough analysis and definition of a group of selected fundamental management principles will the beginning of a needed conceptual framework of management be accomplished. One of the first writers to recommend such an approach was William C. Redfield, an early industrialist and United States Congressman (later appointed Secretary of Commerce). He commented that "if a science were ever needed, meaning definite rules or principles, based on exact knowledge of facts, it is in this very matter of management. . . . There is no uniformity in principles of management, even in the same industry."[11]

Writing four years later, French industrialist Henri Fayol expressed a similar feeling as he bemoaned the absence of management teaching. He felt that "without theory no teaching is possible" and that "the situation might be quite otherwise were there an accepted

---

[10]McFarland, Current Issues, p. 7. Editor's comment.

[11]William C. Redfield, "Scientific Spirit in Management," American Machinist, XXXVI (April 18, 1912), 612.

theory, that is to say, a collection of <u>principles</u>, rules, methods, procedures, tried and checked by general experience."[12]

Over two decades later, Chester I. Barnard voiced similar feelings in his classic work, <u>The Functions of the Executive</u>. Barnard, a past president of both the New Jersey Bell Telephone Company and of the Rockefeller Foundation, criticized several aspects of the business environment--the lack of executive literature; the lack of instruction in the area of organization; and, above all, "the lack of an accepted conceptual scheme with which [executives are able] to exchange their thought."[13]

While there have been innumerable cries for the development of a sound management vocabulary based upon established principles, the climax of this dilemma seems to have been reached in late 1961 with the publication of a paper by Koontz entitled, "The Management Theory Jungle."[14] Koontz's principal thesis in this paper was that the major variances between different schools of management thought needed to be brought into closer agreement. This view aroused much strong

---

[12]Henri Fayol, <u>General and Industrial Management</u>, trans. by Constance Storrs, with a Foreword by Lyndall F. Urwick (London: Sir Isaac Pitman & Sons, Ltd., 1949), pp. 14-15. (Italics mine.) Written in 1916.

[13]Chester I. Barnard, <u>The Functions of the Executive</u> (Cambridge: Harvard University Press, 1933), p. 289.

[14]Koontz, "The Management Theory Jungle," 174-88. Reprinted with minor modifications as "Making Sense of Management Theory," <u>Harvard Business Review</u> (July-August, 1962), 24-48.

controversy within the management field.[15] As a result of this, a

symposium was organized by the Graduate School of Business Administra-

tion at the University of California, Los Angeles (November 8th and 9th,

1962). This seminar was attended by sixty-one participants represent-

ing both industrial and academic interests. Its "specific long-range

---

[15]See for example: Fred E. Case, "Letters to the Editor,"
Harvard Business Review, XL (November-December, 1962), 20, 30, 35, 186;
"Management Pattern: Some Trophies from the 'Jungle'," Business Week,
February 16, 1963, p. 140; Waino W. Suojanen, "Management Theory:
Functional and Evolutionary," Journal of the Academy of Management, VI
(March, 1963), 7-17; Lyndall F. Urwick, "The Tactics of Jungle War-
fare," Journal of the Academy of Management, VI (December, 1963), 316-
29; William C. Frederick, "The Next Development in Management Science:
A General Theory," Journal of the Academy of Management, VI (September,
1963), 212-19; Paul J. Gordon, "Transcend the Current Debate on Admin-
istrative Theory," Journal of the Academy of Management, VI (December,
1963), 290-302; Waino W. Suojanen, "Comments: The Tactics of Jungle
Warfare: Clarification," Journal of the Academy of Management, VII
(September, 1964), 229-30; John W. Darr, "The Management-as-a-Process
Concept: A Consideration," Industrial Management Review (M. I. T.),
VI (Fall, 1964), 41-50; Lyndall F. Urwick, "Have We Lost Our Way in the
Jungle of Management Theory?," Personnel, XLII (May-June, 1965), 8-18;
Donald A. Woolf, "The Management Theory Jungle Revisited," Advanced
Management Journal, XXX (October, 1965), 6-15; Marian V. Sears, "Man-
agement," in Planning and Control Systems: A Framework for Analysis, ed.
by Robert N. Anthony (Boston: Division of Research, Graduate School of
Business Administration, Harvard University, 1965), pp. 117-29; George
S. Odione, "The Management Theory Jungle and the Existential Manager,"
Academy of Management Journal, IX (June, 1966), 109-16; Waino W.
Suojanen, The Dynamics of Management (New York: Holt, Rinehart and
Winston, Inc., 1966); Orlando Behling, "Unification of Management
Theory: A Pessimistic View," Business Perspectives, III (Summer, 1967),
4-9; Jean Boddewyn, "Management: The Trees, the Forest and the Land-
scape," Management International Review, VII, No. 2/3 (1967), 131-36;
Edwin B. Flippo, "Integrative Schemes in Management Theory," Academy of
Management Journal, II (March, 1968), 91-98; Bernard Alpert and Gary
W. Dickson, "Management Theory: Recent Developments Status and
Potential," University of Washington Business Review, XXVIII (Autumn,
1968), 5-17; William L. Williams, "Undergrowth in the Management Theory
Jungle," Business Horizons, XII (February, 1969), 56-58; Hans
Schöllhammer, "The Comparative Management Theory Jungle," Academy of
Management Journal, XII (March, 1969), 81-97; Lyndall F. Urwick, "Are
the Classics Really Out of Date?--A Plea for Semantic Sanity,"
S. A. M. Advanced Management Journal, XXXIV (July, 1969), 4-12.

goal was to make beginnings in clarifying some of the language of management, in integrating the study of management and its underlying disciplines, and in carving out a general theory of management--a conceptual scheme of ideas or statements--that explains or accounts for phenomena of management."[16]

An evaluation of the seminar suggests that it failed to achieve its desired purpose. Semantic difficulties were common throughout the two days of the discussion.[17] Evidence of this was particularly obvious in group discussions involving practitioners and academicians. At one point during the gathering, semantic differences seemed to be so intense that one group discussant commented: "'The terms used were so fantastic I could not understand them.'"[18]

Perhaps one of the most profound contentions of the symposium was forwarded by Englishman Wilfred B. D. Brown of Glacier Metal Company, Ltd. In the opening paragraph of his presentation, Brown voiced the belief that

. . . the vocabulary and the concepts which we use in thinking or talking about industrial organization are lacking in realism, with the consequence that much of our thinking as managers is not as constructive as it could be. This unrealism is evidenced by the lack of a language about organization

---

[16]Harold D. Koontz, ed., Toward a Unified Theory of Management (New York: McGraw-Hill Book Co., Inc., 1964), p. xi.

[17]Harold D. Koontz, "Management Theory and Research: Some Conclusions," in Toward a Unified Theory of Management, ed. by Koontz, pp. 238-39.

[18]Robert Tannenbaum, "Observations on Large Group and Syndicate Discussions," in Toward a Unified Theory of Management, ed. by Koontz, p. 93.

which has been defined in boundary terms. By "boundary terms"
I mean in a manner which enables any reasonable person to
ascertain what falls within or without the ambit of the meaning of the word. Lack of such a vocabulary leaves us unable
to define even our problems with clarity, with the result that
when we discuss them with others, our conversation often turns
into semantic confusion.

Management theory forms the outline from which management
development springs. However, the implications of this outline will
only be fully understood if a common agreement is reached concerning
the meaning of the key fundamental principles of management. Management
thought is still a long way from accomplishing solidarity. Its jargon
is a mess, and in the words of Lyndall F. Urwick: "Every sincere
teacher of the subject should regard it as one of his primary responsibilities to assist in clearing up that mess."[20]

Statement of Purpose

The purpose of this dissertation is to undertake a thorough
analysis of the basic management concepts used in present principles of
management textbooks in an effort to: (1) clarify the meaning of these
concepts by tracing their evolutionary development from past to present, (2) initiate a standardization of the fundamental terminology and
definitions in the field of management, (3) provide a beginning lexical
source for additional future development and compilation of management

---

[19]Wilfred B. D. Brown, "Management Theory from Management Practice: The Concept of Contraction," in Toward a Unified Theory of
Management, ed. by Koontz, p. 122.

[20]Lyndall F. Urwick, "Are the Classics Really Out of Date?--A
Plea for Semantic Sanity," S. A. M. Advanced Management Journal,
XXXIV (July, 1969), 11.

terminology, (4) contribute to the first and perhaps most vital step
in the process of creating a valid and universally accepted general
theory of management. Attention is concentrated upon present principles of management textbooks for a number of important reasons: (1)
it is felt that the initial attack upon the confusion and disagreement
in management must necessarily center upon management's most basic area
of understanding, (2) it is believed that it is at this level of
management, i.e., "principles of management" that the greatest understanding concerning basic management knowledge has been and will be
disseminated, and (3) it is at this level that the clearest and most
detailed discussion of basic management concepts is found.

This dissertation is based upon the general proposition that
the field of management needs explicitly stated concepts. It is
believed that the accomplishment of this proposition will provide a
reference point for the alleviation of a large part of the theoretical
disagreement that exists in management today.

Mention should be made of the fact that the author is aware
that this is only a beginning effort. Management is an active and
evolving field. Being part of a dynamic whole, the definitions to be
developed are in no way meant to be inflexible to future managerial
advancements. They are, however, believed to embody major truths that
time, experience and research have proven to be creditable and pre-
dictable.

Methodology

The methodology followed throughout the body of this dissertation is one of analysis, clarification and recommendation. The

research design used in the solution of the problem is that of a formulative or explanatory study, viz., the type designed "to gain familiarity with a phenomenon or to achieve new insights into" its operation.[21] Such studies are not intended to test or demonstrate hypotheses. Rather, their principal emphasis is on the discovery of ideas and insights. Realizing this, Kaplan has written that as a special form of the heuristic experiment, the exploratory study "is designed to generate ideas, to provide leads for further inquiry or to open up new lines of investigation."[22]

It is, therefore, evident that flexibility is essential in the explanatory study for the consideration of the leads developed throughout the study's investigation. Selltiz and colleagues have noted: "When the purpose of study is exploration, a flexible research design, which provides opportunity for considering many different aspects of a problem, is appropriate."[23]

The soundness and validity of this type of research is noted by one group of researchers who comment:

> Occasionally, there is a tendency to underestimate the importance of exploratory research and regard only

[21]Claire Selltiz, Marie Jahoda, Morton Deutsch, and Stuart W. Cook, Research Methods in Social Relations (Rev. One-volume ed.; New York: Holt, Rinehart and Winston, Inc., 1959), p. 50.

[22]Abraham Kaplan, The Conduct of Inquiry (San Francisco: Chandler Publishing Company, 1964), p. 149.

[23]Selltiz et al., Research Methods, p. 78.

experimental work as 'scientific.' However, if experimental
work is to have either theoretical or social value, it must
be relevant to broader issues than those posed in the
experiment. Such relevance can result only from adequate
exploration of the dimensions of the problem with which the
reader is attempting to deal.[24]

The first phase of each section of the dissertation's main
body involves an analysis dealing with the evolution of management
thought, especially management principles.

To answer the question--what are the commonly agreed upon
"concepts of management"?--a content analysis of ten major "principles
of management" textbooks has been conducted. "Content analysis is a
research technique for the objective, systematic, and quantitative
description of the manifest content of communication."[25] In effect,
it classifies the contents of any communication material (books,
newspapers, documents, etc.) into categories so that their relative
frequency may be determined. More specifically, the contents of the
ten textbooks used in this study have been analyzed to determine what
are the commonly agreed upon (most frequently acknowledged) "principles
of management." Each of these books was selected according to its
popularity as indicated by adoption lists received directly from the
respective publishers. The reasoning for using these books is that
while holding a major portion of the market, they have had a major
influence on the development of management thought. Included in this
group of textbooks is the first principles of management text written

[24]Ibid., p. 52.

[25]Bernard Berelson, Content Analysis in Communication Research
(Glencoe, Ill.: Free Press, 1952), p. 18. (Italics omitted.)

in the United States.[26] Also included in the list is the most recent textbook addition at the principles level--Donnelly, Gibson and Ivancevich's Fundamentals of Management.

The texts analyzed are as follows:

1. George R. Terry, Principles of Management (Homewood, Ill.: Richard D. Irwin, Inc., 1953). Rev. 1956, 1960, 1964, 1968.

2. Harold D. Koontz and Cyril J. O'Donnell, Principles of Management: An Analysis of Managerial Functions (New York: McGraw-Hill Book Co., Inc., 1955). Rev. 1959, 1964, 1968.

3. Dalton E. McFarland, Management: Principles and Practices (New York: Macmillan Company, 1958). Rev. 1964, 1970.

4. Henry H. Albers, Organized Executive Action (New York: John Wiley & Sons, Inc., 1961). Rev. 1965, 1969. Re-entitled Principles of Organization and Management at time of second revision. Re-entitled Principles of Management: A Modern Approach at the time of third revision.

5. William H. Newman and Charles E. Summer, The Process of Management (Englewood Cliffs, N. J.: Prentice-Hall, Inc., 1961). Rev. 1967. Co-authored with E. Kirby Warren at time of second edition.

6. Theo Haimann, Professional Management: Theory and Practice (Boston: Houghton Mifflin Co., 1962). Rev. 1970 at which time it was co-authored by William G. Scott and re-entitled Management in the Modern Organization.

7. Justin G. Longenecker, Principles of Management and Organizational Behavior (Columbus, Ohio: Charles E. Merrill Publishing Co., 1964). Rev. 1969.

---

[26]It should be noted that the first text to be entitled The Principles of Management was written by M. A. Cameron and published in London in 1948 by George Harrop & Co., Ltd. Previously published texts bearing a similar title are: Walter J. Matherly, The Principles of Business Management (Gainesville, Fla.: University Press, 1927). (Mimeographed.) and Edgar A. Allcut, Principles of Industrial Management (Toronto: Sir Isaac Pitman & Sons (Canada), Ltd., 1932). Also, during the same year as the introduction of Terry's text (1953), E. F. L. Brech edited and co-authored The Principles and Practices of Management (London: Longmans, Green and Co., 1953).

8. Ernest Dale, Management: Theory and Practice (New York: McGraw-Hill Book Co., Inc., 1965). Rev. 1969.

9. Henry L. Sisk, Principles of Management: A Systems Approach to the Management Process (Cincinnati, Ohio: South-Western Publishing Co., 1969).

10. James H. Donnelly, Jr., James L. Gibson and John M. Ivancevich, Fundamentals of Management (Austin, Texas: Business Publications, Inc., 1971).

The second phase of each section of the dissertation's main body deals with "clarification." An actual analysis of current terminology usage and definitions at the "principles of management" level is conducted. Also, to aid in the clarification of terms and meanings in question, the development of each concept in the analysis is further discussed. The presentation of this material is in accordance with the most commonly agreed upon functions of the management process, i.e., planning, organizing, and controlling. The belief that these are the most commonly agreed upon functions of the management process is substantiated by an analysis performed by Williams.[27] In dealing with the problem of functional classification, Williams identified and categorized the writings of nineteen different management sources. This investigation concluded that "in most management textbooks today, the functions of planning, organizing, and controlling

---

[27]D. Ervin Williams, "The Management Process from a Functional Perspective POCD? POMC? POIM? POAA?," Atlanta Economic Review, XXI (April, 1971), 26-27.

(POC) appear almost without exception" and seem to be the only functions in which general agreement has been reached concerning classification and content.[28]

The third and final phase of each section of the dissertation's main body is concerned with "recommendations." Following the analysis of each principle, a recommended standard definition is presented. These definitions are collected and presented in the form of a glossary at the end of the dissertation. (See Appendix III.)

Significance of the Study

Since the turn of this century, the field of management has compiled both an impressive and voluminous collection of literature. A search of this literature reveals few previous works contributing to the development of standardized management definitions. Many of these works deal directly with industrial relations, a number deal with the functional areas of personnel management and production management. A few deal with currently used wage terms, but only a limited number deal directly with general management terminology.

This study is significant because in an effort to standardize management terminology, it is the first of its type to specifically

---

[28]Further corroboration for this conclusion may be found in a comparable analysis undertaken by Ronald Greenwood. Greenwood similarly identified and categorized the writings of twenty-two management sources (thirteen of which are not included in the Williams' study) and his findings support those of Williams. See: Ronald Greenwood, "Managerial Functions: A Classification of Major Contributions," Arkansas Business and Economic Review, II (May, 1969), 14-17.

trace the twentieth century development and meaning of the basic
concepts of management. This goal is achieved through analysis, clarification, and recommendation.

Scope and Limitations

With only minor exception, the extent of topic treatment used
in attaining the proposed purposes of the dissertation is concerned
with literature published in the twentieth century. Attention is
primarily paid to major American contributions in the field of
management. However, numerous foreign works that have influenced the
development of American management are included in the analysis. Also,
since the main concern of this dissertation is with basic terminology
at the "principles of management" level, the discussion largely
excludes the majority of advanced periodical contributions in this
area. Further, revised editions of the principles of management textbooks published after 1971 are not included in the analysis.

In its scope, the dissertation pertains exclusively to the
field of management proper. Functional areas such as financial management, personnel management, marketing management, and production
management, as well as their subfunctional areas, are not dealt with.
It is felt that these areas are concerned more with the application of
techniques and practices than with the development of management
proper.

Finally, the methodology that is a part of an explanatory study
of this nature contains a basic limitation. Related to the subjective
value judgments of the writer, it is perhaps most obvious in instances
of varying terminology and in situations where interpretations of

meaning are necessary. Throughout the dissertation, this limitation is continually considered and every effort is made to keep it at a minimum.

Order of Presentation

The present (first) chapter of the dissertation contains: a statement of the dissertation's purpose, its proposed problem, need for a solution to the problem, and a method by which the problem may be solved.

The second chapter is devoted to a discussion of the role of theory in management. It contains material relating to the development of "theory" as it applies to management and also information concerning the importance of terminology in this development. A discussion of the varying types and stages of theory is included.

The third chapter of the dissertation contains a review of previously published literature relevant to the problem presented for solution. A summary and comment concerning each of these contributions is made.

The body of the dissertation (Chapters IV-VI) deals with identified principles as associated with their respective functions of management. Each of these three chapters contains an analysis of the origin and evolution of the principles to be discussed, as well as comments concerning their present state of usage in principles of management textbooks. These discussions are each closed with a recommended definition of the principles in question.

The final chapter of the dissertation (Chapter VII) is concerned with summary and concluding comments. This chapter also includes the recommendations that have developed from the study pertaining to further alleviation of the dissertation problem. Following this chapter and appended to the end of the dissertation is a glossary of the recommended, standardized definitions developed throughout the dissertation.

CHAPTER II

A NOTE ON THE ROLE OF THEORY IN MANAGEMENT

Introduction

Chapter I of the dissertation acknowledged both the absence
of and the need for a general, unified theory of management. It is
the purpose of Chapter II to briefly comment upon the role of theory
in management. Thus, this chapter will briefly discuss: (1) the
structure of theory, (2) the rules of theory-building, (3) the dimensions and levels of management theory, (4) the criteria for evaluating
a theory, and (5) the importance of management theory. Following this
discussion, related remarks will be made concerning the role of terminology in the development of a theoretical management framework.

The Structure of Theory

In beginning a discussion of the structure of theory, it should
be made clear that theory is not something apart from the practical,
but rather, it is a foundation for the practical. Psychologist Melvin
M. Marx has emphasized this point well by noting that theory serves
both as a tool and as a goal. The tool function of theory "is evident
in the generally accepted proposition that theories guide research by
generating new predictions not otherwise likely to occur."[1] As a

---

[1]Melvin H. Marx, "The General Nature of Theory Construction,"
in Theories in Contemporary Psychology, ed. by Melvin H. Marx (New
York: Macmillan Company, 1963), p. 6.

goal, theory is often an end in itself, providing "an economical and efficient means of abstracting, codifying, summarizing, integrating, and storing information."[2]

Derived from the Greek word Θεωρία meaning "contemplation," theory may be more generally defined as the "knowledge of principles."[3] The word principle meaning a statement of fundamental truth is derived from the Latin principium for "beginning." Descartes referred to principles as the "first causes [or source], of all that can be in the world. . . ."[4] Being such, principles are often phrased in the form of causal relationships that attempt to explain phenomena. In reference to the field of management, "if certain conditions are held to be true and . . . new phenomena are in accordance with those which the principle covers, then knowledge of the principle will make it possible to predict the behavior of factors in the new situation."[5]

----

[2]Ibid., p. 6.

[3]W. Stanley Jevons, Elementary Lessons in Logic (New ed.; New York: Macmillan Company, 1882), p. 340.

[4]René Descartes, Discourse on Method, trans. by John Veitch (Chicago: Open Court Publishing Company, 1899), p. 68. Written in 1637.

[5]Theo Haimann, Professional Management: Theory and Practice (Boston: Houghton Mifflin Co., 1962), p. 11. For an excellent discussion of the definition of the word "principle," see: Leonard D. White, "The Meaning of Principles in Public Administration," in The Frontiers of Public Administration, ed. by John M. Gaus, Leonard D. White, and Marshall E. Dimock, Studies in Public Administration, Vol. VI (Chicago: University of Chicago Press, 1936), pp. 13-25.

Principles or "first causes" are derived from hypotheses.
Regarded as "the very essence of scientific method,"[6] hypotheses are
untested propositions regarding relationships that <u>possibly</u> exist
among observed phenomena.[7] Thus, a group of interrelated principles
derived from hypotheses and dealing simultaneously with the same
theme is said to comprise a theory. Vital to the continued evolution
of knowledge in all disciplines, theory is a basic requirement for
the ultimate development of management as a science.[8] As sociologist
Talcott Parsons has noted, "the most important index of the maturity
of a science is the state of its systematic theory."[9]

---

[6]John Locke, <u>An Essay Concerning Human Understanding</u>, abridged
and ed. by Andrew S. Pringle-Pattison (Oxford, England: Clarendon
Press, 1924), p. 33n. Written in 1690.

[7]Henri Poincaré, <u>Science and Hypothesis</u>, trans. by George B.
Halsted (New York: Science Press, 1905), pp. 107-10.

[8]For an informative discussion of the role of theory in the
development of knowledge and of management as a science, see: C. West
Churchman, "Management Science--Fact or Theory?," <u>Management Science</u>,
II (January, 1956), 185. See also: Luther H. Gulick, "Management Is
a Science," <u>Academy of Management Journal</u>, VIII (March, 1965), 7-13;
Marshall A. Robinson, "The Science of Organizations: A Pediatric
Note," <u>Management International Review</u>, VI (July-August, 1966), 3-5;
Stanley I. Hyman, "Management--An Experimental Science?," <u>Management
International Review</u>, X (November-December, 1970), 51-59; John M.
Dutton and William H. Starbuck, "On Managers and Theories," <u>Management
International Review</u>, III (November-December, 1963), 25-35; Thomas M.
Mosson, "Management Theory and the Limits of Common-Sense," <u>Management
International Review</u>, IV (January-February, 1964), 25-37; S. Benjamin
Prasad, "Management Theory and the Limits of Common-Sense: Comment,"
<u>Management International Review</u>, IV (November-December, 1964), 209-13;
John F. Halff, "Applying Scientific Method to the Study of Management,"
<u>Journal of the Academy of Management</u>, III (December, 1960), 193-96.

[9]Talcott Parsons, "The Present Position and Prospects of System-
atic Theory in Sociology," in <u>Twentieth Century Sociology</u>, ed. by
George D. Gurvitch and Wilbert E. Moore (New York: Philosophical
Library, Inc., 1945), p. 42.

Rules of Theory-Building

Developmental efforts in any field of knowledge are greatly aided by the formation of practical rules of theory-building. The field of management is no exception. Drawing from the experiences of the older sciences, social theorist George C. Homans expressed these rules exceptionally well when he wrote:

1. Look first at the obvious, the familiar, the common. In a science that has not established its foundations, these are the things that best repay study.

2. State the obvious in its full generality. Science is an economy of thought only if its hypotheses sum up in a simpler form a large number of facts.

3. Talk about one thing at a time. That is, in choosing your words (or, more pedantically, concepts) see that they refer not to several classes of fact at the same time but to one and one only. Corollary: Once you have chosen your words, always use the same words when referring to the same thing.

4. Cut down as far as you dare the number of things you are talking about. "As few as you may; as many as you must," is a rule governing the number of classes of fact you take into account.

5. Once you have started to talk, do not stop until you have finished. That is, describe systematically the relationships between the facts designated by your words.

6. Recognize that your analysis must be abstract, because it deals with only a few elements of the concrete situation. Admit the dangers of abstraction, especially when action is required, but do not be afraid of abstraction.[10]

---

[10]George C. Homans, The Human Group (New York: Harcourt, Brace & World, Inc., 1950), pp. 16-17. For an earlier statement of these rules, see: Homans, "A Conceptual Scheme for the Study of Social Organization," American Sociological Review, XII (1947), 13-14.

Each of these rules is equally important in its application; however, it should be noted that the third is uniquely pertinent to the stated purpose of this dissertation.

Dimensions of Management Theory

Management theory may be characterized as either prescriptive or descriptive. Prescriptive theory, also called normative theory, is evaluative in form and deals with "what ought to be" or with "what should be." Prescriptive theory is designed for observation and prediction. Because it involves value judgments, it is often moralistic in nature.[11]

Descriptive theory, contrary to prescriptive theory, describes and explains "what is" rather than "what should be." Descriptive theory is also called positive theory. According to Shull, it is "designed to enhance research, description, and measurement."[12]

In the past, some dissension has centered around the prescriptive role of management,[13] but it now appears evident that future

---

[11]See: Rocco Carzo, Jr., "Administrative Science and the Role of Value Judgments," Journal of the Academy of Management, III (December, 1960), 175-82; Robert F. Pethia, "Values in Positive and Normative Administrative Theory: A Conceptual Framework and a Logical Analysis," in Proceedings of the 10th Annual Academy of Management Conference, Midwest Division, (1967), ed. by Alan C. Filley (Carbondale, Ill.: Business Research Bureau, School of Business, Southern Illinois University, 1967), pp. 1-19.

[12]Fremont A. Shull, Jr., "The Nature and Contribution of Administrative Models," Academy of Management Journal, V (August, 1962), 130.

[13]Herbert A. Simon, Administrative Behavior, with a Foreword by Chester I. Barnard (New York: Macmillan Company, 1947), pp. 45-46; W. Jack Duncan, "Fact and Value in Administrative Science: A Reconsideration of Management Theory and Practice," The Southern Journal of Business, VII (February, 1972), 4.

management theory will be both prescriptive and descriptive.[14] Management theory will not only be required to explain what, why and how something happens (descriptive), it also will be called upon to determine the single best way for it to happen (prescriptive).[15]

The Levels of Management Theory

A survey of business literature conducted by R. William Millman has revealed that it is possible to describe three separate levels of theoretical management understanding. The first and most fundamental level is the level of the phenomenon. "A general theory at this level . . . explain [s] the nature of a single phenomenon, the situation under which it occurs, the causal factors, and the way in which the given phenomenon is an effect of these causal factors."[16] In alternate terms, understanding at this level deals with a single or very limited number of principles attempting to explain their associated source hypotheses.

---

[14]W. Jack Duncan, "Methodological Orientation and Management Theory: An Analysis of Academic Opinion," Academy of Management Journal, XIII (September, 1970), 348.

[15]See: Robert F. Pethia, "Some Content Analytic Findings on Values in Normative Administrative Theory," in Academy of Management Proceedings, (1969), ed. by William G. Scott and Preston P. LeBreton (Bowling Green, Ohio, 1970), pp. 145-53.

[16]R. William Millman, "Some Unsettled Questions in Organization Theory," Academy of Management Journal, VII (September, 1964), 190. For a similar alternate classification, see: Bayard O. Wheeler, "Renaissance in Business Theory," University of Washington Business Review, XXIV (February, 1965), 45-46.

The second level of theory is concerned with a class or set of phenomena. "Here the researcher identifies a homogeneous group of phenomena and seeks to explain their operational aspects, individually and collectively."[17] Clearly, this level of theory is the most prominent level in the field of management. Within this level, the operational aspects of associated principles are interrelated and formed into coherent wholes. Examples of scholarly efforts at this level of theory are Pfiffner and Sherwood's Administrative Organization[18] and McGuire's Theories of Business Behavior.[19]

The highest and most complex level of theory is the level of grand (general) theory. "It is at this level that the grandiose claims for the universal theory occur. The theorist suggests that he has formulated the total explanation for a whole family of phenomena, a complex of sets of phenomena, all carefully linked together to provide 'the complete analysis.'"[20] While an accepted "general" theory of management still does not exist, a number of attempts at such an

---

[17]Ibid., 190.

[18]John M. Pfiffner and Frank C. Sherwood, Administrative Organization (Englewood Cliffs, N. J.: Prentice-Hall, Inc., 1960).

[19]Joseph W. McGuire, Theories of Business Behavior (Englewood Cliffs, N. J.: Prentice-Hall, Inc., 1964).

[20]Millman, "Some Unsettled Questions in Organization Theory," 190-91.

accomplishment have been made, e.g., Veblen's The Theory of Business Enterprise[21] and March and Simon's Organizations.[22]

Presently, the field of management is far from the goal of accomplishing a "general theory." It is suffering from what McFarland has termed a severe case of "malnutrition."[23] Because it has been unable to develop its own body of theory, management has been severely handicapped by a lack of speculative strength. According to Forrester, management still does not even possess the underlying structure that is vital to the thorough understanding of the management process.[24]

Criteria for the Acceptability of a Theory

Having thus far discussed the structure of theory, the rules of theory building, and the dimensions and the levels of management theory, it is now appropriate to discuss the criteria for the acceptability of a theory. According to Filley and House, a sound theory

---

[21]Thorstein Veblen, The Theory of Business Enterprise (New York: Charles Scribner's Sons, 1904).

[22]James G. March and Herbert A. Simon, with the collaboration of Harold Guetzkow, Organizations (New York: John Wiley & Sons, Inc., 1958).

[23]Dalton E. McFarland, "Theory As an Angle of Vision in Management Research," in Academy of Management Proceedings, (1965), ed. by Edwin B. Flippo (Bowling Green, Ohio, 1966), p. 3.

[24]Jay W. Forrester, "The Structure Underlying Management Processes," in Academy of Management Proceedings, (1964), ed. by Edwin B. Flippo (Bowling Green, Ohio, 1965), p. 58.

should meet five criteria:

A sound theory should first have internal consistency; that
is, its propositions should be free from contradiction.

Second, a theory should have external consistency; that is, it
should be consistent with observations and measures of real
life. This criteria of theory is called the test of empirical
reference.

Third, it must be possible to prove a theory or its predictions
wrong. If a theory is not stated so that its predictions can
be verified, it may carry unintended bias or error. A theory
is said to be operational when its formulation permits evaluation of its major premises or predictions.

Fourth, a theory should have the characteristic of generality,
in order to provide a wide range of application and an extension
of the field of knowledge. That is, a theory should be capable
of explaining more than isolated, specific incidents. It must
posit a set of relationships within a well-defined class of
events, and these relationships must explain all of the events
that fall within the defined class.

Finally, a practical theory should have the attribute of
scientific parsimony. If two theories both accurately predict
the outcome of events and are equally supported by evidence,
the least complex of the theories--that is, the one involving
the lesser number of hypotheses--should be selected.[25]

A Brief Note on the Importance of Theory

At present, the field of management is beginning to move away

from a reliance upon rules and procedures and towards a fuller

---

[25]Alan C. Filley and Robert J. House, Managerial Process and
Organizational Behavior (Glenview, Ill.: Scott, Foresman and Co.,
1969), pp. 30-31. For earlier statements of these criteria, see:
Filley, "Common Misconceptions in Business Management," Business
Horizons, VII (Fall, 1964), 87-96; House and Filley, "Science, Theory,
Philosophy, and the Practice of Management," Management International
Review, VI (November-December, 1966), 97-107.

utilization of theory.[26] To the practicing manager, the value of theory

is immeasurable. The importance of theory is expressed well by

Richard F. Neuschel, a director of McKinsey and Company, Incorporated,

who said: "Theory is the constant but unseen companion of management.

No manager can function long without it."[27] The late Douglas McGregor

also recognized the importance of theory. In a discussion on

"Management and Scientific Knowledge," he expressed the belief that

"every managerial act rests on . . . theory" and that "theory and

practice are inseparable."[28]

Terminological Conflict

It has been noted that efforts designed to reduce the confu-

sion and controversy in management theory have made only limited

progress. Much of this limited progress can be attributed to the

failure on management's part to develop clear terminological and

conceptual understanding. McFarland, in his 1965 presidential address

before the Academy of Management, noted this by declaring: "Management

theory has not successfully grappled with its terminological and

---

[26]See: Thomas W. Douglas, "Management Theory and the Large
Business Enterprise," Advanced Management Journal, XXXII (July, 1968),
40-50; James S. Hekimian, "The Growing Split Between Management Theory
and Practice," in Academy of Management Proceedings, (1969), ed. by
William G. Scott and Preston P. LeBreton (Bowling Green, Ohio, 1970),
pp. 115-16.

[27]Richard F. Neuschel, "Management's Need for Theory and
Research," in Toward a Unified Theory of Management, ed. by Koontz,
p. 176.

[28]Douglas McGregor, The Human Side of Enterprise (New York:
McGraw-Hill Book Co., Inc., 1960), p. 6.

conceptual difficulties, even at their grossest level."[29] As a result,

management theory suffers severely from a dullness of focus and a lack

of harmony. This type of situation has been diagnosed well by philos-

opher Willard V. Quine:

> The less a science has advanced, the more its terminology
> tends to rest on an uncritical assumption of mutual under-
> standing. With increase of rigor this basis is replaced
> piecemeal by the introduction of definitions.[30]

Conclusion

In conclusion, it is again mentioned that management evolution

is unconditionally dependent upon the continual development of theory.

Theory provides a scheme for studying, predicting and controlling the

managerial environment.[31] It is basic to the actions of all practicing

managers. A more complete understanding of the knowledge that theory

has to offer is at least partially dependent upon the clarification

of the terminological conflict that exists within the field of manage-

ment. A management terminology that is both useful and objective must

be developed. Hopefully, the efforts of this dissertation will lead

towards that direction.

---

[29]McFarland, "Theory As an Angle of Vision in Management
Research," p. 7. (Italics mine.)

[30]Willard V. Quine, "Truth by Convention," in Philosophical
Essays for Alfred North Whitehead, comp. by Otis H. Lee (New York:
Longmans, Green & Co., 1936), p. 90. (Italics mine.)

[31]William Wolf, ed., Management: Readings Toward a General
Theory (Belmont, Calif.: Wadsworth Publishing Co., Inc., 1964), p. 4.
See also: Wolf, "Toward the Development of a General Theory of Manage-
ment," in Comparative Administrative Theory, ed. by Preston P. LeBreton
(Seattle: University of Washington Press, 1968), pp. 179-90.

CHAPTER III

A REVIEW OF THE LITERATURE

Introduction

The history of the efforts to resolve the terminological

conflicts that exist within the field of management is both long and

varied. Its longevity may be traced from the 1927 (May 4th to 23rd)

meeting of the International (World) Economic Conference to the peri-

odical literature of today.[1] It is a conflict that has spanned the

continents of North America, Europe, Asia and Australia.

Initial Efforts

The initial efforts to resolve the terminological conflict

present in the field of management resulted from a proposal forwarded

by the League of Nations at the International Economic Conference of

1927.[2] As part of this proposal, it was recommended that an

---

[1]For prior indication of an awareness of the problem of confu-
sion in management terminology, see: William J. Schulze, "Some Defi-
nitions," Bulletin of the Taylor Society, IV (August, 1919), 3-4;
Morris L. Cooke, "On Mr. Schulze's Definitions," Bulletin of the Taylor
Society, IV (October, 1919), 47-48; "Organization Defined," American
Management Review, XIV (October, 1925), 306-08. See also: Ordway
Tead, The Problem of Terminology in Management Research (New York:
Institute of Management Series No. 5, American Management Association,
1928), pp. 2-12; R. M. Fox, "The Industrial Tower of Babel," The Labour
Magazine, VII (August, 1928), 164; Lyndall F. Urwick, "An Industrial
Esperanto," The Labour Magazine, VII (October, 1928), 259-61.

[2]The World Economic Conference, Final Report. Document C. E. I.
44 (1). (Geneva: League of Nations, 1927), pp. 42-43.

international body be established to study and spread the ideas of management. In fulfillment of this recommendation, a joint agreement was reached between the International Labour Office and the Twentieth Century Fund to support such an undertaking. In mid-1927, the combined efforts of these two groups resulted in the establishment of the International Management Institute at Geneva, Switzerland.[3] Paul E. Devinat, first Director of the Institute undertook as his beginning task the formation of an International Committee on Terminology. Under the direction of the late Frenchman Charles de la Poix de Fréminville, national groups were formed throughout Europe to apply themselves to the task of establishing clear definitions and uniform terminology in the field of management.[4] However, the Committee was unable to achieve positive results before 1933, and with the election of Adolph Hitler to the Chancellorship of Germany and the abandonment of the gold standard by Switzerland, the Twentieth Century Fund withdrew its financial support. As a result, the Institute was forced to close.

------

[3]For additional background information concerning the formation of the International Management Institute, see: Lyndall F. Urwick, "Scientific Management in Europe," Encyclopaedia Britannica, 14th ed., XIV, 125-27; Urwick, "An International Clearing House of Good Management," Factory and Industrial Management, LXXI (February, 1930), pp. 287-89. Urwick was the second and final Director of the Institute, serving from November, 1928 through January, 1934.

[4]See: International Management Institute, Rapport intérimaire sur le terminologie da la rationalisation (Geneva: International Labour office, 1930), (Mimeographed.); International Committee for Scientific Management, C. I. O. S. Manual (Geneva: CIOS, 1949), chap. ii, "Terms and Definitions," pp. 15-23.

Succeeding Efforts

Fortunately, the closing of the Institute did not mark the end
of managerial efforts in the area of terminology. During the years
1933 through 1936 alone, at least four similar major projects were
undertaken. In 1933, the French "Institut D' Organisation Commerciale
et Industrielle" in collaboration with the Paris "Chambre De Commerce"
organized their own special Committee on Terminology for the purpose
of advancing uniform management terms and definitions.[5] Expanding upon
earlier work performed by the "Comité National de l'Organisation
Française,"[6] this undertaking advanced definitions in the areas of
general management, work measurement, marketing, manufacturing,
accounting and finance.

The same year as the formation of the French Committee, the
German "Reichskuratorium für Wirtschaftlichkeit" published recommended
management definitions.[7] Mainly concerned with "rationalisation,"

---

[5]Chambre De Commerce De Paris, Institut D' Organisation Commerciale et Industrielle, Définitions de quelques termes usités dans l'
Organisation commerciale et Industrielle ("Definitions of Some Terms
Used in Commercial and Industrial Organization") (Paris: n. p.,
1934). 61 pages.

[6]Reference is made to Comité National de l'Organisation
Française, Dictionnaire de l'Organisation et de la Science du Travail,
edited by Charles de la Poix de Fréminville (Paris: CNOF, 1926).
Not truly a dictionary, this work consists of a series of 147 index
cards each bearing a definition.

[7]Reichskuratorium für Wirtschaftlichkeit, Wirtschaft, Wirt-
schaftlichkeit, Ständische Wirtschaftsordnung ("Economy, Efficiency,
The Economic Order of the Estates of the Realm"), Veroffentlichung en
Nr. 99 (Berlin: RKW, 1933). 66 pages.

these definitions heavily reflected the reconstruction movement that existed in Germany at that time.

In Czechoslovakia three years later (1936), an analogous effort was made by the Czechoslovak "Na͑rodni Komite͑t Pro Ve͑deckov Organisaci."[8] Established in Prague, this group had earlier provided much valuable assistance in the initial International Management Institute undertaking.

Perhaps the most fruitful and lasting attempts in the area of terminological conflict have come as a result of work performed by the Advisory Committee on Management. Created in 1936 by the Governing Body of the International Labour Office, at its second session held in Geneva on May 28th and 29th, 1937, the Committee unanimously adopted a resolution calling for international attention to the problem of management terminology. At this same session, definitions for the following terms were advanced: (1) management, scientific management; (2) organisation, "Organisation scientifique (du travail)"; (3) rationalisation. These definitions were later translated into ten languages and transmitted to the International Committee on Scientific Management.[9] At its Seventh International Congress on scientific

[8]Csl. Na͑rodni Komite͑t Pro Ve͑deckov Organisaci, Normalisovane Na͑zvoslovi Z Obruv Vedecke͑ Organisace ("Normalized Terminology from the Field of Scientific Organization") (Prague: n. p., 1936). Referenced in Hugo von Haan, "International Aspects of the Terminology and Ideology of Management," International Labour Review, XXXVII (April, 1938), 429.

[9]See: Bureau International du Travail, Commission Consultative de l'Organisation Scientifique du Travail, Definitions Adoptees Par la Commission Consultative de l'organisation scientifique du travail lois de Sa Ze Session, Geneva, 28th and 29th May, 1937, 1 page. Reprinted in "The Terminology of Rationalisation and Scientific Management," International Labour Review, XXXVI (August, 1937), 250-54.

management held in Washington, D. C. on September 22nd and 23rd, 1938,
CIOS recommended the definitions to each of the national committees
present.

Further review of contributions made by other nations reveals
that perhaps none has been as involved in clearing the semantic swamp
as has Great Britain. In 1928, under the editorship of John Lee, the
Dictionary of Industrial Administration was published in London. The
first dictionary of its type, its title page bills it as "A Comprehensive Encyclopaedia of the Organisation, Administration, and Management of Modern Industry." The Dictionary may be the most unique of the
books to be mentioned here.[10] It is a collection of contributions from
over one-hundred of the then best known authorities in the fields of
industrial organization and management. The two volumes (1151 quarto
pages) of the Dictionary are both comprehensive and complete. Among
its "Who's who" of contributors are such authorities as Ralph G.
Hawtrey, Clarence H. Northcott, Thomas G. Rose, Oliver Sheldon, and
Lyndall F. Urwick. American contributors to the volumes include Harvard

---

[10]John Lee, ed., Dictionary of Industrial Administration, Vols.
I, II (London: Sir Isaac Pitman & Sons, Ltd., 1928-1929). In commenting on the Dictionary, Lyndall F. Urwick, ed., The Golden Book of
Management (London: Newman Neame, Ltd., for the International Committee
for Scientific Management, 1956), p. 117, wrote: "The work marked an
epoch. Its only fault was to be in advance of its time. A reprint did
not prove commercially possible [the Dictionary initially sold for
$17.50] and much of the influence it could have had was lost by the fact
that copies were not easily to be found. It continues to be used today
by those fortunate enough to possess it."

Professor Robert F. Forester and Ordway Tead. According to its editor,
the Dictionary "is primarily a work of reference" and hopefully
"indispensable to every industry for day-by-day consultation."[11]

In scope, the Dictionary covers a large variety of subjects
and is supplemented by statistical tables, operating forms and schematic
diagrams. By using the Dictionary, one may find a discussion of such
topics as: (1) the function of administration and organization (sub-
sections: direction, policy, co-ordination, master planning, budgets,
organization charts, "staff and line" organization, departmental organization, etc.); (2) education for industry and commerce; (3) eugenics
in business; (4) fatigue and monotony; (5) the moral duty of management;
(6) repetitive work (sub-sections: repetitive work as a setting for
fantasy, repetition and boredom, review of the literature, attempts to
alleviate boredom in repetitive work; (7) industrial and commercial
research; (8) distribution of responsibility (sub-sections: delegation,
elements of supervision, job analysis, grading, promotion, executive
training and salary standards). More mundane topics covered are:
(1) maintenance of factory buildings (sub-sections: painting and
whitewashing, window cleaning, yard cleaning, etc.); (2) glare; (3)
rest rooms; (4) physical work of women (sub-sections: capacity of
muscular work, special physiological conditions--menstruation and
maternity).

Three of the most interesting sections of the Dictionary have
yet to be mentioned. First, its coverage of "lighting" (both natural

---

[11]Ibid., p. xii.

and artificial) in relation to health and output is strongly reminiscent of the illumination experiments performed at the Hawthorne Works
of the Western Electric Company.[12] Yet at the date of the _Dictionary's_
publication, these studies were only in their beginning phase.

Second, the _Dictionary's_ discussion of "factory reorganization"
seems unusually current in thinking. Often analogous to present
"organizational development" (OD) literature, it makes extended
reference to the "expert organizer" (change agent) and his powers.

The last entry of the _Dictionary_ to be mentioned is possibly
its most famous. Its discussion of the "Principles of Direction and
Control" authored by Urwick has been described by one writer as "at
least a generation ahead of its time."[13] It is in this presentation
that Urwick initially expounded his position on the principles of
management, a position he has modified and defended many times since.

The Nineteen-Forties

With World War II, involvement in the question of management
terminology slowed considerably. In the United States, the Academy
of Management was inactive from 1942 to 1946. In England, the _British_
Management Review, which was then published in collaboration with the
Institute of Industrial Administration, the Institution of Workes

---

[12]See: Fritz J. Roethlisberger and William J. Dickson, with
the assistance and collaboration of Harold A. Wright, _Management and_
the Worker (Cambridge: Harvard University Press, 1939), pp. 14-18.

[13]E. F. L. Brech, _Organisation: The Framework of Management_
(2nd ed.; London: Longmans, Green and Co., Ltd., 1965), p. 506.

Managers and the former Office Management Association, was not published from June, 1940 to September, 1943. After World War II, the
next development of consequence that occurred concerning management
terminology was the Seventh Series of London Lectures on Higher Management. Held in May and June of 1948 under the auspices of the Institute of Industrial Administration (London Centre), the theme of the
lectures was entitled, "Management Principles and Their Application."[14]
Throughout the lectures, a large portion of the discussion centered
upon the question of terminological conflict and the problem of
accurate communication.[15] This group of lectures acted both as an
opportunity for exploring further the principles of management and as
an occasion for re-emphasizing the importance of management terminology.

In the same year, the Melbourne Institute of Industrial Management also dealt with the topic of management terminology. The Management Nomenclature Research Group of the Institute prepared for distribution recommended definitions of ninety-two management terms.[16]

---

[14]Transcripts of the lectures presented are contained in the
British Management Review, VII, No. 3 (1948), 4-102.

[15]See particularly: Lyndall F. Urwick, "Principles of Management," British Management Review, VII, No. 3 (1948), 15-48. "One of the
roots of our lack of our organisation of management knowledge is the
absence of any standardised and agreed terminology. It is of the essence
of any organised body of knowledge that it should be communicable. We
have to use words if we are to communicate with each other. But the
words which we use in discussing management, the very word management
itself, have and has no semantic context. They convey totally different meanings to almost everyone who uses them. There is no adequate
or exact communication, and no possibility of it, till this situation is
corrected." (p. 21.)

[16]Institute of Industrial Management (Melbourne), Definitions
of Terms Used in Industrial Administration (Melbourne: The Institute,
1948).

Divided into four categories, forty-two of the terms dealt with "General Management"; seventeen with "Production Management"; ten with "Personnel Management"; and thirteen with "Supply Management." While not exceedingly broad in scope, the definitions offered by the Institute reflect an interesting combination of British and American management influences. The terms "management" and "administration" are identified as being synonymous.

In the following year (May 5th to 8th), the British Institute of Management held its Seventh Annual Conference Series.[17] Under the direction of Urwick, sectional meeting number five of the Conference directed itself to the question: "Whether there is a need for a standard terminology and nomenclature in management?" A position paper favoring the question was presented by Winston Rodgers of Acton Technical College.[18] Following both pro and con discussion of the issue, a resolution in favor of the question was carried. Presented to the plenary session of the Conference, the resolution reads as follows:

> The BIM is asked to examine existing terms and to publish their current meanings and to encourage standard usage whenever possible. Efforts should be made to extend this work to the international field, initially to the English speaking countries.[19]

---

[17]C. R. Jones, "Management Takes Stock," Scope, VII (July, 1949), 74-85.

[18]Winston Rodgers, Standard Terminology (London: Conference Series No. 7, British Institute of Management, 1949).

[19]Ibid., pp. 21-22.

To implement this resolution, the BIM established an official Committee on Terminology. The result of its efforts--a 174 word multi-lingual management glossary--was presented at the first European Council of CIOS at Torquay, England, October 20-23, 1954.[20]

The Nineteen-Fifties

The early nineteen-fifties saw the first widespread emergence of business dictionaries in the United States.[21] (See Appendices I and II.) The first management vocabulary, however, was not published until the year 1958. It was entitled, Common Vocabulary of Professional Management (COMVOC), and was prepared under the direction of Louis A. Allen, President of Louis A. Allen Associates, Incorporated. Allen explains the purpose of COMVOC as follows: "Ask any two managers precisely what they mean by 'staff,' or 'decentralize,' or 'budget.' The differences in interpretation will make communication difficult. If we are to develop professional practice of management work, seman-tics requires first attention."[22]

Through the three editions (1958, 1963, 1968) of COMVOC, its coverage has expanded from 49 to 194 basic management terms. Its

---

[20]British Institute of Management, Glossary of Management Terms (London: BIM, 1954). Translation of 174 English terms into French and German. For a report of the proceedings and papers of this meeting, see: "Management in Conference," The Manager, XXII (November, 1954), 695-723.

[21]See: David W. Ewing, "Business Dictionaries," Harvard Business Review, XXX (September-October, 1955), 149-59.

[22]Louis A. Allen, Common Vocabulary of Professional Management (3rd ed.; Palo Alto, Calif.: Executive Press, 1968), 37 pages. Quo-tation taken from p. i.

adopters include numerous companies throughout the world, the majority of which have been clients of Allen Associates. Earlier editions of COMVOC are reproduced in two of Allen's earlier publications, Management and Organization[23] and The Management Profession.[24]

Using COMVOC, the reader will quickly note that it follows a functional approach to management. Planning, organizing, leading and controlling are listed as the four functions of management. In line with this, a manager is defined as "a leader who enables people to work most effectively together by performing primarily the work of planning, organizing, leading and controlling." The majority of COMVOC's entries are annotated; and on its last two pages are presented Allen's "Unified Concept of Professional Management" and his "Principles of Professional Management."

The Nineteen-Sixties

In the first half of the nineteen-sixties, more and more practitioners and scholars began working upon the theoretical problem of management terminology. Prepared by Karl E. Ettinger for the Office of Industrial Resources in the International Cooperation Administration,

---

[23]Louis A. Allen, Management and Organization (New York: McGraw-Hill Book Co., Inc., 1958), pp. 300-03.

[24]Louis A. Allen, The Management Profession (New York: McGraw-Hill Book Co., Inc., 1964), pp. 551-56. For an interesting comment on COMVOC, see: "Language of Scientific Management Spoken Here," New York Times, January 6, 1964, p. 55.

Management Glossary was published in 1960.[25] Designed to supplement the
Administration's Management Primer Series, "Principles and Practices of
Productivity," the 370 terms and definitions contained in the Glossary
are freely drawn from all areas of business and economics.

In March of 1961, Factory carried an interesting article
designed "to clear the smoke" and aid in eliminating management meet-
ings that produce "more heat than light because of confusion on terms."[26]
In this article, Eugene J. Benge of Benge Associates defined and
commented upon twenty-five management terms.

Nine months after the publication of Benge's article, Harold
D. Koontz authored an article in the Journal of the Academy of Management entitled, "The Management Theory Jungle."[27] It was reprinted with
minor modifications in the Harvard Business Review as "Making Sense of
Management Theory."[28] Combined, these two articles have provided the
stimulus that has carried the issue of management theory and terminology to its present height and have resulted in a symposium being held
under the auspices of the McKinsey Foundation and the Western Management Sciences Institute on November 8th and 9th, 1962 at the Graduate

---

[25]Karl E. Ettinger, Management Glossary, Management Primer Series:
"Principles and Practices of Productivity," Training Manual No. 201,
Technical Aids Branch, Office of Industrial Resources (Washington, D. C.:
International Cooperation Administration, by the Council for Internation-
al Progress in Managment, 1960).

[26]Eugene J. Benge, "Management Terms Needn't Be Gobbledygook,"
Factory, CXIX (March, 1961), 208. Editor's comment.

[27]Koontz, "The Management Theory Jungle," 174-88.

[28]Koontz, "Making Sense of Management Theory," 24-48.

School of Business Administration of the University of California, Los Angeles. The summarized proceedings of the symposium were published in book form in 1964 under the title, Towards a Unified Theory of Management.[29] This work has been referred to by Urwick as "one of the most stimulating and exciting books about management that . . . he has seen in the last decade."[30]

The initiative provided by Koontz's work has resulted in a host of commentaries regarding management lexicon. Even Business Week has noted the babel to its readers.[31]

In 1966, the first dictionary of general management terminology, Dictionary of Management Terms, was compiled by Albert J. Lindemann, Earl F. Lundgren and H. K. von Kaas.[32] Its introduction states that it "was prepared for two primary classes of users:

a. the professional manager in business as an aid to communi-cation and the development of a common language.

b. the student who has a need to develop a better understanding of management literature." (p. iii.)

---

[29]Harold D. Koontz, ed., Toward a Unified Theory of Management (New York: McGraw-Hill Book Co., Inc., 1964).

[30]Lyndall F. Urwick, "Communications from Readers," review of Toward a Unified Theory of Management, by Harold D. Koontz in the California Management Review, VIII (Fall, 1965), 92.

[31]"Management Pattern: Some Trophies from the 'Jungle'," Business Week, February 16, 1963, p. 140.

[32]Albert Lindemann, Earl Lundgren and H. K. von Kaas, Dictionary of Management Terms (Dubuque, Iowa: Wm. C. Brown Book Co., 1966).

The <u>Dictionary</u> is 81 pages long and contains 139 terms and their associated definitions. A unique feature of the <u>Dictionary</u> is that much of the information in its entries is footnoted. Though not stated, it appears evident that the authors were greatly influenced by Koontz and O'Donnell's <u>Principles</u> <u>of</u> <u>Management</u>: <u>An</u> <u>Analysis</u> <u>of</u> <u>Managerial</u> <u>Functions</u> (3rd ed.)[33] Of the forty-three footnotes that appear in the <u>Dictionary</u>, seventeen refer to this source. In addition, the authors subscribe to the same functional classification as that advanced by Koontz and O'Donnell, i.e., planning, organizing, staffing, directing, and controlling.[34]

At present, the <u>Dictionary</u> <u>of</u> <u>Management</u> <u>Terms</u> is out-of-print and according to its senior author, "less than two dozen copies are now in existence" all of which are in his private possession.[35]

At the same time as the introduction of the first dictionary of general management in the United States, similar progress was being made in Great Britain. Compiled by Hano Johannsen and Andrew Robertson, <u>Management</u> <u>Glossary</u> is described by its publishers as "the first glossary ranging over the whole field of management to be published in Britain."[36]

---

[33](New York: McGraw-Hill Book Co., Inc., 1964).

[34]Lindemann <u>et</u> <u>al</u>., <u>Dictionary</u> <u>of</u> <u>Management</u> <u>Terms</u>, p. 47.

[35]Albert J. Lindemann, personal letter, July 29, 1971. It is not believed that Professor Lindemann was including library owned copies in this comment.

[36]Hano Johannsen and Andrew Robertson, comps., <u>Management</u> <u>Glossary</u>, ed. by E. F. L. Brech (Harlow, England: Longmans, Green and Co., Ltd., 1968). Quotation taken from front inside jacket of dust cover.

Within its format, the Glossary "attempts to include:

(a) Fundamental management terms, normally associated with
    management principles and theory.

(b) The more significant and commonly used terms from each of
    the specialist areas, such as marketing, finance, production,
    personnel.

(c) Terms describing management techniques, though with no
    attempt to cater for the specialist.

(d) Terms from such allied subjects as economics, law, statis-
    tics and sociology, in as far as they are closely associated
    with management." (pp. iv-v.)

While realizing that their work was a pioneering effort, the

authors also recognized that management concepts are in an evolutionary

stage and thus must be treated in a dynamic rather than static manner.

It may be concluded from the previously stated format of the

Glossary that its coverage is wide-spread. In addition to the inclu-

sion of such traditional management concepts as "chain of command,"

"span of control," and "centralisation," the reader may find the mean-

ing of such concepts as the Bedaux (Point) System or the Brisch System

of parts classification and coding. Discussion may also be found for

such terms as bürolandschaft, CAPSTAN, EVOP, rhochrematics and synectics.

While broad in approach, Management Glossary is often incom-

plete in its specific presentations. Absence of the term "unity of

command," for example, or the failure to mention Douglas McGregor's

name in its discussion of Theories of X and Y or Wroe Alderson's name

in its discussion of rhochrematics are just a few instances of this.

Current Conditions

During the past fifty years, there have been a number of

glossaries and dictionaries published in the field of management.

Practically all of these fall into one of two categories. The first
is the full-scale book type which attempts to cover all the terms of
management and its related functional business areas, e.g., The Dictionary of Industrial Administration, Dictionary of Management Terms,
or Management Glossary. The second category is made up of word listings and glossaries in the back of textbooks, e.g., Alvin Brown's two
texts, Organization: A Formulation of Principle (1945)[37] and Organization of Industry (1947)[38] or more recently, Ralph C. Davis' Industrial Organization and Management (1957),[39] Wilfred Brown's Exploration
in Management (1960) and Organization (1971),[40] Dale's Management:
Theory and Practice (2nd ed., 1969)[41] or Donnelly, Gibson and Ivancevich's Fundamentals of Management (1971).[42]

This review of literature has mainly concentrated upon contributions belonging to the first category while totally excluding those
of the second category. The reason for doing so is as follows: The
major and disqualifying criticism of these second-group-compilations

---

[37]New York: Hibbert Printing Co. Glossary, pp. 267-78.

[38]New York: Prentice-Hall, Inc. Glossary, pp. 352-60.

[39]3rd ed.; New York: Harper & Brothers. Glossary, pp. 922-41.

[40]New York: John Wiley & Sons, Inc. Glossary, comp. by J. M.
Hill, pp. 283-92; London: Heineman Educational Books, Ltd. Glossary,
pp. 380-89.

[41]New York: McGraw-Hill Book Co., Inc. Glossary, pp. 755-71.

[42]Austin, Texas: Business Publications, Inc. Glossary, pp.
407-23.

is that they were developed to serve the need of a specific text, and as is true in the majority of cases, the terms supplied are so uniquely used as to make their definition questionable from a general usefulness point of view. Also, if a definition other than those specifically appearing in such a text were needed for a word, another reference would have to be used. This consequently, nullifies any general application such a compilation might have.

It is believed that all major attempts at the solution of the terminological conflict within the field of management have been reviewed. At this point, brief mention will be made of three closely allied efforts in this area. The first concerns the work of Adrian M. McDonough. In his 1963 McKinsey Award-winning book, McDonough developed a computerized retrieval guide for classifying and coding 21,000 elements of the "grammar and vocabulary" of management.[43] Along these same lines but non-quantitative in application are two attempts at the creation of a taxonomy of management theory and work. The first, by Laufer, was hopefully designed "as a means of assisting in the development of a unified theory of management."[44] Within his article, Laufer constructed a taxonomic management matrix fashioned after the Periodic Table with subdivisions for each of the five-functions of management, i.e., planning, organizing, staffing, directing and controlling.

---

[43]Adrian M. McDonough, *Information Economics and Management Systems* (New York: McGraw-Hill Book Co., Inc., 1963).

[44]Arthur C. Laufer, "A Taxonomy of Management Theory: A Preliminary Framework," *Journal of the Academy of Management*, II (December, 1968), 435. Editor's comment.

A second similar effort, forwarded by Allen, proposed "a system for sorting, categorizing, labeling and defining management information."[45] His effort in this area closely parallels the ideas presented in his aforementioned Common Vocabulary of Professional Management.

Conclusion

An overview and appraisal of efforts designed to aid in the alleviation of the terminological conflict within the field of management shows an increasing amount of interest, study and analysis in this area. While the previous works reviewed deserve much applause for their attempts to break the semantic barrier, they have all failed to gain universal acceptance. If this acceptance is to come, more than simple definitions are needed. A clear understanding of the origin, background, and evolving usage of each term to be defined is necessary. It is to aid in this task that the remaining chapters of this dissertation were written.

_____

[45]Louis A. Allen, "A Taxonomy of Management Work," (Palo Alto, Calif.: Louis A. Allen Associates, Inc., 1971). (Mimeographed.)

CHAPTER IV

THE FUNCTION OF PLANNING

Introduction

The first function to be discussed in analyzing the evolutionary development of management is that of planning. As the function of
planning is essential to the performance of any organized task, so are
its four main underlying principles. These principles to be discussed
are as follows: (1) objective, (2) efficiency, (3) balance, and (4)
coordination. The recent emergence of three other principles will
also be presented. These are: (1) primacy of planning, (2) commitment, and (3) flexibility. Because the development of these last
principles does not fall strictly within the framework of discussion
established in the first chapter of the dissertation, a variance in
format will be utilized in their presentation.

After a brief comment on the interrelationships existing among
the four main underlying principles of planning, the development of all
seven principles will be discussed. Statements made by pioneer management writers will first receive attention. These will then be
followed by the comments of later management writers, the views
expressed by current principles of management authors, an analysis of
meaning section and, finally, a formulation of definition.

Interrelationships

The interrelationships that exist among the four main principles of planning selected for discussion are fundamental to the
initiation of the management process. From the first principle,
objective, the second, third, and fourth principles easily follow.
The principle of the objective is based upon the raison d' etre of
an enterprise. The principle of balance reinforces this reason for
existence by seeing that all the parts of the enterprise are properly
proportioned and focused accurately upon its objective(s).

The second principle, efficiency, provides the "why" involved
in proper planning. It is through balance and a singleness of
objective that an enterprise attempts to achieve efficiency in its
operations. Efficiency, that is efficient allocation of an enterprise's resources, enables it to obtain either a maximum output with a
fixed input, or a fixed output with a minimum input.

The principle of the objective, reinforced by the principles
of balance and efficiency, is regulated in its operational involvement by the principle of coordination. Combined, these four principles
initiate the planning phase of the managerial process. The principle
of coordination has been treated with high regard throughout management literature. Its interrelatedness with the first, second, and
third principles may perhaps best be understood from the coming total
analysis of its evolution.

The Principle of the Objective

Background

A review of early management literature reveals a number of descriptive comments that may be considered prerequisites to the acknowledged emergence of the principle of the objective. For example, Taylor observed that: "The first of the four leading principles in management calls for a 'clearly defined and circumscribed task.'"[1]

Writing seven years later, Emerson expressed a similar belief. Being heavily influenced by Taylor,[2] Emerson advanced as the first of his "Twelve Principles of Efficiency" the establishment of "Clearly Defined Ideals."[3]

---

[1]Frederick W. Taylor, "Shop Management," Paper No. 1003 in Transactions (American Society of Mechanical Engineers), XXIV (1903), 1388; Taylor, Shop Management (New York: Harper & Brothers, Publishers, 1911), p. 95.

[2]For Emerson's personal appraisal of the influence Taylor had on his thinking, see: Horace B. Drury, Scientific Management: A History and Criticism, Studies in History, Economics and Public Law, Vol. 65, No. 2; Whole No. 157 (3rd ed.; New York: Columbia University, 1922), pp. 147-48; Sudhi Kakar, Frederick Taylor: A Study in Personality and Innovation (Cambridge, Mass.: MIT Press, 1970), p. 179.

[3]Harrington Emerson, "The Twelve Principles of Efficiency," The Engineering Magazine, XXXIX-XLI (June, 1910 through September, 1911). This series was later published in book form under the same title by Engineering Magazine Co., New York, 1913. See also: Emerson, "Philosophy of Efficiency: An Outline of Its Elements," The Engineering Magazine, XLI (April, 1911), 23-26.

Naval Lieutenant G. J. Meyers was one of the first persons to advance a systematic set of management "laws."[4] He proposed and diagramatically discussed "Seven Laws of Management."[5] Commenting that "it must always be known what object is desired to be accomplished before starting work," Meyers formulated his first law of "What to Do."

LAW I   It is necessary in any activity to have a complete knowledge of what is to be done and to prepare instructions as to what is to be done before the work is started.

Meyers further added that "this law demands that the object of any activity should be stated and instructions covering what to do should be written."[7]   It is interesting to note that all three-- Taylor, Emerson, and Meyers--agreed on the primacy of this principle.

The first explicit formulation of the principle of the objective was made in December, 1918.   Having earlier advanced a "law of objective,"[8] Knoeppel stated the following principle:

The Objective.   A tentative plan of organization should be worked out and decided upon. Owing to the presence of

---

[4]For an earlier set of management "laws," see: Herbert P. Gillette and Richard T. Dana, Cost Keeping and Management Engineering (New York: Myron C. Clark Publishing Co., 1909), chap. i, "The Ten Laws of Management," pp. 1-19.

[5]G. J. Meyers, "The Science of Management," Journal of the American Society of Naval Engineers, XXIII (November, 1911), 994.

[6]Ibid., p. 996.

[7]Ibid.

[8]Charles E. Knoeppel, Organization and Administration, Vol. VI: Factory Management Course and Service (12 Vols.; New York: Industrial Extension Institute, 1917), pp. 73-74.

unknown factors, which cannot be determined in advance, the ultimate objective cannot be agreed upon at the outset, in fact, it will be well toward the completion of the work before the first type of organization can be settled.[9]

The early nineteen-twenties was a period of increased concern for the application of scientific methods to the improvement of industrial practices. Under the auspices of the Federated American Engineering Societies, a subcommittee of the American Engineering Council was formed to investigate the causes of industrial waste. Under the direction of Hoover, the final report of this group demonstrated both the validity of the principle of the objective and its widespread lack of application. A major portion of the Committee's investigation was a listing of responsibilities through which management might aid in reducing industrial waste. Under the heading of the Committee's first recommendation captioned "Improvement of Organization and Executive Control," the following is noted:

> Management control, when properly planned, extends its influence into every activity of an industrial organization and plant, reaching materials, design, equipment, personnel, production, costs and sales policies and coordinating these factors to a common objective.[10]

---

[9]Charles E. Knoeppel, "Industrial Organization As It Affects Executives and Workers," Paper No. 1672 in Transactions (American Society of Mechanical Engineers), XLI (1919), 915.

[10]Committee on Elimination of Waste in Industry of the Federated American Engineering Societies [Herbert C. Hoover, chairman], Waste in Industry (New York: McGraw-Hill Book Co., Inc., 1921), p. 24.

Subsequently, management literature evidenced an increased awareness of the principle of the objective. Lansburgh included as the first of his "primary fundamentals of organization" a "regard for the aim of the enterprise." He further added that such regard "is most important at the time that the first steps are taken in the building or development of the structure which is to be termed the organization of that enterprise."[11]

A similar emphasis was shown by Diemer when he wrote:

> Every business or undertaking has a purpose. To manufacture and sell something at a profit, although in itself is a worthy goal, it is often the means to a bigger one; to manufacture the best article of its kind is frequently the objective.[12]

The above quote is evidence of Diemer's understanding of both the principle of the objective and the cause-effect relationship between a good product and profit.

Dutton's writings represent another example of the increased awareness of the principle of the objective. In a discussion of the "Typical Activities of Business," Dutton remarked:

> All of the activities of control previously described may be regarded as phases of the problem of detailed administration. For successful issue, they must all take place in harmonious and accurate response to the impulse of a single plan.[13]

---

[11]Richard H. Lansburgh, Industrial Management (New York: John Wiley & Sons, Inc., 1923), p. 39.

[12]Hugo Diemer, "The Principles Underlying Good Management," Industrial Management, LXVII (May, 1924), 280.

[13]Henry P. Dutton, Business Organization and Management (Chicago: A. W. Shaw Co., 1925), p. 27.

During the latter part of the nineteen-twenties, the principle

of the objective was generally and explicitly acknowledged. Urwick

explained it as follows:

> The Principle of the Objective. It is a necessary
> preliminary to all activity to have a complete and clear
> statement of the object of such activity in the form of a
> policy or of instructions. Action must be arranged as to
> subordinate all secondary consideration to that object.[14]

Urwick later restated this principle in the following more succinct

form:

> The Principle of the Objective. Every organization
> and every part of every organization must be an expression
> of the purpose of the undertaking concerned or it is mean-
> ingless and therefore redundant.[15]

Reflecting the influence of Urwick, Jones presented a similar

statement of this principle. Speaking before the American Management

Association's "Production Executives' Conference," he gave the

following interpretation:

> Principle of the Objective For any business activity there must
> be a definite and clear knowledge of the objective toward which
> that activity moves, the successive steps necessary to reach
> that objective, and a time schedule in which the various steps
> are assigned definite times for accomplishment.[16]

---

[14]Urwick, "Principles of Direction and Control," p. 178.

[15]Lyndall F. Urwick, Notes on the Theory of Organization (New
York: American Management Association, 1952), p. 19. See also:
Urwick, Organization (The Hague: Publ. 438, Nederlands Instituut
Voor Efficiency, 1966), p. 91.

[16]Thomas R. Jones, Theories and Types of Organizations: Their
History, Industrial and Economic Background, Production Executives'
Series No. 83 (New York: American Management Association, 1929),
p. 28.

Cornell expressed this same concept in this manner:

A prerequisite to the starting of any business enterprise, or to the carrying on of any activity by a concern as
a whole, or by any unit of it, a clear and complete statement
must be made of the objectives in view.[17]

Synthesizing his earlier ideas, Dutton restated his previously

mentioned thoughts under the heading "Principles of the Objective."

It reads simply:

Efforts must be directed toward a specific goal.[18]

Writing on the same topic, Mooney and Reiley expressed the

belief:

Every organization implies an objective of some kind, and
it exists only for one purpose, the attainment of this objective.[19]

Both Gillespie and Alford enlarged upon the reasoning under-

lying this principle. In identifying "principles of industrial man-

agement and organization," Gillespie wrote:

The objective of any inquiry into a business problem must
be clearly and definitely stated so that time and effort
may be a minimum and results a maximum.[20]

---

[17]William B. Cornell, Business Organization, Vol. III: Modern
Business (New York: Alexander Hamilton Institute, 1930), p. 193.

[18]Henry P. Dutton, Principles of Organization As Applied to
Business (New York: McGraw-Hill Book Co., Inc., 1931), p. 26.

[19]James D. Mooney and Alan C. Reiley, Onward Industry! (New
York: Harper & Brothers, 1931), p. 26.

[20]James L. Gillespie, The Principles of Rational Industrial
Management (London: Sir Isaac Pitman & Sons, Ltd., 1938), p. 218.

Alford advanced both a "principle of the objective" and a
"principle of the undertaking."

> Principle of the Undertaking. The necessary preliminary
> to all corporate activity is a clear, complete statement of
> the object of the activity, formulated as a policy or set of
> instructions. The resulting action must subordinate all
> secondary considerations to that of the stated object.[21]

> Principle of the Objective. Each part and subdivision
> of the organization should be the expression of a definite
> purpose in harmony with the objective of the undertaking.[22]

The "principle of the undertaking" simply forms a finer, more distinct

element of the "principle of the objective."

Management literature of the nineteen-forties shows a wide

acceptance of the importance of the principle of the objective. In a

1942 article, Niles listed and discussed the "Principles or Factors

in Organization." At the top of his list, he gave the following

principle:

> Every organization exists to accomplish a purpose or purposes
> which should be: (a) either clearly defined or imagined, or
> both; (b) either understood or accepted by those in the organ-
> ization, or both; (c) considered worthwhile.[23]

Dimock attached similar importance to the principle of the

objective, writing:

> The first step in rounding out your jurisdiction is the clear
> determination of objectives, for you cannot make valid detailed
> plans for either your program or your strategy until you know
> just where you are going. The determination of objectives
> influences policy, organization, personnel, leadership, and

---

[21]Leon P. Alford, Principles of Industrial Management for Engineers (New York: Ronald Press Co., 1940), p. 99. (Italics omitted.)

[22]Ibid., p. 114.

[23]Henry E. Niles, "Principles or Factors in Organization,"
Personnel, XIX (November, 1942), 49. (Italics omitted.)

control. . . . Fixing your objective is like identifying the
North Star--you sight your compass on it and then use it as
the means of getting back on the track when you tend to
stray.[24]

International recognition of this concept is further exhibited
through a statement made by Brech. He commented:

The first stage in management action is setting down
of an aim or objective and the main lines along which the
activity to fulfill that aim is to be directed.[25]

"Principles of Management" Textbooks

The nineteen-fifties witnessed the emergence of the first

"principles of management" textbooks. The content of these books was

basically developed out of earlier management thought. In the first

textbook to be entitled Principles of Management, Terry extensively

dealt with "Management Objectives and Ethics." As part of his analysis,

he advanced a statement of the "Principle of Objective":

A clear and complete statement of the objective is essential,
and it should be made known to all members of an enterprise
affected by it so that management activities can be directed
in a unified, orderly, gainful, and effective manner.[26]

Through numerous revisions, Terry's statement of the principle

of the objective has changed in content and has been modified to

---

[24]Marshall E. Dimock, The Executive in Action (New York:
Harper & Brothers, 1945), p. 54.

[25]Brech, Management (3rd ed., 1953), p. 54.

[26]George R. Terry, Principles of Management (Homewood, Ill.:
Richard D. Irwin Co., 1953, p. 56.

read:

> Objectives are basic in management and a prerequisite to the determining of any course of action; they should be clearly defined and understood by all members of an enterprise affected by them.[27]

Less than two years after the publication of Terry's textbook, Koontz and O'Donnell co-authored the first of four editions of their book. Commenting in their second edition that "if an enterprise is not undertaken to accomplish some objective, there is no need for it,"[28] Koontz and O'Donnell formulated four principles associated with this idea. They are:

1. _Principle of Unity of Objective_: The organization as a whole and every part of it must contribute to the attainment of the enterprise objectives.[29]

2. _Principle of Individual Contribution to Objective_: In guiding and overseeing subordinates, the manager must so communicate the requirements for job performance to subordinates and so motivate them to perform as to assure the most effective contribution possible to group objectives sought.[30]

---

[27]Terry, _Principles of Management_ (5th ed., 1968), p. 25. (Italics omitted.)

[28]Koontz and O'Donnell, _Principles of Management_ (2nd ed., 1959), p. 66.

[29]_Ibid._, 1st ed., 1955, p. 292 (a similar but not identical statement); 2nd ed., 1959, p. 296; 3rd ed., 1964, p. 385. See also: O'Donnell, "Planning Objectives," _California Management Review_, V (Winter, 1963), 3-10; Koontz, "The Rationale of Planning," in _Management: Organization and Planning_, ed. by Donald M. Bowman and Francis M. Fillerup (New York: McGraw-Hill Book Co., Inc., 1963), pp. 67-85.

[30]_Ibid._, 2nd ed., 1959, p. 444; In a modified form, 3rd ed., 1964, p. 530.

3. <u>Principle of Harmony of Objectives</u>: In guiding and overseeing subordinates, the manager must make the attainment of individual subordinates' objectives harmonize with the attainment of group objectives.[31]

4. <u>Principle of Contribution to Objective</u>: Every plan and all its derivative plans must contribute in some positive way to the accomplishment of group objectives.[32]

While the "principle of individual contribution to objective" was dropped after the third edition of Koontz and O'Donnell's book, the remaining three principles were maintained. However, the definition given for each of these principles was changed with the publication of Koontz and O'Donnell's fourth edition. In effect, the "principle of individual contribution to objective" appears to have been merged with the "principle of unity of objective." Compare the following definitions with those previously given:

1. <u>Principle of Unity of Objective</u> An organization structure is effective if it as a whole, and every part of it, make possible accomplishment of [<u>sic</u>] individuals in contributing toward the attainment of enterprise objectives.[33]

2. <u>Principle of Harmony of Objectives</u> Effective directing depends on the extent to which individual objectives in cooperative activity are harmonized with group objectives.[34]

---

[31]<u>Ibid</u>., 1st ed., 1955, pp. 395-96 (a similar but not identical statement); 2nd ed., 1959, p. 397, p. 445; In a modified form, 3rd ed., 1964, p. 475, p. 530.

[32]<u>Ibid</u>., 2nd ed., 1959, p. 453, p. 579; 3rd ed., p. 72, p. 200. See also: Koontz, "A Preliminary Statement of Principles of Planning and Control," <u>Journal of the Academy of Management</u>, I (April, 1958), 45-60.

[33]<u>Ibid</u>., 4th ed., 1968, p. 233, p. 424.

[34]<u>Ibid</u>., 4th ed., 1968, p. 632.

3. <u>Principle</u> <u>of</u> <u>Contribution</u> <u>to</u> <u>Objectives</u>   The purpose
   of every plan and all derivative plans is to contribute
   positively toward the accomplishment of enterprise objectives.[35]

The greatest change in meaning is evident in the altered definition

given for the "principle of unity of objective." The meaning associated

with the principles of "harmony of objective" and "contribution to

objectives" has basically remained the same.

Both Koontz and O'Donnell and Terry formulated explicit state-

ments dealing with the principle of objective. However, succeeding

management writing at the introductory level seemed to enter a period

of unexplained verbal inexactness. Perhaps this condition was actuated

by a desire for academic uniqueness and increased book sales through

product differentiation. Writers such as McFarland, Albers, Newman

and Summer began to shun the usage of the term "principle" in their

writings. For example, McFarland formulated the following statement of

the principle of the objective in the first edition of his book,

<u>Management</u>: <u>Principles</u> <u>and</u> <u>Practices</u>. This statement, however, is

unexplainably absent from both the second and third revisions of his

text.

Principle <u>of</u> the <u>Objective</u>   Objectives are basic elements in the
clear thinking of an executive. They serve the company by providing its employees with guidance, direction, motivation, and
a sense of unity. No business can be well-managed without
explicit statements of its chief objectives.[36]

---

[35]<u>Ibid</u>., 4th ed., 1968, p. 222.

[36]Dalton E. McFarland, <u>Management</u>: <u>Principles</u> <u>and</u> <u>Practices</u>
(New York: Macmillan Company, 1958), p. 96.

In a manner similar to McFarland's, Albers almost completely ignored the concept embodied in the principle of the objective. The first and second editions of his text contain the following statement which is their only referral to the objective principle. It is excluded from the third revision.

> The organization objective may be defined as a synthesis of the totality of actions planned by executives to overcome limitations imposed by environmental and organizational forces.[37]

Newman and Summer are more extensive in their treatment of objectives than is Albers. Nevertheless, neither do they explicitly formulate a principle of the objective. They do feel, however, that "of the various kinds of planning, setting objectives is the most crucial"[38] and that a "clear definition of specific objectives encourages unified planning."[39] At no point is this concept stated as a principle. Newman and Summer come closest to making such a statement in the following comment:

> Company objectives give direction to the operations of an enterprise and take priority over the often diverging interests of various departments.[40]

Shortly after this, Haimann referred to the formulation of objectives as "foremost among the manager's responsibilities" and as

---

[37]Henry H. Albers, Organized Executive Action (New York: John Wiley & Sons, Inc., 1961), p. 311; 2nd ed., 1965, p. 393.

[38]William H. Newman and Charles E. Summer, The Process of Management (Englewood Cliffs, N. J.: Prentice-Hall, Inc., 1961), p. 373.

[39]Ibid., p. 375; 2nd ed., with E. Kirby Warren, 1967, p. 471.

[40]Ibid., p. 376; 2nd ed., 1967, p. 471.

"the first step in planning."[41] In the second edition of his book,

Haimann and his co-author added to this idea. They noted:

> A firm should always state its objectives as clearly
> and simply as possible in order to clarify and point out
> the targets which employees are supposed to reach.[42]

Longenecker only briefly discussed the principle of the objec-

tive. He disposed of it in a single statement:

> Clearly formulated objectives enable all parts of an organi-
> zation to work toward the same goal.[43]

Dale followed a similar pattern. He wrote:

> Finally, there is the matter of objectives. Plans must
> ensure that everything that is done contributes to progress
> toward them.[44]

Dale did, however, provide three pages of discussion on "The

Classical Theorists." At that point, he (without endorsement)

discussed the objective principle as a "classical" concept.

> The organization should have a clearly defined objec-
> tive, and each position should have an objective logically
> related to it in such a way that, if the incumbent of each
> position fulfills his goal, the goal of the entire organi-
> zation will be met.[45]

---

[41]Haimann, _Professional Management_, p. 75.

[42]Theo Haimann and William G. Scott, _Management in the Modern Organization_ (2nd ed.; Boston: Houghton Mifflin Co., 1970), p. 91.

[43]Justin G. Longenecker, _Principles of Management and Organizational Behavior_ (Columbus, Ohio: Charles E. Merrill Publishing Co., 1964), p. 69; 2nd ed., 1969, p. 78.

[44]Ernest Dale, _Management: Theory and Practice_ (New York: McGraw-Hill Book Co., Inc., 1965), p. 351.

[45]_Ibid._, p. 234; In a modified form, 2nd ed., 1969, p. 188.

More recently, Sisk has adopted the same format as that of the original principles of management textbooks. In his book, he enumerates fourteen principles of management. Of these, the first principle to be discussed is the principle of the objective. Sisk writes:[46]

> The requirement that the objective should be predetermined is considered of such significance that it is referred to as the Principle of the Objective. A concise statement of the principle of the objective is that of John F. Mee: "Before initiating any course of action, the objectives in view must be clearly determined, understood, and stated."

An Analysis of Meaning

As the preceding discussion indicates, the first statement of the principle of the objective made an early appearance in management literature. It can also be seen that Knoeppel's definition of the principle of objective was pre-dated by such writers as Taylor, Emerson and Meyers. While Taylor and Emerson stressed "clearly defined plans and tasks," Meyers and Emerson stressed "knowledge of a plan's objective."

In the period following this, the principle of the objective was recognized as a fundamental (Lansburgh) and ubiquitous part of any undertaking (Diemer). Subordination of all phases of the organization to the principle of the objective was first stressed by Dutton and later by Urwick.

---

[46]Henry L. Sisk, Principles of Management (Cincinnati: South-Western Publishing Co., 1969), p. 51, quoting John F. Mee, "Management Philosophy for Professional Executives," Business Horizons, Supplement to the Indiana Business Review, XXXI (December, 1956), p. 7. (Italics not in original.)

Following this point in its development, management thought began to stress both the need for (1) clearness, and (2) specificness in regard to organizational objectives. Cornell and Jones stressed the former need while statements by Dutton and Mooney and Reiley expressed an emphasis on the latter.

In recognition of the need for both qualities, Alford formulated two related principles designed to emphasize these recognized distinctions. His "principle of the undertaking" called for "a clear, complete statement of the object of the activity." In support of this, his "principle of the objective" called for "a definite purpose in harmony with the objective of the undertaking."

The nineteen-forties saw further emphasis on these two aspects of the principle of the objective (H. Niles, Dimock). It also brought further international recognition of the concept involved (Brech).

The appearance of formally entitled "principles of management" textbooks added an additional dimension to management understanding. Terry, in his statement of the principle of the objective, stressed its basicness and need for clear definition. Koontz and O'Donnell, however, by-passed these points, and much like Dutton, Urwick and Alford, stressed the contribution of the organization's secondary efforts to the accomplishment of its over-all major objective. In fact, Koontz and O'Donnell differentiated between "unity of objective," "harmony of objectives" and "contribution to objectives."

The distinction of (1) clear definition of objective, and (2) contribution of derivative efforts to a total objective seem to be the

two over-riding parallel themes utilized in defining the principle of
the objective. Succeeding writers--McFarland, Albers, Newman and
Summer, Haimann and Sisk--stressed one or both of these distinctions.

McFarland saw the definition and identification of objectives
as one of the basic requirements of management. He, like Terry, also
saw objectives as serving to coordinate the plans and behavior of an
organization. In agreement with this, Albers regarded objectives as
synthesizing an organization's plans of action.

In a similar manner, Newman and Summer emphasized both the
formerly acknowledged distinctions used in defining the principles of
the objective. They regarded this principle as "crucial" and felt its
"clear definition" aided unified planning by helping to overcome the
divergent interests of a company's numerous departments.

Authors Haimann, Longenecker, and Dale likewise emphasized the
need for clearness in formulation of objectives, as well as, the
importance of subordinating all plans to a master objective. In contrast to this, Sisk only accentuated the need for clearness of objectives.

Table 1 presents an approximate chronological collection of
statements on the principle of the objective.

Formulation of Definition

The formulation of a definition of the principle of objective
is particularly complicated by different wording of the principle among
various authors. Also, while numerous statements of the principle are
explicit in nature, numerous others are indirect and implied. It
does stand-out, however, that there are two parallel elements most

prevalent in the discussion presented--(1) the necessity of clear statement of organizational objectives, and (2) subordination of all organizational efforts to a common objective.

While not all writers have stressed both these aspects (Terry
and Sisk), other writers have (Dutton and Urwick) and even a few have
logically separated them (Alford, Koontz and O'Donnell). It would
seem best for purposes of clarity to follow the lead of this latter
group. It is with this reasoning and these distinctions in mind that
both a "principle of the objective" and a "principle of unity of
objective" will be forwarded.

Principle of the Objective

The clear statement of desired objectives is basic to
the successful accomplishment of any undertaking.

Principle of Unity of Objective

The efforts of every organization and every part of
every organization should contribute to the accomplishment of
the organization's main objective.

TABLE 1

A COLLECTION OF STATEMENTS
ON THE PRINCIPLE OF THE OBJECTIVE*

Author	Statement
Taylor	"The first of the four leading principles in management calls for a 'clearly defined and circumscribed task.'"
Emerson	A firm must establish "definite plans and ideals."
Meyers	"It is necessary in any activity to have a complete knowledge of what is to be done and to prepare instructions as to what is to be done before the work is started."
Knoeppel	"A tentative plan of organization should be worked out and decided upon."
Lansburgh	A primary fundamental of organization is a "regard for the aim of the enterprise."
Diemer	"Every business or undertaking has a purpose."
Dutton	(a) All activities must "take place in harmonious and accurate response to the impulse of a single plan." (b) "Efforts must be directed toward a specific goal."
Urwick	(a) "It is a necessary preliminary to all activity to have a complete and clear statement of the object of such activity in the form of a policy or of instructions. Action must be arranged as to subordinate all secondary consideration to that object." (b) "Every organization and every part of every organization must be an expression of the purpose of the undertaking concerned or it is meaningless and therefore redundant."
T. R. Jones	"For any activity there must be a definite and clear knowledge of the objective toward which that activity moves. . . ."

TABLE 1--Continued

Author	Statement
Cornell	"A prerequisite to the starting of any business enterprise. . . . a clear and complete statement must be made of the objectives in view."
Mooney and Reiley	"Every organization implies an objective of some kind, and it exists only for one purpose, the attainment of this objective."
Gillespie	"The objective of any inquiry into a business must be clearly and definitely stated so that time and effort may be a minimum and results a maximum."
Alford	"The necessary preliminary to all corporate activity is a clear, complete statement of the object of the activity. . . ."
H. Niles	"Every organization exists to accomplish a purpose or purposes. . . ."
Dimock	"The first step in rounding out your jurisdiction is the clear determination of objectives. . . ."
Brech	"The first stage in management is setting down of an aim or objective. . . ."
Terry	(a) "A clear and complete statement of the objective is essential. . . ." (b) "Objectives are basic in management and a prerequisite to the determining of any course of action."
Koontz and O'Donnell	"The organization as a whole and every part of it must contribute to the attainment of the enterprise objectives."
McFarland	"Objectives are basic elements in the clear thinking of an executive. . . . No business can be well-managed without explicit statements of its chief objectives."
Albers	"The organization objective may be defined as a synthesis of the totality of actions planned by executives to overcome limitations imposed by environmental and organizational forces."

TABLE 1--<u>Continued</u>

<u>Author</u>	<u>Statement</u>
Newman, Summer and Warren	"Company objectives give direction to the operations of an enterprise. . . ."
Haimann and Scott	"A firm should always state its objectives as clearly and simply as possible. . . ."
Longenecker	"Clearly formulated objectives enable all parts of an organization to work toward the same goal."
Dale	Objectives "must ensure that everything that is done contributes to progress toward them."
Sisk	The objective of an enterprise "should be predetermined."

      *The statements included in this listing and those to follow have for the most part been quoted literally. However, for the purpose of brevity, a few particularly long statements have been paraphrased. The absence of quotation marks signifies such cases. The statements are roughly presented in chronological order. To keep the collection as simple as possible, book titles have not been given. A full reference to each author's work(s) may be found in the text of the dissertation.

The Principle of Efficiency

Background

The first two decades of the twentieth century was a period in management development which was characterized by the desire for efficiency. Defined as "the ratio of . . . useful output to the total input in any system," efficiency was the byword of the era.[47] It was this period that first saw mention of the "Taylor System," the Gilbreths' "One Best Way," and Emerson's "Efficiency Engineering."

Emerson's article, "Efficiency As a Basis for Operation and Wages," appeared in 1908. It emphasized the need for waste elimination and efficiency increase. In this article, Emerson declared:

> It is distinctly the business of the engineer to lessen waste--wastes of material, wastes of friction, wastes of design, wastes of effort, wastes due to crude organization and administration--in a word, wastes due to inefficiency.[48]

Emerson enlarged and codified his ideas in a following series of articles. Entitled "The Twelve Principles of Efficiency," these were later combined into book form. To Emerson, his "efficiency system" became a "declaration of a philosophy."[49] He considered his

---

[47]The American Heritage Dictionary of the English Language (1969), p. 416.

[48]Harrington Emerson, "Efficiency As a Basis for Operation and Wages," The Engineering Magazine, XXXV-XXXVI (July, 1908 through April, 1909). This series was later published in book form under the same title by Engineering Magazine Co., New York, 1911. See: p. 17.

[49]Harrington Emerson, The Twelve Principles of Efficiency (New York: Engineering Magazine Co., 1912), p. i.

work part of a "new morality" designed

> . . . to extend the dominion of many over uncarnate [sic]
> energy and its use, to substitute highly paid thinkers and
> supervisors for devitalized toilers, to help each individ-
> ual, each corporation, each government to meet its part
> of the obligation, above all to inspire those executives
> on whose will all progress and all wise performance
> depends [sic].[50]

Emerson was one of management's first professional consultants.

He testified at the Eastern Rate Case,[51] the Taylor Hearings,[52] and

the Commission on Industrial Relations' investigation of scientific

management.[53] In 1912, along with such notables as T. Coleman du

Pont and Henry R. Towne, he helped form the Efficiency Society of

---

[50]Ibid., p. xii.

[51]"Testimony of Harrington Emerson," U. S., Congress, Senate,
Evidence Taken by the Interstate Commerce Commission in the Matter of
Proposed Advances in Freight Rates by Carriers (August to December,
1910), S. Doc. 725 (Ser. Set. 5908), 61st Cong., 3rd sess., 1910-11,
pp. 2823-45; Louis D. Brandeis, Scientific Management and Railroads:
Being Part of a Brief Submitted to the Interstate Commerce Commission
(New York: Engineering Magazine, 1911), p. 83.

[52]"Testimony of Harrington Emerson," U. S., Congress, House,
The Taylor and Other Systems of Shop Management, Hearings Before Special
Committee of the House of Representatives to Investigate the Taylor
and Other Systems of Shop Management Under the Authority of H. Res.
90 [William B. Wilson, chairman] (Washington, D. C.: Government
Printing Office, 1912).

[53]"Testimony of Harrington Emerson," U. S., Congress, Senate,
Final Report and Testimony Submitted to Congress by the Commission on
Industrial Relations [Frank P. Walsh, chairman], S. Doc. 415 (Ser.
Set. 6929), 64th Cong., 1st sess., 1914, pp. 822-33, pp. 1021-24.

New York City.[54] In 1921, he served on the Federated American Engineering Societies' Committee on Elimination of Waste in Industry.[55]

Through Emerson's influence, interest in efficiency spread
rapidly.[56] In 1909, Robb spoke at Harvard University on the "Limits
of Organization." In the presentation of his topic, he expressed the
important relationship existing between organization and efficiency
well. Robb explained:

> A business organization is for the purpose of accomplishing
> definite pieces of work, of arriving at a definite result with
> the least expenditure of labor and material, the smallest
> expenditure for plant, and the shortest time of use of plant;
> and if organization does not prevent wastes or enable us to
> get results attainable in no other way, it has no value.
>
> To increase the efficiency of effort, we must go beyond the
> perfection of the organization machinery as machinery: we
> must know in what directions effort will yield the greatest
> returns, which factors in a result have the greatest bearing
> and will best repay study and attention, which items are
> unimportant and the last that should have consideration.[57]

---

[54]Holbrook F. J. Porter, "Historical Sketch of the Organization
of the Efficiency Society," Transactions, Efficiency Society, I
(1912), 20-28. The stated objective of the Efficiency Society was
"to promote efficiency or percentage of result obtained relative to
effort expended in every activity of man and in everything he employs."
The Society ceased operation shortly before the entry of the United
States into World War I.

[55]Committee on Elimination of Waste, Waste in Industry, p. vii.

[56]For a background discussion of the efficiency movement, see:
Charles B. Going, "The Efficiency Movement. An Outline," Transactions,
Efficiency Society, I (1912), 11-20. See also: Daniel Bell, Work and
Its Discontents: The Cult of Efficiency in America (Boston: Beacon
Press, 1956); Samuel Haber, Efficiency and Uplift (Chicago: University
of Chicago Press, 1964).

[57]Russell Robb, "The Limits of Organization," Stone and Webster
Public Service Journal, IV (May, 1909), 301. Reprinted in Robb,
Lectures on Organization (Boston: Privately printed, 1910), p. 24.

The same year that Robb spoke, Galloway compared an efficient

organization to a machine. He offered the following analogy:

> A business organization is the machine by means of which the
> forces of industry make themselves effective. An efficient
> organization, like a good machine, must work with a minimum
> loss of energy.[58]

Additional evidence of the widespread interest in efficiency

may be found in a report authored by Cooke. Entitled Academic and

Industrial Efficiency, its main purpose was to investigate from a

business viewpoint the operational inefficiencies of American colleges

and universities. The results of this investigation are perhaps best

indicated in the following statement:

> As a result of this inquiry, the writer is convinced
> that there are very few, if any, of the broader principles of
> management which obtain generally in the industrial and
> commercial world which are not, more or less, applicable in
> the college field, as far as was discovered, no one of them
> is now generally observed.[59]

In 1911, both The American Magazine and World's Work (London)

published Taylor's classic paper, "The Principles of Scientific

---

[58]Lee Galloway, Organization and Management, Vol. III: Modern
Business, ed. by Joseph F. Johnson (18 Vols.; New York: Alexander
Hamilton Institute, 1909), p. 1.

[59]Morris L. Cooke, Academic and Industrial Efficiency, Bulletin
No. 5 (New York: Carnegie Foundation for the Advancement of Teaching,
1910), p. 7.

Management."[60] Later published in book form, it was an effort

designed to bring attention to national inefficiencies. Responding

to President Theodore Roosevelt's plea for the conservation of

national resources, Taylor gave the following as two of the reasons

for the preparation of his book:

> First. To point out, through a series of simple
> illustrations, the great loss which the whole country is
> suffering through inefficiency in almost all our daily
> acts.
>
> Second. To try to convince the reader that the
> remedy for this inefficiency lies in systematic management,
> rather than in searching for some unusual or extraordinary
> man.[61]

Unimpressed by the work of Emerson and Taylor,[62] Church and

Alford collaborated in 1912 to advance their own ideas regarding "the

regulative principles of the art of management."[63] The second of the

---

[60]Frederick W. Taylor, "The Gospel of Efficiency: The Principles of Scientific Management," The American Magazine, LXXI (March through May, 1911), and Taylor, same title, World's Work (London), XVII-XVIII (May through July, 1911). For other early similar Taylor presentations, see: Taylor, "The Principles and Methods of Scientific Management," Journal of Accountancy, XII (June and July, 1911); Taylor, "Scientific Management," in New England Railroad Club Proceedings, October 10, 1911 (Boston, Mass.), pp. 138-87; Taylor, "The Principles of Scientific Management," Applied Science (Toronto), VII (N. S.) (January, 1913), 76-80.

[61]Frederick W. Taylor, The Principles of Scientific Management (New York: Harper & Brothers, 1911), p. 7.

[62]A. Hamilton Church, "Has 'Scientific Management' Science?" The American Machinist, XXXV (July 20, 1911), 108-12. See also: Church, "The Meaning of Scientific Management," The Engineering Magazine, XLI (April, 1911), 97-101.

[63]Church and Alford, "The Principles of Management," The American Machinist, XXXVI (May 30, 1912), 857-59.

three principles that they identified was the "principle of economic

control of effort." Using "economic effort" as a synonym for

efficiency, Church later elevated this concept to a "law" with four

supporting sub-principles.

1. Effort Must Be Divided
2. Effort Must Be Co-ordinated
3. Effort Must Be Conserved
4. Effort Must Be Remunerated[64]

Fayol approached the idea of efficiency from the standpoint of

resource optimization. In the final paragraph of the first chapter of

his book, General and Industrial Management, he remarked:

> To govern is to conduct the undertaking towards its objec-
> tive by seeking to derive optimum advantage from all avail-
> able resources.[65]

Later, discussing the different members of a company's corporate body,

Fayol specifically assigned this task to "general management." He

stated:

> The responsibility of general management is to conduct
> the enterprise towards its objective by making optimum use
> of available resources.[66]

In contrast to Fayol, De Haas approached efficiency as a

macroeconomic phenomenon. He held the belief that

> If more men are engaged in loading a ship, in cutting down a
> tree, in selling groceries, or in directing the money

---

[64]A. Hamilton Church, The Science and Practice of Management
(New York: Engineering Magazine, 1914), p. 111. Originally serialized
in six parts in The Engineering Magazine under the title "Practical
Principles of Rational Management," XLIV-XLV (January through June,
1913).

[65]Fayol, General and Industrial Management, p. 6.

[66]Ibid., pp. 61-62.

resources of the community than are absolutely necessary, the total productivity of society is, by that much, less than its maximum. Ultimately every member of society suffers by inefficiency, for if many men are engaged unproductively, there are just as many human wants to satisfy, but less goods to go around than when the same men are engaged in productive work.[67]

Diemer approached the principle of efficiency by associating it with "individual effort and enthusiasm." He explained this approach in the following manner:

Efficiency in organization demands definite knowledge of methods of securing individual effort and enthusiasm as well as departmental co-ordination.[68]

One year later, Diemer expanded on this explanation and added:

By efficiency we mean the ratio of output to intake.[69]

The broad interpretation of efficiency conceives it as the conservation principle in its most general application. It conceives it as the minimum of waste not only in the material and capital of the proprietor, but as the minimum of waste also of human health, energy, and happiness, and as the minimum of waste of the nation's natural materials, as well as the development of the greatest distributed general purchasing power among the community at large.[70]

Lansburgh's explanation of efficiency presupposed a fixed amount of "available energy." He advanced the belief that

The well-constructed organization is like a great power plant

---

[67]J. Anton De Haas, Business Organization and Administration (New York: Gregg Publishing Company, 1920), p. 22.

[68]Hugo Diemer, Factory Organization and Administration, Vol. II: Factory Management (6 Vols.; 2nd ed.; New York: McGraw-Hill Book Co., Inc., 1914), p. 4.

[69]Hugo Diemer, Industrial Organization and Management (Chicago: La Salle Extension University, 1915), p. 12.

[70]Ibid., p. 186.

that is set up in a dam thrown entirely across a river. . . . Every ounce of available energy in the river is utilized.[71]

Using an idea similar to that of Lansburgh's, Sheldon related efficiency to "available effort":

> Organization is the process of so combining the work which individuals or groups have to perform with the faculties necessary for its execution that the duties, so formed, provide the best channels for the efficient, systematic, positive, and co-ordinated application of the available effort.[72]

Brown also commented on efficiency. Sounding much like Sheldon, he wrote:

> Organization, regardless of the place it occupies in an enterprise, is effected in order that the most efficient performance of activities necessary to attain the objectives of the business may be secured.[73]

Mooney and Reiley used numerous approaches in their discussion of efficiency. Recognizing its social implication, they linked efficiency with organization structure, coordination[74] and discipline.[75] Concerning efficiency and line-staff relationships,

---

[71]Lansburgh, Industrial Management, p. 38.

[72]Oliver Sheldon, The Philosophy of Management (London: Sir Isaac Pitman & Sons, Ltd., 1923), p. 32. See also: Sheldon, "The Organisation of Business Control," in Factory Organisation, ed. by Clarence H. Northcott, J. W. Wardropper, Oliver Sheldon, and Lyndall F. Urwick (London: Sir Isaac Pitman & Sons, Ltd., 1928), p. 10.

[73]Percy S. Brown, "Organization of the Manufacturing Division," in Handbook of Business Administration, ed. by William J. A. Donald (New York: McGraw-Hill Book Co., Inc., for the American Management Association, 1931), p. 540.

[74]Mooney and Reiley, Onward Industry!, pp. viii-vix, p. 20.

[75]James D. Mooney and Alan C. Reiley, The Principles of Organization (New York: Harper & Brothers, 1939), p. 13.

they commented:

> Staff efficiency is coming to be recognized as a necessity of
> modern organization, but line efficiency will always remain
> the paramount necessity.[76]

Mooney also later associated efficiency with procedure. He
wrote:

> Organization concerns procedure, and the attainment of any
> human group objective must ever depend in great measure, on
> efficient forms of procedure.[77]

One of the strongest and most explicit statements of the

importance of efficiency was made by Gulick. In an essay especially

written for inclusion in the book Papers on the Science of Administra-

tion, he observed:

> In the science of administration, whether public or
> private, the basic "good" is efficiency. The fundamental
> objective of the science of administration is the accom-
> plishment of the work in hand with the least expenditure
> of manpower and materials. Efficiency is thus axiom
> number one in the value scale of administration.[78]

Perhaps one of the most extensive treatments of efficiency was

undertaken by Simon. In his book, Administrative Behavior (sub-titled:

A Study of Decision-Making Processes in Administrative Organization),

he devoted twenty-five pages to the subject of "The Criterion of

---

[76]Mooney and Reiley, Onward Industry!, pp. viii-vix, p. 20.

[77]James D. Mooney, "The Principles of Organization," in Papers
on the Science of Administration, ed. by Luther H. Gulick and L.
Urwick (New York: Institute of Public Administration, Columbia University, 1937), p. 98.

[78]Luther H. Gulick, "Science, Values and Public Administration,"
in Papers on the Science of Administration, ed. by Gulick and Urwick,
p. 192.

Efficiency." Simon, considered to be a member of the "quantitative management" school,[79] explained the "criterion of efficiency" in the following manner:

> The criterion of efficiency dictates that choice of alternatives which produces the largest result for the given application of resources.[80]

In 1946, Brech (heavily influenced by the early work of Follett and Urwick)[81] formulated and presented a framework of management principles.[82] After an exchange of ideas and a reconsideration of experience, Brech revised his original views.[83] He presented his new thoughts in two works published in 1953.[84] To date, this framework of principles remains unaltered and through its evolution,

---

[79]W. Haynes Warren and Joseph L. Massie, Management: Analysis, Concepts and Cases (2nd ed.; Englewood Cliffs, N. J.: Prentice-Hall, 1969), p. 5, pp. 12-13.

[80]Simon, Administrative Behavior, p. 179. (Italics omitted.)

[81]For Brech's own comments concerning the influences on his thinking, see: "Supplementary Note A. The Determination of the Principles of Organization," in Brech, Organisation: The Framework of Management (2nd ed.; London: Longmans, Green and Co., Ltd., 1964), pp. 155-57.

[82]E. F. L. Brech, The Nature and Significance of Management (London: Sir Isaac Pitman & Sons, Ltd., 1946), pp. 54-61. With the publication of its second edition (1948), this text was re-entitled Management: Its Nature and Significance.

[83]See: E. F. L. Brech, "The Principles of Management," British Management Review, VII, No. 1 (1948), 61-67; Brech, "Summary and Review," British Management Review, VII, No. 3 (1948), 87-102; Brech, "Organisation Structure--Summary and Review," British Management Review, VIII (July, 1949), 104-05.

[84]E. F. L. Brech, "Management in Principle," in The Principles and Practices of Management, ed. by Brech (London: Longmans, Green and Co., Ltd., 1953), pp. 1-82; Brech, Management: Its Nature and Significance (3rd ed.; London: Sir Isaac Pitman & Sons, Ltd., 1953).

Brech's conception of the role of efficiency has remained unchanged.
He considers efficiency to be basic to the management process and
acknowledges this by writing:

> . . . the attainment of efficiency and economy of operations
> is inherent in the essence of the management process. . . .[85]

It is interesting to note that in his analysis, Brech makes no
attempt to differentiate between the words "effectiveness" and
"efficiency." Preferring to use the words synonymously, he wrote:
"No distinction is drawn between them: both are used to convey the
same idea of attaining an optimum performance or result with the
minimum use of resources or at minimum cost."[86]

Following Brech, the importance of efficiency was stressed by
Newman. Using the word administration synonymously with management,
Newman gave the following definition and supplemented it with the
succeeding comment:

> Administration is the guidance, leadership, and control
> of the efforts of a group of individuals toward some common
> goal. Clearly, the good administrator is one who enables
> the group to achieve its objectives with a minimum expendi-
> ture of resources and effort and the least interference with
> other worth-while activities.[87]

Glover was one of the few management authors to quantitatively
express efficiency.[88] He commented that while "ideal efficiency"

---

[85]Brech, "Management in Principle," in The Principles and Practices of Management (2nd ed.; 1963), p. 15. (Italics omitted.)

[86]Ibid., p. 31.

[87]William H. Newman, Administrative Action (New York: Prentice-
Hall, Inc., 1951), p. 1. See also: p. 132, p. 142.

[88]See: Adolph L. De Leeuw, "The Final Measure of Industrial
Efficiency," Management Engineering, I (September, 1921), 141-46.

is yet unobtainable,

> . . . it is the duty of management to operate a business at
> the highest practicable efficiency and efficiency of business
> operations is stated in terms of the fraction:

$$\text{Business Efficiency} \quad \underline{\text{Input}} \quad [89]$$
$$\text{Output}$$

Declaring this relationship "a fundamental criterion of an industrial

operation," Glover further added:

> Profit from business operations is realized when [the]
> "business efficiency" fraction is equal to or less than
> "one" (1) provided the imposed restrictive conditions are
> fulfilled.[90]

"Principles of Management" Textbooks

Terry approached efficiency from a purely structural view-

point. He was of the opinion that organizations characterized by

structural simplicity were most likely to succeed and were the most

effective. He commented:

> For maximum effectiveness, an organization structure
> must be understood, accepted, and utilized by all who are
> affected by it. One of the best ways to gain this under-
> standing and acceptance is to keep the structure free of
> complicated groupings of activities and involved relation-
> ships. A complex structure usually results in managerial
> difficulties. It is axiomatic that the simple way is the
> best way.[91]

---

[89]John G. Glover, Fundamentals of Professional Management
(New York: Republic Book Co., 1954), pp. 308.

[90]Ibid., p. 308.

[91]Terry, Principles of Management, p. 155; 2nd ed., 1956, p.
262.

To this Terry added:

Efficient managers work with simple things; they know from experience that simplicity helps bring the best results.[92]

Koontz and O'Donnell dealt with efficiency much more directly than did Terry. They warned that the principle of efficiency "underlies the measurement of any organization" and "must be applied with judicious balance."[93] They stated the principle of efficiency as follows:

Principle of Efficiency: An organization should attain its objectives with a minimum of unsought consequences, or costs.[94]

In qualifying this statement, they added:

The concept of efficiency so used is employed in the sense of the ratio of output to input, although it goes beyond the usual sense of thinking of these costs entirely in such measurable items as dollars or man-hours. Even though financial or material unit costs are important in measuring organizational efficiency, the principle, as employed here, encompasses such matters as individual and group satisfaction and the contribution of the enterprise to the community.[95]

---

[92]Ibid., 1st ed., 1953, p. 155; 2nd ed., 1956, p. 262.

[93]Koontz and O'Donnell, Principles of Management, p. 293; 2nd ed., 1959, p. 67, p. 68; 3rd ed., 1964, p. 211; 4th ed., 1968, p. 234.

[94]Ibid., 2nd ed., 1959, p. 296; 3rd ed., 1964, p. 385; In a modified form, 4th ed., 1968, p. 222. For a similar statement, see: 1st ed., 1955, p. 292.

[95]Ibid., 1st ed., 1955, p. 292; 2nd ed., 1959, p. 67; In a modified form, 3rd ed., 1964, pp. 73-74.

McFarland vaguely discussed efficiency in the first two
editions of his book, Management: Principles and Practices.[96] He,
however, reversed this trend in the third edition of his book,
declaring:

> Economic, cost, and profit factors are important in
> our society, and resources in any society tend to be scarce.
> Therefore an organization's members wish to maximize the
> output of goods or services resulting from a given input of
> resources, or at least make a respectable showing in that
> direction. Chaos or disorganization work against the ideal
> of efficiency, so there is pressure to develop some measure
> of systematic, orderly, rational, and coordinated effort, and
> to control waste and loss.[97]

Albers related efficiency to innovation, managerial competence,
planning, and enterprise size.[98] In discussing the problem of
general operating efficiency, he remarked:

> The problem is that of technique, or how a given output of
> goods and services can be produced with a lower input of
> resources. A larger output from a given input is another
> way of saying the same thing.[99]

The definition of efficiency provided by Newman, Summer and
Warren is very similar in nature to that implied by Albers. The above

[96]McFarland, Management: Principles and Practices, p. 236;
2nd ed., 1964, p. 323.

[97]Ibid., 3rd ed., 1970, p. 368.

[98]Albers, Organized Executive Action, p. 256, p. 448, p. 305,
pp. 141-43; 2nd ed., 1965, p. 336, p. 602, p. 386, pp. 158-59; 3rd ed.,
1969, p. 339, p. 630, p. 378, pp. 191-93.

[99]Ibid., 1st ed., 1961, p. 277; 2nd ed., 1965, p. 359; 3rd ed.,
1969, p. 361.

authors defined efficiency to mean--"to increase the ratio of output to effort expended."[100]

Dale largely dealt with the topic of efficiency as it related to "classical" management theory. In the first edition of his book, he devoted an entire chapter to "Harrington Emerson and the Twelve Principles of Efficiency."[101] Without endorsement, Dale reported the following interpretation of the "classical" definition of the principle of efficiency:

> Principle of Efficiency. The organization should be so planned that the objective can be attained with the lowest possible cost, which may mean either money costs or human costs, or both.[102]

Sisk related efficiency to planning. In his book, he noted:

> The management of any organization must continuously ask if its action, or its proposed plan, maximizes the efficient utilization of resources in meetings [sic] its goals. When a choice must be made between two or more plans, each of which possesses to the same degree the characteristics of objectivity, structuralization, and flexibility, it is apparent that another measure is needed in order to reach a decision.[103]

The "other measure" referred to by Sisk in the above comment is the criteria of economic effectiveness. The importance he attached

---

[100]Newman and Summer, The Process of Management, p. 516; with Warren, 2nd ed., 1967, p. 615.

[101]Dale, Management, 2nd ed., 1969, pp. 139-42.

[102]Ibid., 1st ed., 1965, p. 234; 2nd ed., 1969, p. 189. It should be realized that Dale is using the words "the organization" to refer to a business or other similar undertaking.

[103]Sisk, Principles of Management, p. 100. (Italics omitted.)

to this measure is reflected in his formulation of the "principle of
economic effectiveness." In it, Sisk combines the concepts of
"effectiveness" and efficiency seeming to indicate that efficiency
results from plans which are "economically effective."

> Principle of Economic Effectiveness: Economic effectiveness
> in planning results in plans that maximize achievement of
> company objectives through the most efficient utilization of
> available resources.[104]

Longenecker related efficiency to employee productivity and
inventory control. He also associated operating efficiency with
employee job attitudes and performance.[105] His discussion of these
topics established their importance for the successful operation of
an organization.

Haimann and Scott[106] and Donnelly, Gibson, and Ivancevich only
briefly discussed efficiency in their respective textbooks.[107]

An Analysis of Meaning

Initially sparked by a Henry R. Towne address in 1886,[108] the
early years of management development testify to the significance

---

[104]Ibid., p. 101.

[105]Longenecker, Principles of Management, p. 518, p. 445;
2nd ed., 1964, p. 445, p. 518.

[106]Haimann and Scott, Management in the Modern Organization,
p. 161.

[107]Donnelly, Gibson, and Ivancevich, Fundamentals of Management,
p. 29.

[108]Henry R. Towne, "The Engineer As Economist," Paper No. 207
in Transactions (American Society of Mechanical Engineers), VII
(1886), 428-32.

attached to the principle of efficiency. The role of efficiency in early management history is personified by the writings of such men as Taylor, Emerson, Robb, Cooke and Church. Its international recognition may be seen in the writings of Fayol and Sheldon.

The early management author De Haas related efficiency to national welfare. Lansburgh associated efficiency with "available energy." Representative of the widely recognized importance of efficiency, Mooney and Reiley related it to social welfare, organization structure, coordination, discipline and line-staff relationships.

Writing six years later, Gulick provided a guideline for measuring efficiency. Similar to Robb's call for the "greatest returns" resulting from "the least expenditure," Gulick called efficiency the "axiom number one," and appealed for "the least expenditure of manpower and materials" in accomplishing work.

Simon, writing in 1945, advanced a "Criterion of Efficiency." Very similar in content to the ideas of Robb and Gulick, it stressed "the largest result for the given application of resources." This same trend of thought is also apparent in later comments by Newman and Glover.

One writer, Brech, confused the term efficiency with the term "effectiveness." Using both words to mean the attainment of "optimum performance" with a "minimum use of resources or at minimum cost," he made no attempt to differentiate between them. Perhaps one of the most famous distinctions between these two items was offered by Barnard. Writing from what he called "common personal experience," he explained:

> When a specific desired end is attained we shall say
> that the action is "effective." When the unsought conse-
> quences of the action are more important than the attainment
> of the desired end and are dissatisfactory, effective action,
> we shall say, is "inefficient." When the unsought conse-
> quences are unimportant or trivial, the action is "efficient."[109]

In restating Barnard's explanation, "effectiveness" may be

defined as actual "goal attainment." However, "efficiency" is only

afforded an outcome when the favorable consequences resulting from

"goal attainment" outweigh the unfavorable consequences.

Slichter shed additional light on the meaning of efficiency

with the following comments:

> Strictly speaking, efficiency is a purely abstract and color-
> less term. It relates simply to the ratio of results achieved
> to the means used. It follows that there is no such thing as
> efficiency in general or efficiency as such--there are simply
> a multitude of particular kinds of efficiency. Actions and
> procedures which are efficient when measured with one measur-
> ing stick may be inefficient when measured with a different
> measuring stick.[110]

Efficiency as indicated by Slichter is a relative term. Its

original meaning, namely "the best ratio of effort and resources

expended to work achieved," does, however, provide a broad aim for

maximum enterprise success.

Combining the thoughts of Barnard and Slichter, it seems

evident that management, to be successful, must be interested in much

---

[109]Barnard, The Functions of the Executive, p. 19.

[110]Sumner H. Slichter, "Efficiency," Encyclopaedia of the Social
Sciences (1934), V, 437-39.

more than "goal attainment." While this is a vital part of management, only through efficient "goal attainment" is continued organizational survival guaranteed.

Following Brech, Terry dealt only indirectly with the principle of efficiency, while Koontz and O'Donnell (reminiscent of Diemer) attacked it in a very broad manner. Using the term "efficiency in the sense of the ratio of output to input," they employed the term not only in financial matters but also in "such matters as individual and group satisfaction and the contribution of the enterprise to the community."

McFarland; Albers; and Newman, Summer and Warren attached the same denotation to the principle of efficiency. Similar to the approach used by Robb, Gulick, Simon and Koontz and O'Donnell, they stressed the establishment of a favorable input-output resource relationship.

Both Dale and Sisk stated principles of efficiency. In keeping with the line of thought established by their predecessors, they also stressed the utilization of resources. In his analysis, Sisk further combined the concept of "efficiency" with "effectiveness," presenting the former as a result of the latter.

Longenecker, while not explicitly formulating a principle of efficiency, stressed its application in such areas as job attitudes and employee performance.

Table 2 presents an approximate chronological collection of statements on the principle of efficiency.

Formulation of Definition

In formulating a definition of the principle of efficiency, one theme seems most predominant in its evolutionary development. Management theorists from Robb to Koontz and O'Donnell have emphasized the importance of a favorable input-output ratio. Furthermore, they have not only stressed this point in financial matters, but also in the areas of human and material resources. With this in mind, it would then seem that an appropriate definition of the "principle of efficiency" should stress: (1) its wide applicability, and (2) a sense of resource measurement.

The Principle of Efficiency

The goals of an enterprise should be attained efficiently, providing the best ratio of resources (human, financial, material or otherwise) expended to work achieved.

TABLE 2

A COLLECTION OF STATEMENTS
ON THE PRINCIPLE OF EFFICIENCY*

Author	Statement
Emerson	"It is distinctly the business of the engineer to lessen waste . . . wastes due to inefficiency."
Robb	"To increase the efficiency of effort . . . we must know . . . what factors in a result have the greatest bearing. . . ."
Fayol	"The responsibility of general management is to conduct the enterprise towards its objective by making optimum use of available resources."
De Haas	"Ultimately every member of society suffers by inefficiency. . . ."
Diemer	"By efficiency we mean the ratio of output to intake."
Gulick	"The fundamental objective of the science of administration is the accomplishment of the work in hand with the least expenditure of manpower and materials. Efficiency is thus axiom number one in the value scale of administration."
Simon	"The criterion of efficiency dictates that choice of alternatives which produces the largest result for the given application of resources."
Brech	" . . . the attainment of efficiency and economy of operations is inherent in the essence of the management process. . . ."
Newman	" . . . the good administrator is one who enables the group to achieve its objectives with a minimum expenditure of resources and effort. . . ."

TABLE 2--Continued

Author	Statement
Glover	" Business Efficiency $\frac{\text{Input}}{\text{Output}}$ "
Koontz and O'Donnell	"An organization should attain its objectives with a minimum of unsought consequences, or costs."
McFarland	" . . . an organization's members wish to maximize the output of goods or services resulting from a given input of resources. . . ."
Albers	"The problem is . . . how a given output of goods and services can be produced with a lower input of resources. A larger output from a given input is another way of saying the same thing."
Newman, Summer and Warren	Efficiency means "to increase the ratio of output to effort expended."
Dale	An "organization should be so planned that the objective can be obtained with the lowest possible cost, which may mean either money costs or human costs, or both."
Sisk	" . . . management . . . must continuously ask if its action, or its proposed plan, maximizes the efficient utilization of resources. . . ."

*See comment at the end of Table 1, p. 70.

The Principle of Balance

Background

Much like the principle of the objective, the concept of balance made an early appearance in management literature. Over seventy years ago, Church wrote of balance:

> The object of modern administrative organization is to readjust the balance of responsibilities disturbed by the expansion of industrial operations, and to enable the central control to be restored in its essential features.[111]

A comment concerning balance may be found in one of the ten volumes of The Library of Business Practice. It advised that in a balanced organization, "neither men, money nor service has undue emphasis; no one department or method is allowed to excel or overtop others, but every part constantly learns from other lines; constantly is kept up to the mark and in proportion with all others."[112]

Another contemporary set of business volumes also stressed the significance of balance. It included balance as one of the four essentials in successful teamwork. This is evident in the following comment:

> One frequent cause of hampered production lines is the failure of an organization to meet the fourth condition of

[111]A. Hamilton Church, "The Meaning of Commercial Organization," The Engineering Magazine, XX (December, 1900), 395.

[112]Carroll D. Murphy, "The Hardest Question in Business," in The Library of Business Practice, Vol. I: Business Management (10 Vols.; Chicago: A. W. Shaw Company, 1914), p. 13.

successful teamwork. If the organization is imperfectly balanced, the production of the whole will be kept down to the level of the production of the weakest department within the whole.[113]

Fayol included balance under his "principle of order." He

expressed the opinion that

Social order demands precise knowledge of the human requirements and resources of the concern and a constant balance between these requirements and resources. Now this balance is most difficult to establish and maintain and all the more difficult the bigger the business, and when it has been upset and individual interests resulted in neglect or sacrifice of the general interest, when ambition, nepotism, favouritism or merely ignorance, has multiplied positions without good reason or filled them with incompetent employees, much talent and strength of will and . . . persistence . . . are required in order to sweep away abuses and restore order.[114]

Writing three years after Fayol and relating different aspects

of production to efficiency, Estes associated balance with occupational

suitability as follows:

Balance should be the aim of every industrial organization and each position should be occupied by a person who has the requisite ability to 'fill' that position, at the same time appreciating the relationship of that position with every other position in the organization.[115]

Jones also dealt with the concept of balance. By taking an

economic viewpoint, he related balance to marginal productivity. This

---

[113]Business Training Corporation, Course in Modern Production Methods, Vol. III: Organization (6 Vols.; New York: Business Training Corporation, 1918), p. 23.

[114]Fayol, General and Industrial Management, pp. 37-38.

[115]Loring V. Estes, "Managing for Maximum Production," Industrial Management, LVII (April, 1919), Part II, 284. Serialized in six parts, March through August, 1919.

is acknowledged in the following statement:

> Balance in Development. The resources of an organization--
> its buildings, personnel, cash, invoices, etc.--will naturally
> be spread over its field operations according to the nature and
> requirements of each function, up to the point which expresses
> in each case the conception of the management as to the impor-
> tance of the function, as compared with the others. To use an
> economic phrase, doses of capital will be applied in each direc-
> tion until an equal marginal productivity is reached through-
> out. . . . As this ideal is approached, it may be said that
> "balance of plant" is achieved for the organization as a whole.[116]

Robinson discussed balance under the heading of "Departmental

Emphasis." His belief in the equality of departments is reflected in

the following remark:

> It cannot be said that one division of the business is superior
> or inferior to another, since each part is essential. The
> maintenance of balance between departments, however, requires
> the concentration of attention upon those activities which the
> type of service rendered and the particular problems faced by
> the business in question make it logical to emphasize.[117]

Robinson also related balance to efficiency. He defined

balance to mean "that coordination of parts which results in the most

efficient operation with the least strain." He further added, "to

preserve this condition, it is essential that no part be over-or-under

emphasized, and that no part be slighted because of stress upon

another."[118]

In essence, Robinson was of the opinion that

> The fundamental idea of balance is the preservation of harmony
> between all the various activities of the business. Control

---

[116]Edward D. Jones, The Administration of Industrial Enterprises
(2nd ed.; New York: Longmans, Green and Co., 1925), p. 155.

[117]Webster R. Robinson, Fundamentals of Business Organization
(New York: McGraw-Hill Book Co., 1925), p. 68.

[118]Ibid., p. 47.

accomplishes this end by eliminating the two principal causes of lack of balance, i.e., neglect of an essential part of the business, and overemphasis on some one part.[119]

Balance was discussed by Dutton, Davis, and Dennison. Dutton related balance to "economical size" and control:

The economical size will depend somewhat on what is required to make a balanced unit.[120]

Various forms of unbalance are apt to be found where the organization is too loosely controlled.[121]

Davis explicitly dealt with the topic of balance. He defined a balanced organization as:

. . . one in which the various organization units have been developed strictly in accordance with the relative importance of their contribution to the achievement of the organization's objectives.[122]

Dennison stressed the importance of enterprise balance:

Like an army a business must move in relative co-ordination. It does not do for one function to be good. It is the business of the chief executive to see that the enterprise is balanced; otherwise its flanks will be exposed with the same disastrous results as in warfare. The great thing is the simultaneous improvement of all functions. It is better that all functions should be improved 10 per cent than that one function should be improved 100 per cent.[123]

---

[119]Ibid., p. 151.

[120]Dutton, Principles of Organization, p. 150.

[121]Ibid., p. 164.

[122]Ralph C. Davis, The Principles of Business Organization and Operation (Columbus, Ohio: H. L. Hedrick, 1934), p. 40. See also: Davis, Industrial Organization and Management (New York: Harper & Brothers, 1940), p. 73; Davis, The Fundamentals of Top Management (New York: Harper & Brothers, 1951), p. 535.

[123]Dennison, quoted in Urwick, "Principles of Direction and Control," p. 174.

Dennison also related balance to the continuing need for reorganization. He stated this need well when he wrote:

A special task of continuous reorganization is to see that the units of the organization are kept in balance--that there is a reasonable apportionment of strength among its departments.[124]

The concept of balance was first stated as a principle in 1928 by Urwick. He explained the principle in the following manner:

The Principle of Balance--each portion and function of the enterprise should operate with equal effectiveness in making its allotted contribution to the total purpose set before the enterprise as a whole.[125]

Urwick has since discussed this principle several times.[126] In continuing to relate balance to effectiveness, he has remarked:

Just as the strength of a chain is the strength of its weakest link and the pace of a fleet is the pace of its slowest ship, so the efficiency of an organization is the efficiency of its least effective function. . . . Hence:

The Principle of Balance It is essential that the various units of an organization should be kept in balance.[127]

The first author in the United States to enunciate a complete statement of the principle of balance was Cornell. Writing for the Alexander Hamilton Institute, he advanced sixteen principles of

---

[124]Henry S. Dennison, Organization Engineering (New York: McGraw-Hill Book Co., Inc., 1931), p. 185.

[125]Urwick, "Principles of Direction and Control," p. 178.

[126]See: Urwick, The Meaning of Rationalisation (London: Nisbet & Co., Ltd., 1929), p. 53, p. 100; and Urwick, Organization in Business (Charlottesville, Va.: The University of Virginia Graduate School of Business Administration, 1958), pp. 15-16.

[127]Urwick, Notes on the Theory of Organization, pp. 57-58. See also: Urwick, Organization, p. 96.

management. The third was that of balance which was stated in this

manner:

> The Principle of Balance. To insure proper development
> of a business, and high efficiency and low cost in its opera-
> tion, a company must be well balanced internally. If one
> function is given attention to the detriment of other functions,
> a business soon gets out of balance.[128]

Niles commented on the principle of balance recommending that

a "well-balanced effect" exist in all organizations. He further noted:

> The organizer must know what to do and how to do it
> to achieve a well-balanced effect, and also when to go contrary
> to general rules.[129]

In a previous article, Niles had formulated a biological

analogy that reinforces this point:

> The various organs of the body are dependent upon
> each other. A weak stomach may paralyze a fine brain; a
> bad heart makes fine muscles useless. There must be balance
> in functioning.[130]

Spriegel also emphasized the importance of balance. Calling

for proper proportionment between the functions of planning, organizing

and control, Spriegel commented:

> Management at all levels requires balance. A lack of balance
> causes vibrations that magnify frictions generating excessive
> heat and resulting in decreased effectiveness and personal
> frustrations and disappointments.[131]

---

[128]Cornell, Business Organization, p. 207.

[129]Niles, "Principles or Factors in Organization," 570.

[130]Henry E. Niles, "Formal and Informal Organization in the Office," NOMA Forum, XV (December, 1939), 24.

[131]William R. Spriegel, Principles of Industrial Organization and Control, Education and Training, Unit 363 (Chicago, Illinois: Harvester Central School, International Harvester Company, n. d.), p. 2. Circa 1947.

To emphasize this point, Spriegel later offered the following example:

Balance in approach and viewpoint is highly desirable in departmental and institutional management. This characteristic is so important that for years one large company made a practice of selecting its president from various divisions of the company so that the development of the company might not become one-sided, but rather give due regard to the requirements of all the respective interests.[132]

Writing in a systems context, Argyris related balance to a steady state (dynamic equilibrium). He commented:

. . . when we begin to study an organization, its parts already exist in a <u>steady state.</u> There is a balance among its parts. The organization will strive to maintain this steady state.[133]

. . . the notion of steady state implies that the dynamic nature and position of each process will vary as is necessary to be in balance with the other processes. Each process may be described as having a certain "strength" or "power," in relation to the other processes. . . . The strength of power in each process at the point of balance among the processes is supposedly the optimum strength. In other words, when a steady state is achieved, we assume that the strength of each process is at its most favorable point. By "favorable" point we mean that point where the organizational processes are such that the best possible results are being obtained under the particular given conditions.[134]

One of the most extensive and unique treatments of balance was provided by Dimock. Devoting a whole chapter to "Balance," he considered it to be "one of the fundamental principles of

---

[132]William R. Spriegel, <u>Principles</u> <u>of</u> <u>Business</u> <u>Organization</u> (Englewood Cliffs, N. J.: Prentice-Hall, Inc., 1946), p. 64.

[133]Chris Argyris, <u>Organization</u> <u>of</u> <u>a</u> <u>Bank</u>: <u>A</u> <u>Study</u> <u>of</u> <u>the</u> <u>Nature</u> <u>of</u> <u>Organization</u> <u>and</u> <u>the</u> <u>Fusion</u> <u>Process,</u> Studies in Organizational Behavior No. 1, Labor and Management Center (New Haven, Conn.: Yale University, 1954), p. 14.

[134]<u>Ibid.</u>, p. 98.

administration, applying equally to the institution and to the

individuals who run the institution."[135]

To Dimock balance meant

. . . the presence of all factors in institutions, in internal
administration, and in the individual, which when integrated
produce health, the growth of personality, and a good life.[136]

In expanding upon his idea of balance, Dimock further

commented:

There are three principal areas of administration in
which the balance factor is important: in the institution
itself, in the integration of its parts, and in the integration of the individual administrator.[137]

"Principles of Management" Textbooks

In his 1953 book, Principles of Management, Terry explicitly

formulated a principle of balance. It reads:

Principle of Balance To insure greatest work accomplishment a proper balance among the essential components of
the entire activity is necessary.[138]

However, he discontinued mention of this principle in the succeeding

editions of his book.

In these volumes, Terry stressed two additional themes. First,

the relationship between balance and the functions of management:

When the managerial work of planning, organizing, actuating,
and controlling are performed properly and adequate consideration is given to their interrelatedness, the results should

---

[135]Marshall E. Dimock, A Philosophy of Administration (New York:
Harper & Brothers, 1958), p. 29.

[136]Ibid., p. 41.

[137]Ibid., p. 29.

[138]Terry, Principles of Management, p. 81. (Italics omitted.)

be an integrated, well-balanced composite of efforts exerted
by an informal and satisfied work group.[139]

Secondly, he warned against organizational imbalance resulting

from improper planning:

. . . it is important that a balance be maintained among the
various plans of an enterprise and that these plans be
integrated.[140]

Unlike Terry's handling of the principle of balance in the

later editions of his text, Koontz and O'Donnell did formulate a

principle of balance. They stated that "the principle of balance is

common to all areas of science and to all functions of the manager"[141]

and they presented it in the following manner:

Principle of Balance: The application of principles or techniques must be balanced in the light of the over-all effectiveness of the structure in meeting enterprise objectives.[142]

Following the lead of Koontz and O'Donnell, McFarland empha-

sized the principle of balance. He commented that "the idea of balance

applies to organization structures as well as to functions and

processes."[143] In the first edition of his text, McFarland summarized

---

[139]Ibid., 2nd ed., 1956, p. 39; 5th ed., 1968, p. 143.

[140]Ibid., 2nd ed., 1956, p. 118; 5th ed., 1958, p. 208.

[141]Koontz and O'Donnell, Principles of Management, 3rd ed., 1964,
p. 388; 4th ed., 1968, p. 427; In a modified form, 2nd ed., 1959,
p. 298.

[142]Ibid., 4th ed., 1968, p. 427; In a modified form, 2nd ed.,
1959, p. 298; 3rd ed., 1964, p. 388.

[143]McFarland, Management, p. 178; 2nd ed., 1964, p. 248.

the principle of balance as follows:

> Principle of Balance Changes in an organization structure
> should be made with full consideration given to balance, by
> avoiding over-reliance upon any single type of structure.
> Horizontal and vertical dimensions should be kept in balanced
> relationship to one another.[144]

Succeeding "principles of management" authors Newman, Summer

and Warren and Haimann related the topic of balance to the definition

and establishment of objectives. Newman, Summer, and Warren wrote:

> Keeping the emphasis on diverse objectives in balance is no
> simple task. A common difficulty is that the tangible,
> measurable ends receive undue attention.[145]

Newman, Summer and Warren also related balance to control.

Commenting that "the greatest opportunities for substantial improve-

ment in the control process lie in designing controls that will

produce balanced results,"[146] they noted:

> Typically, a manager deals with problems of control as
> separate, specific issues. . . . occasionally, however, he
> should consider all these separate controls in their totality.
> What is the combined impact of all controls at work at the
> same time?[147]

Haimann, in a similar manner, commented on objectives and

balance:

> In the process of balancing . . . objectives, the
> manager must first of all establish a proper balance between

---

[144]Ibid., 1st ed., 1958, p. 179.

[145]Newman and Summer, The Process of Management, p. 387; with
Warren, 2nd ed., 1967, p. 481.

[146]Ibid., p. 641; 2nd ed., 1967, p. 757.

[147]Ibid., pp. 639-40; 2nd ed., 1967, p. 756.

objectives to be gained in the immediate future, the next year or so, against objectives to be reached in the long range, perhaps five years hence.[148]

To this Haimann and Scott added the following related comment:

Management's real problem is not so much in selecting objectives as in deciding how to balance various ones.[149]

Dale presented balance as a part of his discussion of "classical" organization theory. Without endorsement, he reported the following interpretation of this "classical" principle:

Balance. The organization must be continually surveyed to ensure that there is reasonable balance in the size of the various departments, between standardization of procedures and flexibility, between centralization and decentralization.[150]

In the second edition of his text, Dale modified this definition slightly by re-wording its last line to read: "Between centralization and decentralization of decision making."[151]

The concept of balance was also discussed by Albers. He commented on the importance of the proper operation and composition of a balanced board of directors.[152]

---

[148]Haimann, Professional Management, p. 80; In a modified form, with Scott, 2nd ed., 1970, p. 94.

[149]Haimann and Scott, Management in the Modern Organization, p. 93.

[150]Dale, Management, p. 236.

[151]Ibid., 2nd ed., 1969, p. 190.

[152]Albers, Organized Executive Action, p. 186; 2nd ed., 1965, p. 202; 3rd ed., 1969, pp. 238-40.

"Principles of management" authors Longenecker; Sisk; and Donnelly, Gibson and Ivancevich[153] did not discuss balance in their textbooks.

An Analysis of Meaning

An appreciation and understanding of balance has been present since the beginning of the development of twentieth century management thought. While the preceding discussion indicates that many divergent approaches were used in discussing the concept of balance, the writings reviewed and their authors may be grouped into four main categories.

Category I--Balance of Departments and Their Activities. This category contains by far the largest number of writers and its explanation of balance is the most popular. Early management authors such as Robinson and Davis emphasized the necessity of developing departments in proportion to their organizational significance. Writings such as those by the Business Training Corporation and Dennison simply stressed that "a reasonable apportionment of strength" exist among all departments.

Cornell and Urwick, members of this category, were the first to state the concept of balance in the form of a principle. Both emphasized the maintenance of proper balance between the departments and activities of an organization. Urwick related balance to "effectiveness," while Cornell related it to "high efficiency and low cost."

---

[153]Longenecker, Principles of Management; Sisk, Principles of Management; Donnelly, Gibson, and Ivancevich, Fundamentals of Management.

Later authors--for example, Niles and Argyris--followed similar patterns. Niles, in a manner reminiscent of the writings of the Business Training Corporation and Dennison, endorsed the achievement of "a well-balanced effect," advising that "there must be a balance in functioning." Argyris, writing in a systems context, endorsed the existence of balance among the parts of an organization so that optimum results might be obtained.

Category II--Balance of Human Requirements and Resources. The writings of the few members in this category are largely limited to the first quarter of this century. Representatives of this group who have been discussed are Fayol and Jones. Fayol was of the opinion that "social order" demanded exact knowledge of an enterprise's human requirements and resources and thus "a constant balance between these requirements and resources." Jones felt that to achieve balance in development, the resources of a concern should be distributed throughout an organization in proportion to the importance of the organization's various functions.

Murphy is the only writer discussed whose works overlap into both Categories I and II. He emphasized the achievement of balance in relationship to both human requirements and resources, as well as, between various departments.

Category III--Balance Through the Proper Performance of the Functions of Management. With the introduction of the first principles of management textbooks, three themes became prevalent in the discussion and definitions of the principle of balance. The first of these themes emphasized the achievement of balance through the proper performance of the functions of management and through a consideration for their interrelatedness. Advanced earlier by Spriegel, this theme was re-stated by Terry.

A second theme was provided by McFarland who commented that "the idea of balance applies to organization structures as well as to functions and processes." This same theme was utilized by Dale in his interpretation of balance as a part of classical organization theory.

The third theme may be found in the writings of Koontz and O'Donnell; Newman, Summer, and Warren; and Haimann and Scott. These authors related the topic of balance to the establishment and meeting of objectives.

Category IV--Unorthodox Views. Of the writings reviewed, two stand-out as being unique. Estes, in his discussion of balance, associated this topic with occupational suitability. Believing that "balance should be the aim of every industrial organization," he also indicated an appreciation of the interrelationships existing between different positions in an organization.

Balance was interpreted in a very unorthodox manner by Dimock. By balance he meant, "the presence of all factors in institutions," in their internal administration, and in the people who run them "which when integrated produce health, the growth of personality, and a good life." No other author reviewed interpreted balance in such a broad manner.

Table 3 presents an approximate chronological collection of statements on the principle of balance.

In retrospect, it should be noted that of the four categories identified in the development of the principle of balance, the first three had the most noticeable influence upon its meaning. Important for definitional purposes, these three categories stress three related themes:

1. A maintenance of balance between departments and their activities.

2. A maintenance of a proper balance of human resources and requirements between organizational units.

3. A maintenance of balance through the proper performance of the functions of management and through a consideration of organization structure, and the establishment and meeting of objectives.

Formulation of Definition

In formulating a definition of the principle of balance, three of the four discussed categories seem to be most predominant. Within and across these three categories, three definitional themes are most identifiable.

Recent "principles of management" writers of Category III have, with little exception, not appreciated the definitional themes forwarded by early management writers of Categories I and II. In comparing the definitional themes of these early writers, the views identified in Category I have over-shadowed those of Category II.

A complete definition of the principle of balance would thus have to include the major theme advanced by those early writers of Category I and reflect in some way the diverse themes of the newer "principles of management" authors of Category III. With these points in mind, the following definition is advanced.

Principle of Balance

Managerial efficiency is increased through the relative development of the organizational units and functions of an enterprise in proportion to their importance.

TABLE 3

A COLLECTION OF STATEMENTS ON
THE PRINCIPLE OF BALANCE*

Author	Statement
Church	"The object of modern administrative organization is to readjust the balance of responsibilities disturbed by the expansion of industrial operations, and to enable the central control to be restored in its essential features."
Murphy	In a balanced organization "neither men, money, nor service has undue emphasis; no one department or method is allowed to excel or overlap others, but every part . . . constantly is kept up to the mark and in proportion with all others."
Business Training Corporation	Balanced is a "condition of successful teamwork."
Fayol	"Social order demands a precise knowledge of the human requirements and resources of the concern and a constant balance between these requirements and resources."
Estes	"Balance should be the aim of every industrial organization and each position should be occupied by a person who has the requisite ability to 'fill' that position, at the same time appreciating the relationship of that position with every other position in the organization."
E. D. Jones	"The resources of an organization . . . will naturally be spread over its field operations according to the nature and requirements of each function . . . as compared with the others."

TABLE 3--Continued

Author	Statement
Robinson	(a) "The maintenance of balance between departments . . . requires the concentration of attention upon those activities which the type of service rendered and the particular problems faced by the business in question make it logical to emphasize." (b) Balance is accomplished "by eliminating the two principal causes of lack of balance, i.e., neglect of an essential part of the business, and overemphasis on some one part."
Dennison	Balance is an organization seeing "that there is a reasonable apportionment of strength among its departments."
Urwick	" . . . each portion and function of the enterprise should operate with equal effectiveness in making its allotted contribution to the total purpose set before the enterprise as a whole."
Cornell	"To insure proper development of a business, and high efficiency and low cost in its operation, a company must be well balanced internally. If one function is given attention to the detriment of other functions, a business soon gets out of balance."
R. C. Davis	"A balanced organization may be defined as one in which the various organization units have been developed strictly in accordance with the relative importance of their contribution to the achievement of the organization's objectives."
Spriegel	"Management at all levels requires balance. A lack of balance causes vibrations that magnify frictions generating excessive heat and resulting in decreased effectiveness and personal frustrations and disappointments."
Dimock	"There are three principal areas of administration in which the balance factor is important: in the institution itself, in the integration of its parts, and in the integration of the individual administrator."

TABLE 3--Continued

Author	Statement
Terry	"To insure greatest work accomplishment a proper balance among the essential components of the entire activity is necessary."
Koontz and O'Donnell	"The application of principles or techniques must be balanced in the light of the over-all effectiveness of the structure in meeting enterprise objectives."
McFarland	"Changes in an organization structure should be made with full consideration given to balance, by avoiding over-reliance upon any single type of structure. Horizontal and vertical dimensions should be kept in balanced relationship to one another."
Newman, Summer and Warren	"Keeping the emphasis on diverse objectives in balance is no simple task. A common difficulty is that the tangible, measurable ends recieve undue attention."
Haimann	"In the processing of balancing . . . objectives, the manager must first of all establish a proper balance between objectives to be gained in the immediate future, the next year or so, against objectives to be reached in the long range, perhaps five years hence."
Dale	"The organization must be continually surveyed to ensure that there is reasonable balance in the size of the various departments, between standardization of procedures and flexibility, between centralization and decentralization of decision making."

*See comment at the end of Table 1, p. 70.

The Principle of Coordination

Background

Writing at the turn of this century, Church, a consultant and a specialist in costing systems, was one of the first authors to comment upon the importance of coordination in management. Defined, coordination means "harmonious adjustment or interaction."[154] In a 1900 article, Church advised:

> Co-ordination is the keynote of modern industry, but it is a word of which the meaning is too often ignored by would-be reformers. . . . Coordination is the very antithesis, the irreconcible opposite, of rule of thumb. . . .[155]

In two later compositions, Church made clear exactly what he meant by the word coordination. Regarding coordination as a subprinciple of the law of effort, he explained:

> By coördination is meant the prearrangement of a number of separate efforts in such a manner as to produce a definite end.[156]

> Coördination is the synthetical principle. It requires that all the divided units of effort, taken together, shall amount to the result desired exactly, i.e., without gap or overlays.[157]

---

[154]The American Heritage Dictionary of the English Language (1969), p. 293.

[155]Church, "The Meaning of Commercial Organization," 393.

[156]Church and Alford, "The Principles of Management," 858.

[157]Church, The Science and Practice of Management, p. 131.

One of the first academicians to write in the field of management was Kimball. In his pioneering textbook, Principles of Industrial Organization, he identified coordination as an independent principle of management.[158] Kimball felt that the need for coordination increased with aggregation and division of labor and commented accordingly:

It is obvious that any plan of organization to be highly effective must be definite; that is, it must define clearly every man's duties and coördinate every man's efforts toward the desired result. The duties of every man and every department should be outlined as clearly as possible and the authority and responsibility of every man definitely fixed.[159]

In 1916, Fayol considered coordination (along with planning, organizing, command, and control) to be one of the major functions of management. He defined coordination to mean the

. . . binding together, unifying and harmonizing [of] all activity and effort. . . . of a concern so as to facilitate its working, and its success.[160]

Fayol later expanded this definition in an address before the Second International Congress of Administrative Science at Brussels in 1923. He commented:

To co-ordinate is to bring harmony and equilibrium into the whole. It is to give to things and to actions their proper

---

[158]Dexter S. Kimball, Principles of Industrial Organization, Vol. I: Factory Management (6 Vols.; New York: McGraw-Hill Book Co., Inc., 1913), p. 67.

[159]Ibid., p. 76. See also: Kimball, "Economic Principles," in Management's Handbook, ed. by Leon P. Alford (New York: Ronald Press Co., 1924), p. 1212.

[160]Fayol, General and Industrial Management, p. 6, p. 103.

proportion. It is to adapt the means to the end and to unify disconnected efforts and make them homogeneous. It means establishing a close liason among services specialized as to their operations, but having the same general objective.[161]

At the same time that Fayol was writing in France, Jones was writing in the United States. He approached the principle of coordination from an economic viewpoint. He related coordination to marginal utility in the following comment:

Each agency in an organization, whether that agency be a gang in a shop, or a corps in an office, or a stand of machines adapted to a process, should be brought to such a degree of productive power as to be able to perform as much of its kind of work as the functioning of the other agencies will render necessary. The test of perfect coördination is equivalent marginal utility. The last doses of labor force, executive attention or invested capital applied to the various functions of an enterprise should bring in substantially equivalent profitable returns.[162]

Coordination was related to functionalization by Feiss. Writing in the Bulletin of the Taylor Society, he regarded coordination to be an essential outgrowth of functionalization. Feiss observed:

Just in so far as functionalization brings the necessary and effective decentralization for action, so does functionalization of itself make essential another function. Where there are separate entities of an organization, each responsible for action and results in its own line, and all aiming at

---

[161]Henri Fayol, "The Administrative Theory in the State," in Papers on the Science of Administration, ed. by Gulick and Urwick, p. 103.

[162]Jones, The Administration of Industrial Enterprises (1st ed., 1916), p. 144.

the same ultimate object, it is necessary, in order to obtain harmonious and effective action, to recognize the necessity for co-ordination, and to treat it as a distinct and basic function of the organization.[163]

Dutton associated coordination with system. Warning against "disintegration and disorder," he commented:

One great instrument of coordination is system, an orderly outline of procedure which makes it possible for perfectly effective work to be done by men who may have no comprehension of why they are doing it, and which holds the activities of all in an ordained and orderly relationship to each other.[164]

Cornell related coordination to efficiency. He stated that "organization means cooperation and coordination" and added that the two combined "make possible maximum results with a minimum of expense and effort."[165]

Urwick also advanced a statement of the principle of coordination. Obviously influenced by Fayol's "gang plank,"[166] it read:

The Principle of Co-ordination--the specialized conduct of activities necessitates arrangements for the systematic interrelating of those activities so as to secure economy of operation. Reference from one activity to another should always take the shortest possible line.[167]

---

[163]Richard A. Feiss, "Centralization of Administrative Authority, Discussion: First Session," Bulletin of the Taylor Society, VI (April, 1919), 15.

[164]Dutton, Business Organization and Management, p. 69.

[165]William B. Cornell, Industrial Organization and Management (New York: Ronald Press Co., 1928), p. 20.

[166]Fayol, General and Industrial Management, p. 35.

[167]Urwick, "Principles of Direction and Control," 178.

Urwick, who was later heavily influenced by the work of Mooney and Reiley,[168] restated this principle on numerous occasions.[169] It subsequently was stated as follows:

The Principle of Coordination The purpose of organizing per se, as distinguished from the purpose of the undertaking, is to facilitate coordination, i.e., unity of effort.[170]

Speaking before the American Management Association's "Production Executives' Series," Jones identified coordination as one of fourteen principles of management. He stated:

Principle of Coordination Definite mechanisms and routines must be provided to the end of causing all groups within an organization to function harmoniously toward the attainment of the common objective.[171]

Bangs also commented on coordination. His comments closely paralleled earlier remarks made by Kimball.

If a plan of organization is to be highly effective it must be specific and concrete, clearly defining the duties of each individual and coordinating every effort toward the ultimate

---

[168]John Child, British Management Thought, Studies in Management No. 5 (London: George Allen and Unwin, Ltd., 1969), p. 89.

[169]See: Urwick, Management of Tomorrow (London: Nisbet and Co., Ltd., 1933), p. 63; Urwick, Scientific Principles and Organization, Institute of Management Series No. 19 (New York: American Management Association, 1938), p. 8; Urwick, Notes on the Theory of Organization, p. 20.

[170]Urwick, Organization, p. 92.

[171]Jones, Theories and Types of Organization, p. 30.

objective. The duties of each executive and the functions of every department should be clearly stated in written form, with authority and responsibility definitely fixed.[172]

Onward Industry! by Mooney and Reiley was first published in 1931. Mooney and Reiley considered coordination to be the first principle of organization. They believed that coordination was the "internal" objective of organization and they felt that all other principles were contained in it. In their discussion of coordination, they explained:

. . . we mean that this term [coordination] expresses the principles of organization in toto; nothing less. This does not mean that there are no subordinated principles; it simply means that all the others are contained in this one of coordination. The others are simply the principles through which coordination operates, and thus becomes effective.[173]

To this Mooney later added:

Co-ordination, as we have noted is the determining principle of organization, the form which contains all other principles, the beginning and the end of all organized effort.[174]

Follett, writing about the same time as Mooney and Reiley, also placed the principle of coordination in high regard. An organization expert and an advocate of professionalized management, she emphasized

---

[172]John R. Bangs, Factory Management, in collaboration with Charles D. Hart, Vol. VIII: Modern Business (New York: Alexander Hamilton Institute, 1930), p. 55. Although Bangs used identical topic headings and quoted the same material as Kimball, he, for unexplained reasons, did not acknowledge this earlier source.

[173]Mooney and Reiley, Onward Industry!, p. 19.

[174]Mooney, "The Principles of Organization," p. 93. See also: Mooney, "Organizing the Small Plant," in Small Plant Management, ed. by Edward H. Hempel (New York: McGraw-Hill Book Co., Inc., for the Small Plant Committee, Management Division, American Society of Mechanical Engineers, 1950), p. 147.

the importance of complete coordination. In a lecture at the 1925

annual Conference of the Bureau of Personnel Administration, she

remarked:

> It seems to me that the first test of business administration,
> of industrial organization, should be whether you have a busi-
> ness with all its parts so coordinated, so moving together in
> their closely knit and adjusting activities, so linking, inter-
> locking, interrelating, that they make a working unit, that
> is, not a congeries of separate pieces, but what I have called
> a functional whole or integrative unity.[175]

Follett subsequently formulated the following four principles

of organization:

1. Co-ordination by direct contact of the responsible people
   concerned
2. Co-ordination in the early stages
3. Co-ordination as the reciprocal relating of all the factors
   in a situation
4. Co-ordination as a continuing process[176]

Tead included coordination among the typical tasks of an

executive.[177] In his discussion of "The Leader As Executive," Tead

stated a principle of coordination. He explained it by writing:

---

[175]Mary Parker Follett, "Business As an Integrative Unity," in
Scientific Foundations of Business Administration, ed. by Henry C.
Metcalf (Baltimore: Williams and Wilkins Co., 1926), p. 150. See
also: Follett, "The Illusion of Final Authority," Bulletin of the
Taylor Society, XI (December, 1926), 245; Follett, "The Meaning of
Responsibility in Business Management," in Business Management As a
Profession, ed. by Metcalf (Chicago: A. W. Shaw Co., 1927), p. 331;
Follett, "Co-ordination," in Freedom and Co-ordination, ed. by Lyndall
F. Urwick (London: Management Publication Trust, Ltd., 1949), p. 61.

[176]Mary Parker Follett, "Individualism in a Planned Society,"
in Dynamic Administration--The Collected Papers of Mary Parker Follett,
ed. by Metcalf and Urwick (New York: Harper & Brothers, Inc., 1942),
p. 297.

[177]Ordway Tead, The Art of Leadership (New York: Whittlesey
House, McGraw-Hill Book Co., Inc., 1935), pp. 14-15.

In general the principle underlying success at the
coordinative task has been found to be that every special and
different point of view in the group effected by major executive decisions should be fully represented by its own exponents
when decisions are being reached.[178]

In succeeding textbooks, Tead clarified his meaning of coordi-

nation. Designating it as a function, he defined coordination as

--the work of assuring that production, sales, finance,
personnel, as well as the lesser functional activities are
interpreted and interrelated, in terms of both appropriate
structure and attitudes, in order to achieve most smoothly
the desired end result.[179]

--the orderly synchronization of efforts of the subordinates
to provide the proper amount, timing, and quality of execution, so that their unified efforts lead to the stated objective, namely, the common purpose of the enterprise.[180]

Balderston, Karabasz and Brecht related coordination to "jobs

and departments." They considered coordination to be "the most funda-

mental principle" and basic to effective and harmonious operations.

They expressed these beliefs in the following comment:

Coördination is the most fundamental principle to be considered
in developing an organization. It may be thought of as the
harmonious and effective teamwork of various portions of an

---

[178]Ibid., p. 118.

[179]Ordway Tead, The Art of Administration (New York: McGraw-Hill
Book Co., Inc., 1951), p. 102. See also: chap. xii, "Administration
for Coordination," pp. 179-94.

[180]Ordway Tead, Administration: Its Purpose and Performance
(New York: Harper & Brothers, 1959), p. 36.

of an enterprise so that work which must receive the attention
of numerous departments and individuals may be properly synchronized. The act of coördinating implies the harmonizing of
divergent interests and points of view, and is somewhat analogous to the frictionless meshing of gears.[181]

Davis presented coordination as an important part of planning.
In explaining the meaning of coordination, he remarked:

Coordination may be defined as the correlation of
functions with one another, from the standpoint of time and
order of performance. Its purpose is the maximum cumulation
of efforts and results leading to maximum accomplishment.[182]

In 1957, Davis identified "thought" and "action" as the two

main phases of coordination and he consequently modified its defini-

tion as follows:

Coördination: The development and maintenance of a proper
relation of activities, either mental or physical.[183]

As a member of the 1936 President's Committee on Administrative

Management, Gulick commented on the importance of coordination.

Gulick, who considered coordination to be "the major purpose of organ-

ization,"[184] advised that:

---

[181]C. Canby Balderston, Victor S. Karabasz, and Robert P. Brecht,
Management of an Enterprise (New York: Prentice-Hall, Inc., 1935), p.
406.

[182]Davis, The Principles of Business Organization and Operation,
p. 67.

[183]Davis, Industrial Organization and Management (3rd ed., 1957),
pp. 924-25 and p. 125. See also: Davis, The Fundamentals of Top
Management, p. 405, p. 634.

[184]Luther H. Gulick, "Notes on the Theory of Organization," in
Papers on the Science of Administration, ed. by Gulick and Urwick, p.
33. See also: Gulick, "Principles of Administration," National
Municipal Review, XIV (July, 1925), pp. 400-03.

Co-ordination is not something that develops by accident. It must be won by intelligent, vigorous, persistent and organized effort.[185]

Gulick, discussing the work of the chief executive, identified coordination as one of the seven functional elements of management. He coined the famous nonce word, POSDCORB, from the initial letters of the following managerial functions: (1) planning, (2) organizing, (3) staffing, (4) directing, (5) co-ordinating, (6) reporting and (7) budgeting. His entry for coordination reads:

Co-ordinating, that is the all important duty of interrelating the various parts of the work.[186]

Barnard considered coordination to be "the creative side of organization" and he equated its quality with organization survival. Barnard further felt that coordination was indispensable to cooperation and accordingly commented:

The securing of the appropriate combination of the elements of the organization to produce utilities is the basis for the endurance of coöperative systems.[187]

White used an analogy to compare the coordination of an organization as a "complex organism" to that of a machine. As a student of public administration, he commented:

In any complex organism the parts have to work in coordination with each other in order to produce useful results. In a mechanical device, the machine stalls if

---

[185]Ibid., p. 6.

[186]Ibid., p. 13.

[187]Barnard, The Functions of the Executive, p. 256.

its parts do not gear together; in an organism the consequence
of imperfect coordination is reduced efficiency.[188]

Further elaborating, White defined coordination as

. . . the adjustment of the functions of the parts to each
other, and of the movement and operation of parts in time
so that each can make its maximum contribution to the
product of the whole.[189]

Influenced by the ideas of Urwick,[190] Alford presented a
statement of the principle of coordination in 1940. Emphasizing the
close relationship between efficiency and coordination, it reads:

Principle of Coordination: The smooth, frictionless,
effective attainment of the objective of an organization is
secured through the coordination of all activities performed.[191]

Appearing in the December, 1940 issue of The American Political Science Review, "An Approach to a Science of Administration" by
Stene was as its title indicates, an attempt to aid in the development of a science of administration. Stene, strongly influenced by

---

[188]Leonard D. White, Introduction to the Study of Public Administration (Rev. ed.; New York: Macmillan Co., 1939), p. 46.

[189]Ibid., p. 46.

[190]William J. Jaffe, L. P. Alford and the Evolution of Modern
Industrial Management (New York: New York University Press, 1957),
p. 313.

[191]Leon P. Alford, Principles of Industrial Management for
Engineers (New York: Ronald Press Co., 1940), p. 169; (Italics
omitted.) Alford and John R. Bangs, eds., Production Handbook (New
York: Ronald Press Co., 1944), p. 1386.

Mooney and Reiley, was of the opinion "that all . . . phenomena which serve to promote attainment of organizational objectives operate through coördination."[192]   In his analysis, he developed three axioms and five supporting propositions. The first axiom that Stene advanced was the principle of coordination:

> Axiom I: The degree to which any given organization approaches the full realization of its objectives tends to vary directly with the coördination of individual efforts within the organization.[193]

In 1941, Petersen and Plowman associated coordination with leadership. Defining coordination as "to regulate and combine so as to produce harmonious results,"[194] Petersen and Plowman extended the view that coordination

> . . . is based on the just adaptation of all parts of the whole, and the proportioning of each part to all others for the purpose of securing agreement in action. . . . [it] is signified by concurrence in purpose and performance resulting in successful harmonious action toward a common objective.[195]

One year later than Petersen and Plowman, Niles also discussed coordination. Naming coordination a principle of management, Niles linked it with organizational size and complexity, Niles used

---

[192]Edwin O. Stene, "An Approach to a Science of Administration," The American Political Science Review, XXXIV (December, 1940), 1129.

[193]Ibid., p. 1128.

[194]Elmore Petersen and E. Grosvenor Plowman, Business Organization and Management (Chicago: Richard D. Irwin, Inc., 1941), p. 57, p. 62.

[195]Ibid., p. 57.

coordination to

> . . . mean the orderly arrangement of the group efforts to
> provide unity of action in pursuit of a common purpose.[196]

Spriegel connected coordination with organization. Calling
coordination "a common principle in all organizations," Spriegel
defined it as "the process of tying the various activities of a company
together so that they will synchronize as to time, place, and objective."[197]

First writing in 1946, Brech identified co-ordination as a key
element of management. He later associated coordination with both
balance and unification.[198] Brech used coordination to mean:

> Co-ordination: balancing and keeping together the
> team, by ensuring a suitable allocation of tasks to the
> various members, and seeing that the tasks are performed
> with due harmony, among the members themselves.[199]

In his 1951 book, Administrative Action, Newman devoted an
entire chapter (14 pages) to the topic of coordination. He described
a coordinated operation as

> . . . one in which the activities of the employees are harmo-
> nious, dovetailed, and integrated toward a common objective.[200]

---

[196]Niles, "Principles or Factors in Organization," 575.

[197]Spriegel, Principles of Business Organization and Operation,
(2nd ed., 1952), p. 40.

[198]Brech, Management, 1st ed., 1946, p. 57; 3rd ed., 1953, p. 59.

[199]Ibid., p. 59.

[200]Newman, Administrative Action, p. 390.

In defining what coordination deals with, Newman commented: "Coordination deals with synchronizing and unifying the actions of a group of people."[201] He further added:

> [It] is concerned with harmonious and unified action directed toward a common objective. It is not a separate activity, but a condition that should permeate all phases of administration.[202]

"Principles of Management" Textbooks

In a manner similar to Newman's, Terry also devoted an entire chapter to the subject of coordination. Terry defined coordination as:

> . . . the orderly synchronization of efforts to provide the proper amount, timing, and directing of execution resulting in harmonious and unified actions to a stated objective.[203]

He stated the following principle:

> Principle of Co-ordination Co-ordination helps maximize the achievement of a group by means of obtaining a balance among, and a smooth blending of, the essential component activities, encouraging the group's participation in the early stages of planning, and winning acceptance of the group's goal from every member.[204]

By the time of the publication of the fifth edition of his book, Terry had discontinued mention of this principle.

---

[201]Ibid., p. 390.

[202]Ibid., p. 403.

[203]Terry, Principles of Management, p. 81; 2nd ed., 1956, p. 33. (Italics omitted.)

[204]Ibid., 1st ed., 1953, p. 84; 2nd ed., 1956, p. 39. (Italics omitted.)

Koontz and O'Donnell did not state a principle of coordination per se.[205] In regard to this, they later remarked:

Many analysts of managership separate coordination as an essential function of the manager. It seems more accurate, however, to regard it as the essence of managership, for the achievement of harmony of individual effort toward the accomplishment of group goals is the purpose of management.[206]

The first edition of McFarland's textbook, Management: Principles and Practices, contained a statement of the principle of coordination. However, the second and third editions did not. McFarland defined coordination as

. . . the process whereby an executive develops an orderly pattern of group effort among his subordinates, and secures unity of action in the pursuit of common purposes.[207]

The statement of the principle of coordination found in his first edition relies very heavily upon authroity, pointing out a two-fold relationship:

Principle of Coordination Coordination relates to lines of authority in two ways. First, coordination tends to require clear lines of authority and a minimum of overlapping authority in the units coordinated. Second, where overlapping authority is desirable, coordination is required to minimize undesirable effects which might otherwise ensue.[208]

---

[205]It should be noted that Koontz and O'Donnell, in their first edition, mention coordination as a criterion in the assignment of activities to different departments. Koontz and O'Donnell, Principles of Management, pp. 130-31.

[206]Ibid., 2nd ed., 1959, p. 38; In a modified form, 3rd ed., 1964, p. 41; 4th ed., 1968, p. 50. For a similar but not identical statement, see: 1st ed., 1955, p. 37.

[207]McFarland, Management, p. 268; 2nd ed., 1964, p. 385; 3rd ed., 1970, p. 238.

[208]Ibid., 1st ed., 1958, p. 275.

Albers also discussed coordination. While he did not give a definition or principle of coordination, Albers did relate its importance to functional departmentation and the operation of committees.[209]

Authors Newman, Summer and Warren did not place as much importance upon coordination as did earlier "principles" writers. While they did associate coordination with departmentation and clear objectives, it was in a very brief manner.[210]

Haimann and Scott approached the subject of coordination in much the same way as did Koontz and O'Donnell. They used the word coordination to mean:

. . . the conscious process of assembling and synchronizing differentiated activities so that they function harmoniously in the attainment of organization objectives.[211]

In commenting upon the persuasiveness of coordination, they remarked:

Coordination is not a separate and distinct activity of management; it is a part of all the managerial functions. It transverses the entire process of management.[212]

A different view of coordination was taken by Dale. He did not agree with the contention that coordination transverses all of

---

[209]Albers, Organized Executive Action, p. 96, p. 161; 2nd ed., 1965, p. 108, p. 178; 3rd ed., 1969, p. 133, p. 215.

[210]Newman and Summer, The Process of Management, p. 33, p. 377; with Warren, 2nd ed., 1967, p. 56, p. 473.

[211]Haimann and Scott, Management in the Modern Organization p. 163. (Italics omitted.)

[212]Ibid., p. 166.

management. Instead, Dale felt that

> . . . coordination is . . . an essential part of organization
> rather than . . . a function in itself.[213]

Dale presented the following definition for the term coordination:

> Coordination Ensuring that all efforts are bent toward a
> common objective and that there is no duplication of work
> that results in wasted effort. Includes resolution of
> differences of opinion.[214]

Remaining "principles of management" authors Sisk; Longenecker;
and Donnelly, Gibson and Ivancevich either very briefly discussed
coordination or did not mention it at all. Sisk related coordination
to committees;[215] Donnelly, Gibson and Ivancevich mentioned coordination in relation to the work of Mooney and Reiley.[216] Longenecker did
not mention or discuss coordination.[217]

An Analysis of Meaning

The concept of coordination has played an important role
throughout the entire development of twentieth century management
thought. Church, in 1900, referred to it as "the keynote of modern
industry." Pioneer management textbook writer Kimball linked effective

---

[213]Dale, Management, pp. 5-6; 2nd ed., 1969, p. 6.

[214]Ibid., p. 717; 2nd ed., 1970, p. 758.

[215]Sisk, Principles of Management, p. 344.

[216]Donnelly, Gibson, and Ivancevich, Fundamentals of Management,
p. 47.

[217]Longenecker, Principles of Management.

management to the need to "coordinate every man's efforts toward the desired result."

Succeeding textbook authors Jones, Dutton and Cornell related coordination to such topics as marginal utility, system and efficiency. While the preceding discussion indicates that many divergent approaches were used in analyzing the concept of coordination, the majority of writings reviewed and their authors may be broken down into three main categories.

The authors who when taken together form the largest category are those who present coordination as a principle of management. The writings of this group stretch from the early work of Kimball to the current work of Terry.

Included in the second category are those authors who regard coordination as a function of management. Building upon the legacy of Fayol, this group is the smallest in number.

The third category is made-up of those authors who regard coordination to be the essence of managership. Like the first category, the influence of this group also has a long history.

While each of these three main categories will be discussed separately and their members identified with particular themes, this is not meant to indicate that there has not been any overlapping in their writings. It can be assumed that they were partially influenced by the writings of their forerunners and by each other.

Table 4 presents an approximate chronological collection of statements on the principle of coordination.

Category I--Coordination As a Principle. Building upon an early statement made by Kimball, this category's explanation of coordination as a principle has become the most popular. Prominent management authorities such as Urwick, T. R. Jones, Tead and Alford have explicitly stated a principle of coordination. In their statements, each has similarly stressed the belief that coordination involves harmonious and synchronized activity.

Later authors--for example, Balderston, Karabasz and Brecht; Brech; H. Niles; and Spriegel--followed this same pattern. The first two authors mentioned emphasized harmony in their definitions, while the last two wrote of synchronization and order.

Of the current "principles of management" authors, Terry and McFarland have both stated a principle of coordination. However, the definitions offered by each are to a certain extent dissimilar. Terry's definition is concerned with the synchronization of group activity to achieve a goal; McFarland's, while implying a similar idea, heavily stresses the use of authority.

Category II--Coordination As a Function. The first member of this group to be mentioned is Henri Fayol. Recognized as the first writer to divide management into functions, Fayol defined coordination to mean the "binding together, unifying and harmonizing of all activity and effort."

Later writers--Feiss and Gulick--also subscribed to the belief that coordination is a function of management. Like Fayol, they also related coordination to "harmonious and effective action." As part of

Gulick's famous nonce word, POSDCORB, coordination was defined to mean the "duty of interrelating the various parts of . . . a work."

Of the "principles of management" authors analyzed, none currently presents coordination as a function of management. In fact, Dale specifically refutes this contention by holding that while coordination is an essential part of management, it is not a function in itself.

Category III--Coordination As the Essence of Managership. Included in this group are those authors who regard coordination as the most important aspect of successful management. As early as 1900, Church referred to coordination as "the keynote of modern industry." This idea was similarly stressed by Follett and Mooney and Reiley. The former considered coordination to be "the first test of business administration," while Mooney and Reiley referred to it as "the beginning and the end of all organized effort."

Barnard and Stone also wrote of the importance of coordination. Combined, their writings associated an enterprise's effectiveness and survival to the degree of its coordination.

More recent members of this category are "principles of management" authors Koontz and O'Donnell and Haimann and Scott. Both sets of writers have advanced remarks which have placed them in this group. Koontz and O'Donnell directly stated that coordination is the "essence of managership," while Haimann and Scott referred to coordination as transversing the entire management process.

In retrospect, it should be noted that each of the three categories identified with the concept of coordination has been surprisingly consistent in the meaning it assigns to the word coordination itself. Important for definitional purposes, the statements analyzed, irrespective of category, largely stress one or more of three related themes:

1. Coordination involves harmonious and interrelated activity.

2. Coordination is designed to lead to effective action or goal attainment.

3. Coordination is of utmost importance in the operation of an enterprise.

Formulation of Definition

In formulating a definition of the principle of coordination, three categories of discussion seem to be most predominant in its evolutionary development. Within and across these categories, three definitional themes are identifiable.

The preference of considering coordination to be a principle rather than a function or the essence of management is based not only upon popularity of usage, but also upon the belief that coordination is an essential part of management, but not a function in itself.

Drawing upon the identified themes and upon the associated expertise of their advocates, it is possible to forward a definition of the principle of coordination.

Principle of Coordination

The successful attainment of enterprise goals is vitally dependent upon harmonious and interrelated organizational activity.

TABLE 4

A COLLECTION OF STATEMENTS
ON THE PRINCIPLE OF COORDINATION*

Author	Statement
Church	(a) "Co-ordination is the keynote of modern industry . . . the very antithesis, the irreconcible opposite, of rule of thumb. . . ." (b) "By coördination is meant the prearrangement of a number of separate efforts in such a manner as to produce a definite end."
Kimball	" . . . any plan of organization . . . must define clearly every man's duties and coordinate every man's efforts toward the desired result."
Fayol	"To co-ordinate is to bring harmony and equilibrium into the whole."
E. D. Jones	"The test of perfect coördination is equivalent marginal utility."
Feiss	" . . . it is necessary, in order to obtain harmonious and effective action, to recognize the necessity for co-ordination. . . ."
Urwick	" . . . the specialized conduct of activities necessitates arrangements for the systematic interrelating of those activities so as to secure economy of operation."
T. R. Jones	"Definite mechanisms and routines must be provided to the end of causing all groups within an organization to function harmoniously toward the attainment of the common objective."
Bangs	"If a plan of organization is to be highly effective it must be specific and concrete, clearly defining the duties of each individual and coördinating every effort toward the ultimate objective."
Mooney	Coordination is "the beginning and the end of all organized effort."

TABLE 4--Continued

Author	Statement
Follett	" . . . the first test of business administration . . . should be whether you have a business with all its parts . . . coordinated. . . ."
Tead	"Coordination is the orderly synchronization of efforts of the subordinates . . . so that their unified efforts lead to the stated objective. . . ."
Balderston, Karabasz and Brecht	"Coordination is the most fundamental principle to be considered in developing an organization."
R. D. Davis	Coordination is "the development and maintenance of a proper relation of activities, either mental or physical."
Gulick	"Co-ordinating . . . is that all important duty of interrelating the various parts of the work."
Barnard	Coordination is "the creative side of organization" and "the basis for the endurance of cooperative systems."
White	"In any complex organism the parts have to work in coordination with each other in order to produce useful results."
Alford	"The smooth, frictionless, effective attainment of the objectives of an organization is secured through the coordination of all activities performed."
Stene	"all . . . phenomena which serve to promote attainment of organizational objectives operate through coordination."
Petersen and Plowman	Coordination "is based on the just adaptation of all parts of the whole, and the proportioning of each part to all others for the purpose of securing agreement in action. . . ."
H. E. Niles	Coordination means "the orderly arrangement of . . . group efforts to provide unity of action in pursuit of a common purpose."

TABLE 4--Continued

Author	Statement
Spriegel	"Coordination is the process of tying the various activities of a company together so that they will synchronize as to time, place, and objective."
Brech	Coordination means "balancing and keeping together the team, by ensuring a suitable allocation of tasks to the various members, and seeing that the tasks are performed with due harmony. . . ."
Newman	" . . . coordination deals with synchronizing and unifying the actions of a group of people."
Terry	"Co-ordination is the orderly synchronization of efforts to provide the proper amount, timing, and directing of execution resulting in harmonious and unified actions to a stated objective."
Koontz and O'Donnell	Coordination is the "essence of managership."
McFarland	"Coordination is the process whereby an executive develops an orderly pattern of group effort among his subordinates, and secures unity of action in the pursuit of a common purpose."
Haimann and Scott	"Coordination is the conscious process of assemblying and synchronizing differentiated activities so that they function harmoniously in the attainment of organization objectives."
Dale	Coordination means "ensuring that all efforts are bent toward a common objective and that there is no duplication of work that results in wasted effort."

*See comment at the end of Table 1, p. 70.

Newer Principles of Planning

The methodology established in the initial chapter of the dissertation was designed to deal with the evolutionary development of management thought. Falling outside the strict design of this methodology but within the boundaries of an exploratory study, a number of newly recognized planning principles have emerged. These newer principles, which appeared with the introduction of the first principles of management textbooks, have achieved varying degrees of acceptance. The most notable and those to be discussed are: (1) primacy of planning, (2) commitment, and (3) flexibility. Each of these principles was originally formulated by Harold D. Koontz. All have experienced a measure of general acceptance within the field of management.

The Principle of Primacy of Planning

The first statement of the principle of primacy of planning made by Koontz in 1956 was part of an attempt to formulate a preliminary framework of management planning principles.[218] Koontz stressed the "unique role" played by the function of planning in initiating the management process which he identified as consisting of the planning, organizing, staffing, directing and controlling functions:

---

[218]Harold D. Koontz, "A Preliminary Statement of Principles of Planning and Control," Journal of the Academy of Management, I (April, 1958), 45-60.

The Principle of the Primacy of Planning This principle
states that planning is a primary requisite to the managerial
functions of organization, staffing, direction, and control.[219]

The most recent formulation of the principle reads:

Principle of Primacy of Planning Since managerial operations
in organizing, staffing, directing, and controlling are designed
to support the accomplishment of enterprise objectives, planning
is the primary requisite of these functions.[220]

An attempt to establish an evolutionary trend of development

leading to the sudden emergence of the principle of primacy of planning

has met with negative results. Two of the earliest statements of a

"principle of planning" demonstrate a recognition of the need for

planning **prior** to performance. However, they give no indication as to

whether or not planning was considered to be a requisite for the

execution of the other functions of management.[221] In partial expla-

nation of this fact, two points must be remembered:

1. Planning was recognized in France as a function of manage-
    ment as early as 1916;[222] however, this same idea was not
    popularly introduced in the United States until 1936.[223]

2. The functional approach to managerial analysis did not gain
    widespread popularity in this country until the early nineteen-
    fifties.[224]

---

[219]Ibid., 49.

[220]Koontz and O'Donnell, Principles of Management, 4th ed.,
1969, p. 222. For similar but not identical statements, see: 2nd ed.,
1959, p. 579; 3rd ed., 1964, p. 200.

[221]Urwick, "Principles of Direction and Control," p. 178;
Cornell, Business Organization, p. 213.

[222]Fayol, General and Industrial Management, p. 43.

[223]Gulick, "Notes on the Theory of Organization," p. 43.

[224]See, for example: Newman, Administrative Action, p. 4.

Recognition of the principle of primacy of planning did not immediately follow its 1956 formulation. To date it has still not been recognized by half of the authors of the "principles" textbooks surveyed in this analysis. This group of writers includes McFarland; Albers; Newman, Summer and Warren; Dale; and Donnelly, Gibson, and Ivancevich. Of this group, McFarland specifically questioned the validity of the principle of primacy of planning. He even went so far as to question the entire scheme of functional analysis.[225] Noting the interrelatedness of the phases of management, Newman, Summer and Warren, for reasons of "convenicence in exposition," discussed planning as the second of four functions of management.[226]

On the other hand, the principle of primacy of planning has been favorably recognized by other writers. Terry has termed planning "the first essential function to be performed by a manager"[227] and has advanced a "principle of planning" to support this belief:

> Principle of Planning To accomplish a goal most effec-
> tively, adequate planning, or mental effort, should take
> place before the doing, or physical effort.[228]

In a manner similar to Terry's, Haimann and Scott have referred to planning as the "foremost among management's five functions"[229] and

---

[225]McFarland, Management, 2nd ed., 1964, p. 73; 3rd ed., 1970, p. 137.

[226]Newman and Summer, The Process of Management, p. vi; 2nd ed., with Warren, 1967, p. vi.

[227]Terry, Principles of Management, 2nd ed., 1956, p. 22.

[228]Ibid., 5th ed., 1968, p. 161; In a modified form, 2nd ed., 1956, p. 111. (Italics omitted.)

[229]Haimann and Scott, Management in the Modern Organization, p. 91.

as a prerequisite for the intelligent performance of any other function.[230] While Haimann and Scott did not explicitly state a principle
of primacy of planning, the importance that they assigned to the
planning function is readily clear.

The primacy of planning is also discussed by Longenecker.
While acknowledging Koontz's original formulation of the primacy
principle, Longenecker provided the following explanation for this
concept:

> The idea of primacy of planning . . . stresses the fact that
> goal setting and operational planning are necessary before
> any intelligent consideration can be given to organizational
> relationships, staffing, direction, or control.[231]

Sisk is the last author in this analysis to mention the
primacy of planning. Noting the "pervasiveness" of planning, Sisk
considered it to have "a position of primacy among the management
functions."[232]

Table 5 presents an approximate chronological collection of
statements on the principle of primacy of planning.

An Analysis of Meaning and a Formulation of Definition

An analysis of the meaning associated with the principle of
primacy of planning reveals a brief history of development. In the

---

[230]Ibid., p. 111. See also: p. 18.

[231]Longenecker, Principles of Management, p. 109; 2nd ed., 1969,
p. 125.

[232]Sisk, Principles of Management, p. 84.

fifteen years since its introduction, it has met with a mixed degree of
acceptance. Of the ten books included in this study, five appear to
have given it recognition. The definitions or explanations offered
by these five have been very consistent in meaning. Each has stressed
the role of the planning function in initiating the management process.
This consistency of meaning may be due to the relatively short period
of development the principle of primacy of planning has experienced.

It is with the concepts found in this short period of development and the original Koontz statement in mind that the following
definition is offered.

Principle of Primacy of Planning

Planning is a prerequisite for the proper execution of
each of the other managerial functions.

TABLE 5

A COLLECTION OF STATEMENTS ON
THE PRINCIPLE OF PRIMACY OF PLANNING*

Author	Statement
Terry	"To accomplish a goal most effectively, adequate planning, or mental effort, should take place before the doing, or physical effort."
Koontz and O'Donnell	"Since managerial operations in organizing, staffing, directing, and controlling are designed to support the accomplishment of enterprise objectives, planning is the primary requisite of these functions."
Longenecker	"The idea of primacy of planning . . . stresses the fact that goal setting and operational planning are necessary before any intelligent consideration can be given to organizational relationships, staffing, direction, or control."
Sisk	Planning occupies "a position of primacy among the management functions."

*See comment at the end of Table 1, p. 70.

The Principle of Commitment

The commitment principle was also developed by Koontz at the same time as the principle of primacy of planning. It was designed "to answer the oft-raised question as to how far into the future plans should extend."[233] According to Koontz, the application of the commitment principle "indicates . . . that there is no uniform or arbitrary length of time into the future that a given company should plan or for which a given program or any of its parts should be planned."[234] The wording of this principle in the Koontz and O'Donnell text reads:

> The Commitment Principle Logical planning covers a period of time in the future necessary to foresee, through a series of actions, the fulfillment of commitments involved in a decision.[235]

While such topics as the continuity and stability of planning were previously discussed in management literature,[236] no record of an earlier attempt to establish a guideline for the proper length of the planning period could be traced.

---

[233]Koontz, "A Preliminary Statement of Principles of Planning and Control," 56.

[234]Ibid., 56.

[235]Koontz and O'Donnell, Principles of Management, 3rd ed., 1964, p. 202; 4th ed., 1968, p. 224; In a modified form, 2nd ed., 1959, p. 581.

[236]Urwick, "Principles of Direction and Control," p. 178; Davis, The Fundamentals of Top Management, p. 49.

Five of the ten principles of management texts used in this analysis indicate an awareness of the concept embodied in the commitment principle. Perhaps the strongest awareness was exhibited by Terry who has also stated a principle of commitment. In a manner similar to Koontz's, Terry noted that "periods of commitment vary considerably among enterprises" and "that an arbitrary universal length of time for a planning period is not feasible."[237] The following is his statement of the commitment principle:

> Principle of Commitment The time period covered by the
> planning of a program should preferably include sufficient
> time to fulfill the managerial commitment involved.[238]

Other authors who have noted the commitment principle include McFarland; Albers; and Haimann and Scott. McFarland related his discussion of commitment to decision making. He remarked that "decisions in an organization cannot be erratic, haphazard, or too unrelated to the ongoing current stream of effort," and "acquire a degree of permanence that may be described as commitment."[239]

The commitment principle was discussed only superficially by Albers who posed the following question: "How far should an organization plan into the future? A day, a week, a month, a year, a decade?"

---

[237]Terry, Principles of Management (5th ed., 1968), p. 234.

[238]Ibid., p. 234. (Italics omitted.)

[239]McFarland, Management (2nd ed., 1964), p. 163; 3rd ed., 1970, p. 78.

In response to his own question, Albers advised: "The answer depends upon the nature of the environmental and organizational forces that are involved. A planning period of less than a day may be appropriate in some situations; a decade might not be sufficient for others."[240]

In their discussion of "Planning and Commitments," Haimann and Scott acknowledged Koontz as the original source of the commitment principle. They commented that "the length of the planning cycle should be intimately connected with the commitments a firm has made."[241] In addition, they remarked that a firm's "planning period should cover at least the period for which the manager has committed the firm and that planning should encompass the time required to fulfill the commitments involved."[242]

Table 6 presents an approximate chronological collection of statements on the principle of commitment.

An Analysis of Meaning and a Formulation of Definition

An analysis of the meaning associated with the commitment principle indicates a strong consistency of meaning. Both Koontz and Terry have forwarded a principle of commitment. The commitment principle

---

[240]Albers, Organized Executive Action, p. 300; 2nd ed., 1965, p. 381; 3rd ed., 1969, p. 373.

[241]Haimann, Professional Management, p. 70; In a modified form, with Scott, 2nd ed., 1970, p. 115.

[242]Ibid., 1st ed., 1962, pp. 70-71; In a modified form, 2nd ed., 1970, p. 115.

has also been discussed by McFarland; Albers; and Haimann and Scott.
In all cases, determination of the proper length of the planning period
has been stressed. It has been the consensus of each writer that the
plans of a firm should extend through that period in time in which all
of its commitments are fulfilled.

It is with this most important point in mind that the following definition is offered.

The Principle of Commitment

The planning period of a firm should extend through that
future time in which all of its commitments will be fulfilled.

TABLE 6

A COLLECTION OF STATEMENTS ON
THE PRINCIPLE OF COMMITMENT*

Author	Statement
Terry	"The time period covered by the planning of a program should preferably include sufficient time to fulfill the managerial commitment involved."
Koontz and O'Donnell	"Logical planning covers a period of time in the future necessary to foresee, through a series of actions, the fulfillment of commitments, involved in a decision."
Haimann and Scott	A firm's "planning period should cover at least the period for which the manager has committed the firm and that planning should encompass the time required to fulfill the commitments involved."

*See comment at the end of Table 1, p. 70.

The Principle of Flexibility

Flexibility has long been recognized as a desirable characteristic of a plan. It was listed as a "broad feature of a good plan" as early as 1916 by Fayol.[243] In his 1942 study of the "elements of administration," Urwick identified flexibility as both a characteristic of a good plan and as a planning principle.[244] However, Urwick's statement of this principle reveals that it is simply a retitling of a principle previously identified as the "principle of mobility."[245] Interestingly enough, it more closely resembles a later Koontz and O'Donnell organizing principle (also referred to as the "principle of flexibility") rather than its planning counterpart of the same name.[246] In a manner similar to both Fayol's and Urwick's, Davis listed flexibility as a "general characteristic" of a good plan.[247] However, it was not until Koontz stated it as a planning principle that it became a standard part of management literature.[248]

---

[243]Fayol, General and Industrial Management, p. 45.

[244]Lyndall F. Urwick, The Elements of Administration (New York: Harper & Row, Publishers, Inc., 1943), p. 34, p. 121.

[245]Urwick, "Principles of Direction and Control," p. 178.

[246]Koontz and O'Donnell, Principles of Management (2nd ed., 1959), p. 299; 3rd ed., 1964, p. 389; 4th ed., 1965, p. 428.

[247]Davis, The Fundamentals of Top Management, p. 46.

[248]Koontz, "A Preliminary Statement of Principles of Planning and Control," 55.

While the wording of the principle of flexibility has changed
in each of the last four editions of the Koontz and O'Donnell textbook,
its conceptual content has remained basically the same. It has most
recently been expressed in the following words:

> Principle of Flexibility The more that flexibility can
> be built into plans, the less danger of losses incurred through
> unexpected events, but the cost of flexibility should be
> weighed against its advantages.[249]

Of the texts included in this analysis, that authored by Koontz
and O'Donnell is the only one to explicitly state a principle of
flexibility. All of the remaining texts surveyed, with the exception
of Dale's, associate flexibility with planning. Terry regarded flexibility to be a "major consideration" in the operation of a plan and
a "stipulation" all plans should meet.[250] McFarland acknowledged
Urwick's identification of flexibility as one criterion of a good
plan.[251] Albers,[252] and Newman, Summer and Warren[253] stressed the
importance of flexibility in adjusting plans to external conditions.

Like Fayol, Urwick, Davis, and McFarland, Haimann and Scott
identified flexibility to be a characteristic of a good plan. That is,

---

[249]Koontz and O'Donnell, Principles of Management (4th ed.,
1968), p. 224; In a modified form, 2nd ed., 1959, p. 581; 3rd ed.,
1964, p. 202.

[250]Terry, Principles of Management (5th ed., 1968), p. 165.

[251]McFarland, Management, p. 91; 2nd ed., 1964, p. 98; In a
modified form, 3rd ed., 1970, p. 156.

[252]Albers, Organized Executive Action, p. 302; 2nd ed., 1965,
p. 383; 3rd ed., 1969, p. 375.

[253]Newman and Summer, The Process of Management, p. 425; 2nd
ed., with Warren, 1967, p. 519; 3rd ed., 1972, p. 450.

a plan that "can be smoothly adjusted without delay and without serious loss of economy or effectiveness to the requirements of changing conditions."[254] Longenecker considered flexibility to be a necessity of a long-range plan.[255] Sisk even argued that flexibility is "the characteristic that contributes most to the stability and probable success of a plan. . . ."[256] Finally, Donelly, Gibson and Ivancevich linked plans to flexibility by listing it as a characteristic of effective policy-making.[257]

Table 7 presents an approximate chronological collection of statements on the principle of flexibility.

An Analysis of Meaning and a Formulation of Definition

A review of the principles of management texts included in this study indicates wide recognition of the need for flexibility in a plan. As originally stated by Koontz, the principle of flexibility stresses the establishment of a balance between the benefits and costs of a predetermined plan. Thus, acknowledging that flexibility is a desired characteristic of a good plan and that the advantages and disadvantages

---

[254]Haimann and Scott, Management in the Modern Organization, p. 117.

[255]Longenecker, Principles of Management, p. 110; 2nd ed., 1969, p. 126.

[256]Sisk, Principles of Management, p. 95.

[257]Donnelly, Gibson, and Ivancevich, Fundamentals of Management, p. 72.

of flexibility must be counterbalanced, the following definition is
offered.

Principle of Flexibility

    The more flexible a plan, the more likely it will be
able to respond to unforeseen events; however, the benefits
of flexibility must be balanced against the resulting costs.

TABLE 7

A COLLECTION OF STATEMENTS ON
THE PRINCIPLE OF FLEXIBILITY*

Author	Statement
Fayol	Flexibility is "a general feature of a good plan."
Davis	Flexibility is a "general characteristic" of a good plan.
Terry	Flexibility is a "major consideration" in the operation of a plan and a "stipulation" all plans should meet.
Koontz and O'Donnell	"The more that flexibility can be built into plans, the less danger of losses incurred through unexpected events, but the cost of flexibility should be weighed against its advantages."
McFarland	Flexibility is one criterion of an effective plan.
Sisk	Flexibility is "the characteristic that contributes most to the stability and probable success of a plan. . . ."

*See comment at the end of Table 1, p. 70.

Summary

A review of the principles associated with the function of planning reveals that the evolution of its four main underlying principles--objective, efficiency, balance, and coordination--may be traced to the first decade of this century. However, three "newer" planning principles--primacy of planning, commitment and flexibility-- have a past of less than two decades. An analysis of the definitions associated with each, particularly in regard to the older principles, discloses varying degrees of accepted meaning. The largest areas of confusion exist regarding the principle of objective (as distinguished from the principle of contribution to objective) and in clarifying the meanings associated with the terms "efficiency" and "effectiveness."

CHAPTER V

THE FUNCTION OF ORGANIZING

Introduction

The preceding chapter contained a discussion of seven basic
principles of management associated with the function of planning. This
chapter (Chapter V) will focus its attention upon some of the more
important and generally recognized principles of organizing. Many of
these principles have raised provocative issues. The meaning associated with some of them has evolved over a period of time and, as a
result, this is an area of management in which great terminological
conflict exists. The principles selected for discussion are: (1)
division of labor, (2) scalar, (3) parity of authority and responsibility, (4) span of management, and (5) unity of command.

After a brief consideration of the interrelationships among
them, the background of each principle will be reviewed. Statements
made by pioneer management writers will first receive attention.
These will then be followed by: (1) comments of later management
writers, (2) views expressed by current principles of management
authors, (3) an analysis of meaning section, and (4) a formulation of
definition.

Interrelationships

Each of the interrelationships that exist among the five principles of organizing selected naturally emerges in the normal process

of enterprise growth. The division of labor or the subdividing of
work into smaller tasks is a logical form of institutional expansion.
As a firm's business increases, work must be divided. One person's
continued performance of all a company's activities is circumscribed
by two limitations: (1) Physical limitations--the physical inability
of a single person to perform all duties, and (2) Mental limitations--
the natural knowledge boundaries of the human mind.

The scalar chain of authority is immediately derived from the
principle of division of labor. Relating to the vertical growth of an
enterprise, it automatically exists whenever an individual is made a
subordinate of a superior. The scalar chain refers to the differing
levels of authority and scales or grades of duties that exist within
an enterprise. It is a natural outcome of the granting of authority
to a superior over a subordinate. The principle of parity of authority and responsibility is a corollary to the scalar principle. It
maintains that the delegation of authority through the scalar chain,
a subsequent result of the division of labor, should be accompanied by
equal responsibility.

As the scalar principle relates to the vertical growth of an
enterprise, the span of management principle relates to its horizontal
growth. Just as the business of a firm grows to a point where it is
impossible for one person to handle all the work, some point is
reached where the manager cannot effectively supervise all the
employees assigned to him. As a result, what normally occurs is that
the original total supervisory job is split and an additional person
is hired to share in the managerial task.

The principle of unity of command acts as a limitation upon the authority implied in both the scalar principle and the span of management principle. The unity of command principle relates a single subordinate to a single superior. Its limiting influence can thus be seen in both the scalar principle and the span of management principle. The first principle indicates that there should be a single line of authority running completely through an enterprise. The latter principle implies that there is a limit to the number of subordinates a single manager can effectively supervise.

The Principle of Division of Labor

The principle of division of labor is an exceptionally old concept. Two of the earliest studies dealing with this topic were reported by Smith and Babbage. Smith analyzed and described the manufacture of pins. It is indicative of the importance that he attached to the principle of division of labor that his Wealth of Nations begins with these words:

> The greatest improvements in the productive powers of Labour, and the greater part of the skill, dexterity, and judgment with which it is anywhere directed or applied, seem to have been the effects of the division of labour.[1]

Referencing the works of Smith and Melchiore Gioja, Babbage also reported an early study that dealt with pin-making. Performed by Jean Rodolphe Perronet, this study was remarkably similar in nature to the original Smith study. In agreement with Smith concerning the

---

[1]Adam Smith, An Inquiry into the Nature and Causes of the Wealth of Nations (2 vols.; London: A. Strahan and T. Cadell, 1776), I, 5. See also: Vol. I: bk. i, chapter i-iii; bk. iii, chapter i.

importance of the division of labor, Babbage opened his chapter, "On

the Division of Labour," with the following statement:

> Perhaps the most important principle on which the econ-
> omy of a manufacture depends, is the <u>division of labour</u>
> amongst the persons who perform the work.[2]

While Smith was an economist and Babbage a mathematician, the

managerial importance attached to the principle of the division of

labor is immediately obvious from the views of a few selected writers.

They refer to the division of labor as:

> The most fundamental principle underlying all organization
> of every kind. . . .[3]
>
> Probably the most important single concept in analyzing
> organizations. . . .[4]
>
> . . . without doubt the cornerstone . . . of classical
> organization theory.[5]
>
> [one of] the most stimulating concepts for the management
> movement in the twentieth century.[6]

---

[2]Charles Babbage, <u>On the Economy of Machinery and Manufactures</u>
(Philadelphia: Carey & Lea, 1832), p. 121.

[3]Edward H. Anderson and Gustav T. Schwenning, <u>The Science of
Production Organization</u> (New York: John Wiley & Sons, Inc., 1938),
p. 203.

[4]Joseph A. Litterer, <u>The Analysis of Organizations</u> (New York:
John Wiley & Sons, Inc., 1965), p. 157.

[5]William G. Scott, <u>Organization Theory: A Behavioral Analysis
for Management</u> (Homewood, Ill.: Richard D. Irwin, Inc., 1967), p. 103.

[6]John Mee, <u>Management Thought in a Dynamic Economy</u> (New York:
New York University Press, 1963), p. 15. See also: Mee, "Management
Movement," in <u>International Handbook of Management,</u> ed. by Karl E.
Ettinger (New York: McGraw-Hill Book Co., Inc., 1965), p. 477.

Background

As early in this century as 1903, Taylor stressed the importance of the division of management work. In his endorsement of
"functional management," he advocated

. . . dividing the work of management [so] that each man
from the assistant superintendent down shall have as few
functions as possible to perform. If practicable the work
of each man in the management should be confined to the
performance of a single leading function.[7]

In 1911, Taylor expanded these thoughts to include
non-managerial work. He identified his fourth principle of scientific management as "the principle of the division of work."[8] Writing
first in The American Magazine and later in his book, The Principles
of Scientific Management, Taylor phrased this principle as follows:

There is an almost equal division of the work and the
responsibility between the management and the workman. The
management take over all work for which they are better
fitted than the workmen, while in the past almost all of
the work and the greater part of the responsibility were
thrown upon the men.[9]

In 1906, Sparling commented that "the extent to which the
principle of the division of labor can be applied to any given business will determine the efficiency of the organization."[10] Three

[7]Taylor, "Shop Management," p. 1391; Taylor, Shop Management,
p. 99.

[8]Frederick W. Taylor, "The Principles of Scientific Management," Bulletin of the Taylor Society, II (December, 1916), 18.

[9]Frederick W. Taylor, "The Gospel of Efficiency: The Principles of Scientific Management," Part I, 577; Taylor, The Principles
of Scientific Management, p. 37.

[10]Samuel E. Sparling, Introduction to Business Organization
(New York: Macmillan Co., 1906), p. 28.

years later, Mason referred to the division of labor as "the greatest factor in increasing the efficiency of labor and in lowering the cost of production . . . since the beginning of economic and industrial time."[11] In the same year, Galloway credited the division of labor with furthering "the mass production which was possible only with the advent of the machine."[12]

Robb also commented about this principle. Speaking on the topic of "Industrial Organization," Robb described division of labor as a key factor in organizational success. He remarked:

> As undertakings become more complex, the factor of division of labor, of specialization, grows in importance. We use great care in choosing men for their different duties according to their fitness, and we increase this fitness and create special skill by narrowing duties so that all attention and study and practice are confined in one direction. In division of labor, advantage is taken of a natural tendency. Men do most readily what they can do best. It increases their interest and enthusiasm and efficiency.[13]

A statement by Church and Alford in which "division of effort" is used synonymously with the phrase division of labor signifies the early wide acceptance achieved by this concept. Church and Alford dealt with the "division of effort" as a base for their principle of "economic control of effort." They remarked: "'Division of effort' is a universal principle throughout all the activities of manufacturing."[14]

---

[11]Frank R. Mason, Business Principles and Organization (Chicago: Cree Publishing Co., 1909), p. 51.

[12]Galloway, Organization and Management, p. 32.

[13]Russell Robb, "Organization As Affected by Purpose and Conditions," Stone and Webster Public Service Journal, IV (April, 1909), 231. Reprinted in Robb, Lectures on Organization, pp. 18-19.

[14]Church and Alford, "The Principles of Management," 858.

Corporate executive Enoch B. Gowin listed the division of labor as one of six advantages of organization. Considering specialization to be a result of the division of labor, he commented:

> By Organization the Division of Labor is made Possible.
> It is not alone in amount of work, merely more men; effective management also means graduation of work with a consequent graduation of men. Under such conditions, men specialize.[15]

While Gowin considered specialization to be a result of the division of labor, numerous authors of this era limited their discussions solely to the concept of specialization.

Examples of such authors and the importance they attached to specialization may easily be seen. Going referred to specialization as one of the "three great tendencies" that resulted from the replacement of the handicraft system by power and machinery.[16] Duncan considered specialization to be "one of the greatest possible aids to industrial economy."[17] Diemer and Knoeppel both advanced statements of explanation concerning the concept of specialization. Diemer referred to it as a principle of "economic necessity," while Knoeppel

---

[15]Enoch B. Gowin, The Executive and His Control of Man (New York: Macmillan Co., 1915), p. 74.

[16]Charles B. Going, Principles of Industrial Engineering (New York: McGraw-Hill Book Co., Inc., 1911), p. 19. It should be noted that not all writers shared Going's feelings. See: J. Slater Lewis, "The Mechanical and Commercial Limits of Specialisation," The Engineering Magazine, XX (Jan., 1901), 709; Charles D. Hine, "Modern Organization," The Engineering Magazine, XLII (March, 1912), Part III entitled "Over-Specialization," 869-72. Originally serialized in seven parts, XLII-XLIII (January through July, 1912) and published later in book form under the same title by Engineering Magazine Co., New York, 1912. See: pp. 47-55.

[17]John C. Duncan, The Principles of Industrial Management (New York: D. Appleton & Co., 1911), p. 74.

considered it to be a "law of organization":

> Specialization--The principle of specialization demands
> that all similar duties, handicrafts and trades be selected
> and performed by one man or group of men so far as proc-
> esses and classes of activity permit.[18]

> Specialization. Dividing work up so that a man may
> operate in limited fields rather than cover many diver-
> sified fields, in order that a few things may be done
> well rather than a large number superficially.[19]

One of the earliest writers to enunciate a list of management

principles was Fayol--he identified division of work as the first

of fourteen principles of management.[20] Distinguishing between the

two concepts, Fayol considered specialization to be a result of the

division of work and conceived of it as being rooted in nature. He

---

[18]Diemer, Factory Organization and Administration (2nd ed.;
1914), p. 24. See also: Diemer, "The Principles Underlying Good
Management," 281; Diemer, Industrial Organization and Management, p.
8. Diemer referred to specialization as one of "the two great underlying principles of modern industry."

[19]Charles E. Knoeppel, "Laws of Industrial Organization,"
Industrial Management, Part I, LVIII (October, 1919), 268. See also:
Knoeppel, "Industrial Organization As It Affects Executives and
Workers," 915.

[20]It should be noted that the J. A. Coubrough translation of
Fayol's work, Industrial and General Administration (Geneva: International Management Institute, 1930), pp. 19-20, interpreted this
principle as "division of labor" rather than "division of work."
Apparently Fayol's use of the phrase "division du travail" is the
point of variance. It may be validly translated as either "work" or
"labor." See: Fayol, "Administration Industrielle et Générale,"
Bulletin de la Société de l' Industrie Minérale," X (5th Ser.), No. 3
(1916), p. 26; or Fayol, Administration Industrielle et Générale
(Paris: Dunod Press, 1947), pp. 20-21. For an additional analysis
and translation of Fayol's work, see: Norman P. Glass, "Administration and Administrative Management: A Critique of Henri Fayol's
Administration Industrielle et Générale" (unpublished M.A. thesis,
George Washington University, 1957). Glass interpreted the phrase in
question as "division of work."

observed:

> Specialization belongs to the natural order; it is
> observable in the animal world, where the more highly
> developed the creature the more highly differentiated its
> organs. . . .
> The object of division of work is to produce more and
> better work with the same effort. . . . Division of work
> permits of reduction in the number of objects to which
> attention and effort must be directed . . . it results
> in specialization of functions and separation of powers.[21]

Like Gowin and Fayol, Kimball also distinguished between
specialization and division of labor. By division of labor he meant:

> . . . subdividing work so that each worker has but a single
> or very few manual or mental operations to perform.[22]

In contrast to this, he defined specialization to mean

> . . . the confining of human activity to a limited field.
> . . . the limitation of an enterprise to a portion of the
> field and to the production of a limited line of products.[23]

In clarification of this distinction, Kimball stated:

> . . . the term division of labor has become associated with
> the individual worker, whereas specialization is, in general,
> far reaching in its effects, and influences industrial enter-
> prises of all kinds.[24]

The division of labor was related to functionalization and
economic "comparative advantage" in the mid-1920's. Robinson gave
division of labor as one reason for functionalization while Black

---

[21]Fayol, General and Industrial Management, p. 20.

[22]Kimball, "Economic Principles," p. 1206.

[23]Kimball, Principles of Industrial Organization, p. 41.

[24]Ibid., p. 37. See also: Kimball, Plant Management, Vol.
IV: Modern Business, ed. by Joseph F. Johnson (24 vols.; New York:
Alexander Hamilton Institute, 1918), p. 11, p. 20.

considered economic "comparative advantage" to be the basis for special-

ization. They explained their respective views as follows:

> Functionalization . . . is undoubtedly the greatest factor
> in getting maximum results from division of labor. From
> the standpoint of the organization analyst, its advantages
> fall into two classes: those derived from specialization
> of effort; and those accompanying specialization of task.[25]

> Each person tends to do that work in which his ratio of
> advantage is greatest as compared with other persons, or
> his ratio of disadvantage is least, up to the point when
> his services are needed for work which he does less well,
> in order to meet the demand for this work at the prices
> that will come to prevail under such circumstances.[26]

Following this period, specialization was defined and

expressed as a principle by such writers as Alford, Jones, Cornell and

Urwick. With the exception of Urwick, the statements of each of these

authors stressed the economic advantages to be derived from

specialization:

> Law of Division of Work, or Specialization of the Job. Sub-
> dividing work so that one or a very few manual or mental
> operations can be assigned to a worker improves the quality
> and increases the quantity of output.[27]

> Principle of Specialization The functions of, or opera-
> tions performed by, any business or group within a busi-
> ness should be so separated, segregated and grouped that
> attainment of efficiency from repetitive experience may

---

[25]Robinson, Fundamentals of Business Organization, p. 43.

[26]John D. Black, Introduction to Production Economics (New York:
Henry Holt & Co., 1926), p. 137.

[27]Leon P. Alford, "Laws of Manufacturing Management," Paper No.
2014 in Transactions (American Society of Mechanical Engineers),
XLVIII (1926), p. 399. See also: Alford, Laws of Management Applied
to Manufacturing (New York: Ronald Press Co., 1928), p. 82, p. 88.
See also: Alford, ed., Cost and Production Handbook (New York:
Ronald Press Co., 1934), p. 1332; Alford, Principles of Industrial Man-
agement for Engineers, p. 53; Alford and Bangs, eds., Production
Handbook (New York: Ronald Press Co., 1944), p. 1386.

result and that full advantage may be obtained from special human aptitudes, abilities, and educational specializations, and from the intensive application of human effort to a single problem.[28]

The Principle of Specialization. Scientific distribution of work results in specialization of effort and specialization of task, with the resultant advantages derived from concentration.

Specialization of effort develops experts in any particular field of activity and greatly increases productivity, quality and accuracy, whether the work be mental or manual.[29]

The Principle of Specialization The work of every person in the organization should be confined as far as possible to the performance of a single leading function.[30]

Additional recognition of the significance of the division of labor may be found in the works of Balderston, Karabasz and Brecht; Gulick and Hopf. Observing that "the division of work into separate duties is found in all types of organization, and is centuries old," Balderston, Karabasz and Brecht declared:

If the problem of how best to accomplish the total amount of work that a company needs to have done is considered, the classic concept of the subdivision of labor is immediately encountered.[31]

Gulick, in what has become a "classic" discussion of "the reasons for and the effect of division of work," stressed the

------

[28]Jones, Theories and Types of Organizations, p. 29.

[29]Cornell, Business Organization, p. 250.

[30]Urwick, Scientific Principles and Organization, p. 8. For a reconsideration of this principle, see: Urwick, Organization, pp. 92-94.

[31]Balderston, Karabasz, and Brecht, Management of an Enterprise, p. 394.

pervasiveness of work division:

> Every large-scale or complicated enterprise requires
> many men to carry it forward. Whenever many men are thus
> working together the best results are secured when there is
> a division of work among these men. . . . it is not possible
> to determine how an activity is to be organized without,
> at the same time, considering how the work in question is to
> be divided. Work division is the foundation of organization;
> indeed, the reason for organization.[32]

In a different manner, Hopf noted the role of division of work

in organization:

> The primary step in organization is to determine and to
> establish as separate entities, the smallest number of
> dissimilar functions into which the work of an institu-
> tion may be divided.[33]

Specialization was uniquely distinguished as a "refinement" of

the principle of division of labor by Bethel, Atwater, Smith and

Stackman. In explaining the meaning of the division of labor, they

commented:

> In its simplest form, division of labor means dividing
> up the work either by the devotion of labor to particular
> activities and products, or to the minute operations
> required in the making of a single product.[34]

By the beginning of the 1950's, specialization had long

achieved the status of a principle of management. Newman commented:

---

[32]Gulick, "Notes on the Theory of Organization," p. 3.

[33]Harry A. Hopf, "Organization, Executive Capacity, and
Progress," Advanced Management Journal, XI (June, 1946), 35-36.

[34]Lawrence L. Bethel, Franklin S. Atwater, George Smith, Harvey
A. Stackman, Jr., Industrial Organization and Management (New York:
McGraw-Hill Book Co., Inc., 1945), p. 2. See also: p. 132.

"Specialization is such a widely recognized characteristic of modern enterprise that it needs little emphasis. . . ."[35] In a parallel statement, Niles remarked: "The enormous increase of specialization is an outstanding characteristic of modern business."[36]

"Principles of Management" Textbooks

Terry did not confront directly the topic of specialization. In the first edition of his book, he made no mention of it. In his second edition, he linked specialization with coordination. He explained:

> Co-ordination implies that specialization is being followed, i.e., each management member is performing his managerial work in a prescribed area which has been determined either on a functional, product or service, geographical, or physical basis.[37]

In the third and following editions of his book, Terry did not include the above statement.[38]

Koontz and O'Donnell explicitly stated a principle of division of work in each of the four editions of their book. Their discussion and definition of division of work was heavily related to the concept of departmentation. The following definition is representative of

---

[35]Newman, Administrative Action, p. 132.

[36]Mary Cushing Niles, The Essence of Management (New York: Harper & Brothers, Inc., 1958), pp. 117-18.

[37]Terry, Principles of Management (2nd ed., 1956), p. 36.

[38]Ibid. See, for example: 3rd ed., 1960, p. 105.

their earlier ideas:

> Principle of Division of Work: The structure of organ-
> ization should so divide and group the activities of the
> enterprise that they contribute most effectively and effi-
> ciently to enterprise objectives.[39]

This concept was modified in their fourth edition at which

time they differentiated between "occupational" specialization and

"organization" specialization. They remarked:

> It should be emphasized that division of work--in
> the sense of occupational specialization--is an economic
> principle and not a management principle. In other
> words, it has been found in many cases that when work is
> specialized, people learn the task more easily and
> perform it more efficiently.[40]

In the form of an explanation, Koontz and O'Donnell formulated

a new statement for the meaning they attached to the principle of

division of work. It reads:

> Given a system of tasks or activities required economically
> to attain enterprise goals, the better an organization
> structure reflects a classification of these tasks and assists
> in their coordination through creating a system of interrelated
> roles, and the more these roles are designed to fit the capa-
> bilities and motivations of people available to fill them, the
> more effective and efficient it will be.[41]

In contrast to Koontz and O'Donnell, McFarland defined special-

ization without differentiating between types of specialization. He

commented that "specialization arises out of the complexities of

---

[39]Koontz and O'Donnell, Principles of Management (2nd ed.,
1959), p. 298. For an earlier statement, see: 1st ed., 1955, p.
294. For a later statement, see: 3rd ed., 1964, p. 248.

[40]Ibid., 4th ed., 1968, p. 277.

[41]Ibid., 4th ed., 1968, p. 278.

modern business enterprise" and added that "specialization thus

pertains both to jobs or functions in a business and also to the skills

and abilities of people."[42]

Division of work and specialization were approached in yet

another manner by Albers. He related specialization to job enlarge-

ment, centralization and organization size.[43] More importantly, he

presented specialization as a corollary of the division of work. He

observed:

> Work division has its corollary in specialization.
> Work is divided; persons specialize. Individual differ-
> ences caused by heredity and environmental factors form a
> basis for both work division and specialization. Work divi-
> sion makes possible a more efficient utilization of the
> diverse capabilities available in a society. On the other
> hand, individuals tend to specialize in tasks for which they
> are best suited. Much of the specialization that exists in
> modern industrial civilization results from work division
> that takes place in organization. Men learn skills and
> acquire knowledge that will fit them into one of the niches
> made in the work division process.[44]

Authors Newman, Summer and Warren also distinguished between

division of work and specialization. Using the phrases division of

labor and division of work synonymously, they wrote:

> . . . an administrator should always at least consider a
> division of labor that permits persons to become special-
> ists in certain kinds of work.[45]

---

[42]McFarland, Management, p. 174; 2nd ed., 1964, p. 388.

[43]Albers, Organized Executive Action, p. 99, p. 145, p. 93; 2nd ed., 1965, p. 111, p. 161, p. 105; 3rd ed., 1969, p. 195, p. 135, p. 130.

[44]Ibid., p. 4n; 2nd ed., 1965, p. 5n; 3rd ed., 1969, p. 5n.

[45]Newman and Summer, The Process of Management, p. 32; with Warren, 2nd ed., 1967, p. 55.

Showing a broadness similar to that of McFarland's, they added:

> Usually we think of specialization by function. But
> we should not overlook the possibility that an employee
> may become an expert on a product or on a particular type
> of customer.[46]

In his book, Professional Management, Haimann related special-

ization to coordination in a manner similar to Terry's. Haimann

referred to specialization as "another source from which problems of

coordination stem."[47] In the second edition of his book which was

co-authored with Scott, a like pattern was again followed. Haimann

and Scott remarked: "Division of labor and coordination are the

'natural imperatives' of organization management."[48]

Haimann and Scott also separated division of labor and special-

ization as distinct phenomena. They remarked:

> Through the division of labor tasks are broken down as
> naturally as possible to allow the specialization of both
> mental and physical labor.[49]

Haimann and Scott, sounding similar to the quoted comments at the

beginning of this chapter, concluded: "The division of labor is the

reason for organization."[50]

---

[46]Ibid., p. 32; 2nd ed., 1967, p. 55.

[47]Haimann, Professional Management, p. 30.

[48]Haimann and Scott, Management in the Modern Organization,
p. 162.

[49]Ibid.

[50]Ibid., p. 163.

Longenecker associated specialization with increasing organization complexity, efficiency, and job enlargement.[51] Referring to
division of labor as a principle, Longenecker considered it a
phenomena separate from specialization. He held that "the continued
utilization of the principle of division of labor is a matter of
common knowledge" and in part that it has made possible the impressive
growth of modern industry.[52]

Specialization was treated strictly as a "traditional" management principle by Dale. After reviewing the work of Fayol, he
referred to specialization as one of the most commonly cited "classical"
principles of organization.[53] In his "classical" interpretation of
this principle, he also incorporated the concept of departmentation.
He reported (without endorsement) the following statement:

> So far as possible, the work of each person should be confined
> to a single leading function and related functions should be
> grouped under one head.[54]

Donnelly, Gibson, and Ivancevich also identified specialization
as a classical principle of organization.[55] While it is not

---

[51]Longenecker, Principles of Management, pp. 149-51; 2nd ed.,
1969, pp. 175-79.

[52]Ibid., p. 150; 2nd ed., 1969, pp. 176-77.

[53]Dale, Management, p. 197; 2nd ed., 1969, p. 170.

[54]Ibid., p. 234. For a modified statement, see: 2nd ed.,
1969, p. 188.

[55]Donnelly, Gibson, and Ivancevich, Fundamentals of Management,
p. 75.

exactly clear what relationship they expounded as existing between division of labor, division of work and specialization, they do use these words separately.[56] It does, however, seem as if the phrases division of labor and division of work are used interchangeably.

Sisk did not discuss division of labor, division of work or specialization.[57]

An Analysis of Meaning

While it is true that the principle of division of labor is a relatively old concept, it is also an extremely confusing one. As is evident from the preceding background discussion, the terms division of labor, division of work and specialization are often used both synonymously and separately, but seldom consistently. However, the writings reviewed and their authors may be broken down into three categories. This is not meant to imply that a clear-cut classification is possible. In fact, a number of the authors previously discussed overlap the categories that will be identified and thus form a bridge between groups.

The authors who fall into the first category are those who limit themselves solely to the use of the phrase "division of labor." Coined by Smith[58] and further popularized by Babbage, this phrase

---

[56]Ibid., p. 76, p. 211.

[57]Sisk, Principles of Management.

[58]Adam Smith is credited with using the phrase "division of labor" for the first time in his Lectures on Justice, Police, Revenue and Arms in a section entitled, "That Opulence Arises from the Division of Labour." Reported by a student in 1763, Edwin Cannan, ed. (Oxford, England: Clarendon Press, 1896), p. 161.

encompasses the idea of subdividing work into smaller tasks. Those writers, such as Gulick and Hopf, who make use of the variant phrase "division of work" also fall into this group.

Included in the second category are those authors who predominantly make use of the term "specialization." Of uncertain origin, this term represents a concept apart from division of labor. It incorporates the notion of an individual or organization that confines his (its) activities to a limited area thereby becoming a specialist at them. Included in this group are writers such as Going, Robb, Diemer, Jones and Urwick.

The third category is made-up of those authors who distinguish between specialization and division of labor. Although smaller in number than either of the other two groups, the writings of this group are perhaps the clearest and most complete. Representatives of this group are writers such as Gowin, Fayol, Kimball and Bethel et al.

Table 8 presents an approximate chronological collection of statements on the principles of division of work and specialization.

Category I--Division of Labor. Carrying forth the legacy of Smith and Babbage, this group of writers found its twentieth century mentor in Frederick W. Taylor. Taylor, although using the phrase division of work in place of division of labor, popularized this concept through his advocation of scientific management. Division of work was the basis for his scheme of "functional management," and in turn became his fourth principle of scientific management.

Many of Taylor's contemporaries stressed the importance of this concept. Writers such as Mason, Sparling and Galloway all wrote on the significance of the division of labor. Later authors--for example, Robinson and Balderston, Karabasz and Brecht--also used the phrase division of labor in their writings.

Following the lead of Taylor and contrary to the last set of authors mentioned, a separate group of scholars helped popularize the phrase "division of work." Notables such as Gulick and Hopf each used the wording division of work in their writings. Perhaps the most prominent authors who still exclusively cling to the phrase division of work with only a minor mention of specialization are Koontz and O'Donnell. They hold the position that "occupational specialization-- is an economic principle and not a management principle."

Category II--Specialization. The first member of this group to be mentioned is Going. He regarded specialization as one of the "three great tendencies" that resulted from the replacement of the handicraft system by power and machinery. Going's definition of specialization, however, is quite vague. It actually borders upon an explanation of the division of labor.

Robb and Diemer also advanced early but similarly vague explanations for specialization. Robb appears to use the phrases division of labor and specialization interchangeably, while Diemer actually describes more of what specialization does than what it is.

In contrast to the above authors, Knoeppel was one of the first management writers to incisively define specialization. His explanation of this concept emphasized the dividing of work "in order that a few things may be done well rather than a large number superficially." A similar line of reasoning was also advanced by Jones.

Numerous other management authors have employed the word specialization in their writings. Of those mentioned--Cornell, Newman, and Niles--all have emphasized either the essentiality or the wide acceptance of specialization.

Of the current "principles of management" authors discussed, three predominantly dealt with specialization. Terry linked specialization broadly as arising "out of the complexities of modern business enterprise." He added that "specialization thus pertains both to jobs or functions in a business and also to the skills and abilities of people." Dale offered a traditional "Tayloristic" definition of specialization incorporating the idea of the performance of a "single leading function."

Category III--Specialization and Division of Labor. Included in this group are those management authors who in their writings distinguish between specialization and division of labor. As early as 1915, Gowin presented specialization as a result of the division of labor. This same view was shared by later authors such as Fayol, Kimball and Bethel et al.

Of the current "principles of management" authors discussed, four separate specialization and division of labor in their analyses. Included in this number are Albers; Newman, Summer and Warren; Longenecker and Haimann and Scott. Perhaps the clearest distinction was offered by Albers. He presented specialization as a corollary of the division of work, contending that "work is divided; persons specialize."

The preceding analysis has attempted to establish that while often used interchangeably, a valid distinction can be and for clarity's sake must be made between division of labor and specialization.

Succeeding the work of Gowin, Fayol, and Kimball, such present-day authors as Albers; Newman and Warren; Haimann and Scott and Longenecker have all emphasized an existing difference between division of labor and specialization.

Other present-day authors such as Terry, McFarland, and Dale have only dealt with specialization while Koontz and O'Donnell restricted their discussion to the division of work.

For the purpose of further clarity and for a more complete documentation, the view of one other writer will be presented. Barnard has offered a statement of notable clarity in this area. His views, while not exactly the same as those advanced here, do closely parallel them. Barnard observed:

> Three terms are in current use to denominate the same subject: "division of labor," "specialization," "functionalization." Each of these terms implies the other at least in considerable degree, with some variations in meaning of local or personal preference. There is, however, some approach to consistency of usage in that "division of labor" seems usually to connote a general social setting and an aspect of large economic systems, whereas "functionalization" is used within large organizations with emphasis upon a particular kind of work as a function of an organic system of work; and "specialization" places the emphasis upon the person or groups of persons. Thus men specialize, but work is functionalized. In either event, there is a division of labor--and of necessity a corresponding division of work.[59]

---

[59]Barnard, The Functions of the Executive, p. 127.

Thus, Barnard distinguishes division of labor as "an aspect of large economic systems," "functionalization" as an internal phenomena; and specialization as applying to "persons or groups of persons." The influence of Barnard's thinking upon Albers can immediately be seen. Whereas Barnard commented that "men specialize, but work is functionalized," Albers paraphrased this to read: "Work is divided; persons specialize."

It should be also noted that while this analysis has been treating division of work as a variant of division of labor, Barnard appears to have distinguished between them. However, the view is advanced here that if the word "labor" is used generically (as it has been historically) to mean "all workers collectively" rather than simply "manual exertion," the two are the same.[60] Following this line of thought and in consideration of the fact that "division of labor" is the original and most popular phrase in use, it is favored over "division of work."

Formulation of Definition

The formulation of a definition of the principle of the division of labor is particularly complicated by the misuse of this concept. There is no general agreement upon its meaning, nor any general disagreement--there simply exists an area of linguistic indeterminateness.

---

[60]For a related discussion of this point, see: Max Weber, The Theory of Social and Economic Organization, trans. by A. M. Henderson and Talcott Parsons (New York: Free Press of Glencoe, 1947), p. 219. Written circa 1904-1905.

The interchangeable use of the terms division of labor and specialization has led to a classic case of "schizosemantia." Its victims most often seem unconscious of their malady. Considering these circumstances and bearing in mind the distinctions offered by Barnard, it would thus seem best to advance both a "principle of the division of labor" and a "principle of specialization."

Principle of the Division of Labor

The labor of an enterprise should be subdivided into separate tasks to allow specialization.

Principle of Specialization

The restriction of the work of each person or group of persons to one or a limited number of tasks permits specialization of knowledge and skill.

TABLE 8

A COLLECTION OF STATEMENTS ON THE PRINCIPLES
OF DIVISION OF WORK AND SPECIALIZATION*

Author	Statement
Taylor	" . . . the work of each man in the management should be confined to the performance of a single leading function."
Mason	Division of labor is "the greatest factor in increasing the efficiency of labor and in lowering the cost of production . . . since the beginning of economic and industrial time."
Sparling	" . . . the extent to which the principle of the division of labor can be applied to any given business will determine the efficiency of the organization."
Robb	"In the division of labor, advantage is taken of a natural tendency. Men do most readily what they can do best. It increases their interest and enthusiasm and efficiency."
Gowin	"It is not alone in amount of work, merely more men; effective management also means graduation of work with a consequent graduation of men. Under such conditions, men specialize."
Going	Specialization is one of the "three great tendencies" that resulted from the replacement of the handicraft system by power and machinery.
Diemer	"The principle of specialization demands that all similar duties, handicrafts and trades be selected and performed by one man or group of men so far as processes and classes of activity permit."
Duncan	Specialization means "dividing work up so that a man may operate in limited fields rather than cover many diversified fields, in order that a few things may be done well rather than a large number superficially."

TABLE 8--Continued

Author	Statement
Fayol	"The object of division of work is to produce more and better work with the same effort. . . . it results in specialization of functions and separation of powers."
Kimball	(a) Division of labor means "subdividing work so that each worker has but a single or very few manual or mental operations to perform." (b) Specialization means "the confining of human activity to a limited field."
Black	"Each person tends to do that work in which his ratio of advantage is greatest as compared with other persons, or his ratio of disadvantage is least, up to the point when his services are needed for work which he does less well, in order to meet the demand for this work at the prices that will come to prevail under such circumstances."
Alford	"Subdividing work so that one or a very few manual or mental operations can be assigned to a worker improves the quality and increases the quantity of output."
T. R. Jones	"The functions of, or operations performed by, any business or group within a business should be so separated, segregated and grouped that attainment of efficiency from repetitive experience may result and that full advantage may be obtained from special human aptitudes, abilities, and educational specializations, and from the intensive application of human effort to a single problem."
Cornell	"Specialization develops experts in any particular field of activity and greatly increases productivity, quality and accuracy, whether the work be mental or manual."
Urwick	"The work of every person in the organization should be confined as far as possible to the performance of a single leading function."

TABLE 8--Continued

Author	Statement
Balderston, Kara-basz and Brecht	"If the problem of how best to accomplish the total amount of work that a company needs to have done is considered, the classic concept of the subdivision of labor is immediately encountered."
Gulick	"Work division is the foundation of organization, indeed, the reason for organization."
Hopf	"The primary stop in organization is to determine and to establish as separate entities, the smallest number of dissimilar functions into which the work of an institution may be divided."
Bethel et al.	" . . . division of labor means dividing up the work either by the devotion of labor to particular activities and products, or to the minute operations required in the making of a single product."
Terry	Specialization involves "each management member . . . performing his managerial work in a prescribed area which has been determined either on a functional, product or service, geographical or physical basis."
Koontz and O'Donnell	"The structure of organization should so divide and group the activities of the enterprise that they contribute most effectively and efficiently to enterprise objectives."
McFarland	" . . . specialization arises out of the complex-ities of modern business enterprise" and " . . . pertains both to jobs or functions in a business and also to the skills and abilities of people."
Albers	"Work division has its corollary in specializa-tion. Work is divided; persons specialize."
Newman, Summer and Warren	" . . . an administrator should always at least consider a division of labor that permits per-sons to become specialists in certain kinds of work."

TABLE 8--Continued

Author	Statement
Haimann and Scott	(a) "Through the division of labor tasks are broken down as naturally as possible to allow the specialization of both mental and physical labor."
	(b) "The division of labor is the reason for organization."
Dale	"So far as possible, the work of each person should be confined to a single leading function and related functions should be grouped under one head."

*See comment at the end of Table 1, p. 70.

The Scalar Principle

Background

An appreciation of the scalar principle is perhaps as old as the first discussion of organization. Indications of its operation have been found in early Greek and Roman history.[61] It has provided a core for the development of both classical and modern organization theory.

Early management thought in this area was greatly influenced by the military concept of the chain-of-command. Recognizing the influence that a superior has upon a subordinate, Arthur L. Wagner, a Captain in the United States Army, stated the nature of the scalar process well in the following comment:

> . . . the proper direction of an army requires that it should be divided primarily into units small enough to be controlled by the voice, and influenced by the example of their leaders. These units are grouped into larger units, and these again into still larger ones, each group under its special commander; steps being thus formed, as it were, by which the will of the commander of the army can descend to touch the lowest soldier.[62]

Evidence of a military influence may easily be seen in the work of Mason. Mason compared industrial organization to military

---

[61]Mooney and Reiley, The Principles of Organization, pp. 57-58.

[62]Arthur L. Wagner, Organization and Tactics (New York: B. Westmann Co., 1895), p. 3.

organization. He wrote:

> The industrial army is patterned more or less after
> the military type. There are divisions of men into sep-
> arate departments. These larger units may be still further
> subdivided into smaller units, and the smaller units again
> may be marked off into "gangs." So, too, with the
> officers; there must be an executive head or president.
> Under him come superintendents, managers, foremen, and job
> bosses.[63]

Robb also directed himself to the question of the scalar prin-

ciple. He believed that certain universal principles of management

common to all organizations could be identified. In line with this,

he explained:

> As authority tapers down, it relieves from responsibility
> except in the fields for which men are fitted. It provides
> a definite court of appeal in case of difficulty, and thus
> saves endless disputes and arguments and consequent confu-
> sion. This tapering authority never leaves affairs with-
> out a head, and it assures the steady progress of the
> undertaking because it provides a properly trained supply
> of new men to fill vacated superior positions.[64]

A viewpoint partially similar to Robb's was expressed by

Emerson. Using an amusing simile, Emerson wrote:

> There is, of course, authority running from top to
> bottom, authority commensurate with responsibility,
> greater and stronger authority than that inspired by fear,
> but though the cubs obey the mother and the father, the
> organization is one of defense, of up-building.[65]

---

[63]Mason, Business Principles and Organization, p. 133.

[64]Robb, "Organization As Affected by Purpose and Conditions,"
231. Reprinted in Robb, Lectures on Organization, p. 18.

[65]Emerson, The Twelve Principles of Efficiency, p. 46.

In a discussion of the "traditional" type of management,
Gilbreth related the scalar principle to the principle of unity of
command. In doing so, she remarked:

> . . . the power of managing lies, theoretically at least,
> in the hands of one man, a capable "all-around" manager.
> The line of authority and responsibility is clear, fixed
> and single. Each man comes in direct contact with but one
> man above him. A man may or may not manage more than one
> man beneath him, but, however this may be he is managed by
> but one man above him.[66]

Perhaps the earliest use of the term scalar is found in the
work of Fayol.[67] Listing scalar chain as his nineth principle of
management, Fayol provided the following definition:

> The scalar chain is the chain of superiors ranging
> from the ultimate authority to the lowest ranks. The
> line of authority is the route followed--via every link
> in the chain--by all communications which start from or
> go to the ultimate authority.[68]

Sounding very much like Fayol, Lansburgh directed himself to
the question of "lines of supervision" (authority). He helpfully

---

[66]Lillian M. Gilbreth, The Psychology of Management (New York:
Sturgis & Walton Co., 1914), p. 8. Originally serialized in Industrial
Engineering and the Engineering Digest, XI-XIII (May, 1912 through May,
1913). See: Part I, p. 343.

[67]It should be noted that the 1930 Coubrough translation of
Fayol's work interpreted this principle as "hierarchy" rather than
"scalar chain." See: Fayol, Industrial and General Administration,
pp. 28-29. The point of variance is Fayol's use of the word "hierarchie."
See: Fayol, "Administration Industrielle et Générale," p. 45; or
Fayol, Administration Industrielle et Générale, p. 27. For an additional
translation, see: Glass, "Administration and Administrative Management." Glass interpreted the phrase in question as "scalar chain."

[68]Fayol, General and Industrial Management, p. 34.

observed:

> Definiteness of control through the establishment of
> lines of supervision implies the idea of tapering authority.
> It implies the development of a group of executives along
> this line of supervision, each one down the line having some-
> what less authority in scope, and somewhat more direction of
> detail.[69]

Reflecting a similar reasoning, but in a more explicit manner,

Jones discussed "lines of authority" as follows:

> The Lines of Authority--There will exist, in intelligent
> organizations, an unbroken line of authority from head-
> quarters down to the persons ultimately responsible for
> each act. And an equally unbroken line of responsibility
> will extend upwards in the reverse direction.[70]

The idea of the scalar principle was linked to the subject of

discipline by Robinson. As a part of his discussion on authority and

responsibility, he remarked:

> Since discipline is dependent upon authority, each of the
> heads responsible for the performance of the multitudinous
> duties of the business must be given proper authority to make
> his direction and control effective. This definitely fixed
> authority should extend from the owners of the business in a
> tapering system down to every employee of the concern, for
> the efficient performance of any task depends upon the posses-
> sion of the full authority requisite to facilitate its proper
> execution.[71]

The military background of the scalar principle was recognized

by Williams. Commenting on its development "from the military

---

[69]Lansburgh, Industrial Management, p. 41.

[70]Jones, The Administration of Industrial Enterprises (2nd ed., 1925), p. 151.

[71]Robinson, Fundamentals of Business Organization, p. 185.

experience of mankind," he explained this principle as follows:

Each member of an organization is responsible to his immediate superior. All orders must pass from superior to immediate subordinate.[72]

The management literature of the 1930's shows wide acceptance

of the importance of the scalar principle. This is particularly

evident in the writings of Mooney and Reiley who identified the scalar

process as one of the three basic principles of organization. The

following is an indication of the emphasis they placed upon this

concept:

The supreme coordinating authority must rest somewhere and in some form in every organization. . . . It is equally essential to the very idea and concept of organization that there must be a process, formal in character, through which this coordinating authority operates from the top throughout the entire structure of the organized body. This process is not an abstraction; it is a tangible reality observable in every organization. It appears in a form so distinct and characteristic that it practically names itself,--hence the term Scalar Process.[73]

Florence also showed an appreciation of the scalar principle.

Noting that "there are certain principles proper to the hierarchical

system which must be obeyed on pain of loss of efficiency and confusion

---

[72]Henry H. Williams, "The Art of Organizing," Factory and Industrial Management, LXXIX (May, 1930), 1082.

[73]Mooney and Reiley, Onward Industry!, p. 31. See also: Mooney, "The Principles of Organization," p. 94; Mooney, "Organizing the Small Plant," p. 148.

in all rule and work relations," he concluded:

> Commands should only be given to subordinates through their
> immediate superior. There should be no skipping of links in
> the chain of command.[74]

Greatly influenced by the works of Fayol and Mooney and

Reiley,[75] Urwick identified the sixth principle of management as the

scalar principle. He defined it thus:

> . . . the supreme co-ordinating authority must rest somewhere
> and in some form in every organization . . . there should be
> a process formal in character, through which this co-ordinating
> authority operates from the top throughout the entire structure
> of the organized body.[76]

Urwick has since restated this same idea referring to it as

the "principle of authority."[77] He, however, noted:

> This principle has been called "The Scalar Principle" (J. D.
> Mooney and A. C. Reiley, "Onward Industry"), "The Hierarchi-
> cal Principle" (Henri Fayol, "Administration Industrielle et
> Générale") and "The Chain of Command" (military writers,
> passim).[78]

---

[74]P. Sargant Florence, The Logic of Industrial Organisation
(London: Kegan Paul, Trench, Trubner and Co., Ltd., 1933), p. 120.
See also: Florence, "Management and the Size of Firms: A Reply,"
The Economic Journal, XLIV (December, 1934), 727.

[75]See: Urwick, "Organization As a Technical Problem," p. 51 or
"The Function of Administration," p. 49 both in Papers on the Science
of Administration, ed. by Gulick and Urwick; Urwick, The Elements of
Administration; Urwick, "Principles of Management," 43.

[76]Urwick, Management of Tomorrow, p. 63. (Italics omitted.)
See also: Urwick, Scientific Principles and Organization, p. 8.

[77]Urwick, Notes on the Theory of Organization, p. 22. See also:
Urwick, Organization in Business, p. 13. For a reconsideration of this
principle, see: Urwick, Organization, pp. 92-93.

[78]Ibid.

In a manner similar to Urwick's, Alford referred to the scalar concept as the principle of authority and identified it in the following manner:

Principle of Formal Authority. A clear line of formal authority must run from the top to the bottom of an organization for control.[79]

Reminiscent of the earlier works of Gilbreth, Jones, Fayol, and Lansburgh, Spriegel related the scalar principle to "lines of supervision." Like his predecessors, he stated:

Carefully established lines of supervision facilitate definite control of the company. In the line organization, the "scalar" principle involves the idea of tapering authority. Each executive at every level is responsible for all of the functions to be performed directly below him.[80]

Brech, also, appreciated the significance of the scalar principle. In his interpretation of the fundamentals of management, he presented the following principle:

There must be a clear line of authority running through the organisation, such that policy and instructions can be transmitted from top management to the lowest subordinate groups.[81]

Tead, a prolific writer on the topic of administration, was another commentator on the scalar principle. He wrote:

What has been called the "scalar principle" and what is here called the "hierarchical principle" is another useful concept in administration. For as soon as an organization

---

[79]Alford, Principles of Industrial Management for Engineers, p. 115. See also: Alford and Bangs, eds., Production Handbook, p. 1386.

[80]Spriegel, Principles of Business Organization (1st ed., 1946), p. 42.

[81]Brech, Management (1st ed., 1946), p. 58.

reaches a size where each major function is carried by a person who has others reporting to him as assistant heads and as operatives, a hierarchy of authority and responsibility begins to emerge. This hierarchy operates through successive levels of executives in what are known as <u>lines of authority</u>.[82]

"Principles of Management" Textbooks

Terry approached the scalar principle in a manner similar to Robinson's. He discussed the "vertical growth of organization structure,"[83] and related the scalar principle to authority by commenting:

Authority is delegated in the amount required to perform satisfactorily the assigned task. This creates a so-called "tapering concept" of authority. In going from top to bottom of an organization structure, the delegated authority becomes smaller and smaller with each successive level, thus causing a tapering characteristic.[84]

In each of the four editions of their book, Koontz and O'Donnell advanced a statement of the scalar principle. Heavily influenced by Fayol, they recognized the necessity of the scalar principle for effective decision making and communications.[85] Stated in essentially the same manner in each of their editions, perhaps Koontz and O'Donnell's clearest formulation of this principle is contained in

---

[82]Tead, <u>The Art of Administration</u>, p. 103.

[83]Terry, <u>Principles of Management</u> (2nd ed., 1956), p. 255; 5th ed., 1968, pp. 400-01.

[84]<u>Ibid</u>., 2nd ed., 1956, p. 272.

[85]Koontz and O'Donnell, <u>Principles of Management</u>, p. 295; 2nd ed., 1959, p. 88; 3rd ed., 1964, p. 63.

their fourth edition:

> The Scalar Principle The more clear the line of
> authority from the ultimate authority for management in
> an enterprise to every subordinate position, the more
> effective will be responsible decision making and organ-
> ization communication.[86]

The scalar concept was held in similar high regard by McFarland.

Referring to it as the basic component of the vertical organization

dimension, McFarland discussed scalar levels in each of the three

editions of his textbook.[87] However, he only advanced this idea as a

principle in his first edition:

> A business organization consists of levels of authority which
> are graded in a scale of decreasing importance from the chief
> executive to the workers' positions. The work to be done in
> the organization is distributed among the levels through the
> authority relationships involved.[88]

Evidence of the early military influence upon the scalar prin-

ciple is found in the work of Newman, Summer and Warren. Preferring to

use the phrase "chain of command," they related the scalar principle to

delegation:

> In any efficient administrative organization, we find
> a chief executive--commander-in-chief of an army, president
> of a corporation, executive secretary of a charitable organ-
> ization, or a top executive under some other title. . . .
> Since a chief executive cannot do all the work himself, he
> delegates large blocks of duties to his immediate subordinates.

---

[86]Ibid., 4th ed., 1968, p. 425.

[87]McFarland, Management, p. 165; 2nd ed., 1964, pp. 240-42;
3rd ed., 1970, pp. 340-41.

[88]Ibid., 1st ed., 1958, p. 165.

Each of these men, in turn, redelegates to his subordinates,
and the process of delegating and redelegating continues
until all the work . . . is assigned. . . . Each time an
executive delegates work, he forges a new link in the chain
of command.[89]

The scalar principle was also associated with delegation by

Haimann and Scott. They referred to the scalar principle as being

"of utmost importance to every manager" and explained that it is under-

stood to mean "the grading of duties not according to different func-

tions, but according to the amount of authority and corresponding

responsibility."[90] In an effort to define the scalar principle, the

following definition was offered:

The scalar principle states that within an organization there
is a line of superior-subordinate relationship which runs
from the top of the organization down to the bottom.[91]

One of the more extensive discussions of the scalar principle

included in the "principles of management" textbooks reviewed is that

offered by Longenecker. Reflecting a military flavor similar to that

which influenced Newman, Summer and Warren, Longenecker identified

authority, responsibility, and communication as three distinguishable

characteristics of the "chain of command." In explaining the "chain of

---

[89]Newman and Summer, The Process of Management, p. 59; with
Warren, 2nd ed., 1967, pp. 83-84.

[90]Haimann and Scott, Management in the Modern Organization, p.
23. See also: Haimann, Professional Management, p. 3.

[91]Ibid., 1st ed., 1962, p. 194; 2nd ed., 1970, p. 207.

command," Longenecker wrote:

> In its simplest form, a chain of command is the rela-
> tionship between a superior and subordinate. Starting at
> the top with the chief executive, we may visualize a series
> of lines connecting him with his subordinates. These
> subordinate managers, in turn, are connected with their
> subordinates. . . . The total network of relationships
> constitutes the organization's chain (or, more technically,
> chains) of command.[92]

Influenced by Urwick,[93] Dale stated the scalar concept as the

principle of authority. Referring to it as a "classical" principle

of organization, he reported (without endorsement) the following

"classical" interpretation:

> The organization must have a supreme authority, and a clear
> line of authority should run from that person (or group) to
> every individual in the organization, a principle sometimes
> known as the scalar principle and sometimes the chain of
> command. The scalar hierarchy or the chain of command, is
> of course, one method of providing coordination.[94]

Sisk used the phrase "chain of command" to refer to the scalar

principle. Noting that "it is a command relationship extending from

the top of the organization to the lowest echelon,"[95] he provided the

following explanation:

> [A] . . . military phrase, chain of command, is used to
> describe the means of transmitting the president's author-
> ity so that ultimately production employees produce the

---

[92]Longenecker, Principles of Management, p. 166; 2nd ed., 1969, p. 194.

[93]Dale does not acknowledge this influence, but it is evident by comparing his discussion with: Urwick, Notes on the Theory of Organization, pp. 18-22.

[94]Dale, Management, p. 234. For a similar but not identical statement, see: 2nd ed., 1969, p. 189.

[95]Sisk, Principles of Management, p. 295.

desired work. Authority is transmitted through a chain of command, the successive levels of management, between the president and the production worker.[96]

The scalar principle was viewed by Donnelly, Gibson and Ivancevich "as a series of superior-subordinate relationships" that run from the top of an organization to its lowest level. They also indicated that this series of relationships must be accompanied by an "unbroken chain of command."[97] Donnelly, Gibson and Ivancevich formally defined the scalar chain as follows:

> Scalar Chain. The graded chain of authority through which all communications flow.[98]

An Analysis of Meaning

In retrospect it may be seen that in its development the scalar principle has experienced a pattern of continual acceptance. Emerging in a definite form from early military writings, the importance of the scalar principle was quickly appreciated by pioneer management theorists. Mason and Robb emphasized the importance of authority "tapering down" in an organization. Scholars such as Emerson, Gilbreth, and Jones wrote about the necessity of "lines of authority" flowing from the top to the bottom of an enterprise.

The first formulation of the scalar concept as a principle was made by Fayol. His definition of this concept stressed the existence

---

[96]Ibid., p. 242.

[97]Donnelly, Gibson, and Ivancevich, Fundamentals of Management, pp. 85-86.

[98]Ibid., p. 420.

of a chain of authority flowing from the highest to the lowest ranks
of an organization. A similar pattern was emphasized by Fayol's
successors, Lansburgh and Robinson. They each wrote of "tapering
authority" in their explanations of the scalar concept.

With the 1931 publication of Mooney and Reiley's Onward
Industry!, the scalar principle received its widest and most publi-
cized recognition. Mooney and Reiley presented the scalar principle
as one of the three basic principles of organization and believed it
to be essential to the concept of organization.

After the first edition of Mooney and Reiley's Onward Industry!
and its two revisions in 1939 and 1947,[99] the influence of their
ideas spread rapidly. The effect of these ideas may be seen in the
work of writers such as Urwick and Alford. While both men referred to
the scalar concept as the "principle of authority," each made note of
the term scalar principle. Much like those of earlier writers, their
definitions of this concept centered around the "line of authority"
theme.

Management literature of the 1940's which dealt with the scalar
principle can largely be classified as integrative. It was integrative
in the sense that discussion of the scalar principle reached a point of
fixed understanding and its successive treatments merely took the form

---

[99]At the time of its second edition, Onward Industry! was
re-entitled, The Principles of Organization. Its third edition was
authored singularly by Mooney.

of restatements or rewordings. The works of Spriegel, Brech and Tead, each of whom stressed "lines of supervision/authority" or tapering "authority," offer examples of this period.

With the introduction of "principles of management" books in the early nineteen-fifties, the scalar principle became more firmly entrenched in management theory than ever before. The ideas of "tapering authority" and "lines of supervision/authority" continued to form a center of emphasis for its discussion.

Terry wrote explicitly of "tapering authority." Koontz and O'Donnell utilized the "line of authority" theme in defining the scalar principle. McFarland wrote of "levels of authority which are graded in a scale of decreasing importance from the chief executive to the workers' positions."

In a manner similar to Koontz and O'Donnell's and McFarland's, Dale also made use of the "line of authority" theme in his explanation of the scalar concept. The remaining "principles of management" authors--Newman, Summer, and Warren; Haimann and Scott; Longenecker; Sisk; and Donnelly, Gibson and Ivancevich--all employed a variant of the "tapering authority" theme. In their writings, each made use of the phrase (or a form of the phrase) "chain of command."

Newman, Summer and Warren associated the scalar principle with delegation and remarked: "Each time an executive delegates work, he forges a new link in the chain of command." Haimann and Scott commented: "There must be a chain of direct authority relationships from superior to subordinate throughout the entire organization."

Longenecker followed the same vein of thought, declaring:
" . . . a chain of command is the relationship between a superior and
a subordinate. . . . The total network of relationships constitutes
the organization's chain . . . of command." In a like manner,
Donnelly, Gibson and Ivancevich remarked that all superior-subordinate
relationships must be accompanied by an "unbroken chain of command."

Lastly, Sisk saw the chain of command as "a command relationship extending from the top of the organization to the lowest
echelon. . . ."

In reviewing the history of the development of the scalar principle, a number of points immediately stand out. First, as is true of
the principle of division of labor, the scalar principle, being
borrowed from military organization, made an early appearance in management literature. Second, with only minor exception, the scalar
principle achieved a stage of relative fixed understanding by the late
nineteen-thirties. At that time, it entered an "integrative" period
that stressed its two historically established themes: (1) tapering
authority, and (2) lines of authority from the top to the bottom of
the organization. Third, the limited semantical confusion that has
been associated with the scalar principle has been largely in connection with the terms "principle of authority" and "chain of command."
However, the majority of authors that have employed the term "chain of
command" have done so in the form of a definitional synonym, thereby
eliminating much unnecessary babel.

In regard to the three authors who were reported as using
"principle of authority" in place of scalar principle (Urwick, Alford,

and Dale), each more than fully recognized the alternate dual phraseology. Because these writers are in the minority and because it is
felt that the term scalar principle is more accepted and more
descriptive of the concept involved, it is considered to be a preferred
expression.

Table 9 presents an approximate chronological collection of
statements on the scalar principle.

Formulation of Definition

The formulation of a definition of the scalar principle is in
part simplified by the unusual stability of meaning it has achieved
over the past four decades. Of the definitions analyzed, the
"tapering authority" and "lines of authority" themes are most prominent.
It is with this in mind and in recognition of the wide acceptance the
term scalar has enjoyed that the following definition is offered.

The Scalar Principle

Within every enterprise there should exist a clear line
of tapering authority (a chain of command) from the top of
the enterprise to its lowest level.

TABLE 9

A COLLECTION OF STATEMENTS ON
THE SCALAR PRINCIPLE*

Author	Statement
Wagner	"There is a limit . . . to the size of the command that can be controlled by one man . . . units are grouped into larger units, and these again into still larger ones, each group under its special commander; steps being thus formed . . . by which the will of the commander . . . can descend to touch the lowest soldier."
Mason	"The industrial army is patterned more or less after the military type. There are divisions of men into separate departments. These larger units may be still further subdivided into smaller units, and the smaller units again may be marked off into 'gangs'."
Robb	"As authority tapers down, it . . . never leaves affairs without a head and it assures the steady progress of the undertaking. . . ."
Emerson	"There is . . . authority running from top to bottom . . . greater and stronger authority than that inspired by fear . . . the organization is one of defense, of up-building."
L. Gilbreth	"The line of authority and responsibility is clear, fixed and single. Each man comes in direct contact with but one man above him. A man may or may not manage more than one man beneath him, but, however, this may be he is managed by but one man above him."
E. D. Jones	"There will exist, in intelligent organizations, an unbroken line of authority from headquarters down to the person ultimately responsible for each act."
Fayol	"The scalar chain is the chain of superiors ranging from the ultimate authority to the lowest ranks."

TABLE 9--Continued

Author	Statement
Lansburgh	" . . . lines of supervision implies the idea of tapering authority. . . . of a group of executives . . . each one down the line having somewhat less authority in scope. . . ."
Robinson	" . . . fixed authority should extend from the owners of the business in a tapering system down to every employee of the concern. . . ."
Williams	"Each member of an organization is responsible to his immediate superior. All orders must pass from superior to immediate subordinate."
Mooney and Reiley	"The supreme coordinating authority must rest somewhere and in some form in every organiza- tion. . . . It is equally essential . . . that there must be a process . . . through which this coordinating authority operates from the top throughout the entire structure of the organized body."
Florence	"Commands should only be given to subordinates through their immediate superior. There is no skipping of links in the chain of command."
Urwick	" . . . the supreme co-ordinating authority . . . operates from the top throughout the entire structure of the organized body."
Alford	"A clear line of formal authority must run from the top to the bottom of an organization for control."
Spriegel	" . . . the 'scalar' principle involves the idea of tapering authority. Each executive at every level is responsible for all the functions to be performed directly below him."
Brech	"There must be a clear line of authority running through the organisation, such that policy and instructions can be transmitted from top man- agement to the lowest subordinate groups."

TABLE 9--Continued

Author	Statement
Tead	" . . . as soon as an organization reaches a size where each major function is carried by a person who has others reporting to him as assistant heads and as operatives, a hierarchy of authority and responsibility begins to emerge."
Terry	"Authority is delegated. . . . This creates a so-called 'tapering concept' of authority. In going from top to bottom of an organization structure, the delegated authority becomes smaller and smaller with each successive level, thus causing a tapering characteristic."
Koontz and O'Donnell	"The more clear the line of authority from the ultimate authority for management in an organization enterprise to every subordinate position, the more effective will be responsible decision making and organization communication."
McFarland	"A business organization consists of levels of authority which are graded in a scale of decreasing importance from the chief executive to the workers' positions."
Newman, Summer and Warren	"Each time an executive delegates work, he forges a new link in the chain of command."
Haimann and Scott	"The scalar principle states that within an organization there is a line of superior-subordinate relationships which runs from the top of the organization down to the bottom. . . ."

*See comment at the end of Table 1, p. 70.

The Principle of Parity of Authority and Responsibility

Background

The developmental stage of the principle of parity of authority and responsibility closely parallels that of the scalar principle
of which it is a corollary. Not quite as old as the scalar principle,
the principle of parity of authority and responsibility initially
appeared in its present form in the first decade of this century.

The importance of authority and responsibility, however, was
appreciated by at least one earlier writer. Writing in 1856,
McCallum observed that "sufficient power [should be] conferred to
enable the same to be fully carried out, that such responsibilities
may be real in their character."[100]

Taylor was perhaps the first writer of this century to place
an emphasis on the necessity of corresponding authority and responsibility. While discussing the improvement of systems within a plant
and the duties of those in charge of this improvement, he noted:

> The respective duties of the manager and the man in charge of
> improvement, and the limits of the authority of the latter
> should be clearly defined and agreed upon, always bearing
> in mind that responsibility should invariably be accompanied
> by its corresponding measures of authority.[101]

───────────────

[100]Daniel C. McCallum, "Superintendent's Report," March 25, 1856,
in Annual Report of the New York and Erie Railroad Company for 1855
(New York, 1856), partially reprinted in Alfred D. Chandler, Jr.,
comp. and ed., The Railroads: The Nation's First Big Business (New
York: Harcourt, Brace & World, Inc., 1965), p. 102.

[101]Taylor, "Shop Management," 1415; Taylor, Shop Management, p.
136.

Both Ennis and Kimball attached similar importance to the

concept of authority and responsibility. In the identification of

twelve "organization axioms," Ennis advanced the following guide:

> Authority and responsibility should be clearly defined and
> coordinated. If A is responsible for the cost of repairs,
> B must not be allowed to order a new roof.[102]

Kimball, writing in what was later to become known as the

"bible of management,"[103] stressed the inseparability of authority and

responsibility:

> The duties of every man and every department should be out-
> lined as clearly as possible and the authority and respon-
> sibility of every man definitely fixed. Authority and
> responsibility are inseparable and are essential to effec-
> tive service.[104]

Succeeding authors such as Fayol, Robinson, Jones, Follett,

White and Hopf each expressed a realization of the relationship

existing between authority and responsibility. Fayol listed authority

and responsibility as the second of his fourteen principles of man-

agement. Robinson presented "delegation and coordination of authority

and responsibility" as one of eight "fundamentals" of business.

He considered authority and responsibility to be complementary, neither

---

[102]William D. Ennis, Works Management (New York: McGraw-Hill Book Co., 1911), p. 119.

[103][William J. Arnold], Milestones of Management, I (New York: Business Week, 1965), 14.

[104]Kimball, Principles of Industrial Organization, p. 76. Kimball later repeated this statement verbatim in Kimball, "Economic Principles," p. 1212.

being singularly sufficient for efficient operation. Jones, Follett,

White and Hopf all stressed the importance of reasonable parity

existing between authority and responsibility.

Fayol--

> Authority is not to be conceived of apart from responsibility.
> . . . Responsibility is a corollary of authority, it is its
> natural consequence and essential counterpart, and wheresoever
> authority is exercised responsibility arises.[105]

Robinson--

> . . . authority and responsibility must be <u>coexistent</u> and
> conterminous. One without the other is useless. The dele-
> gation of authority for the performance of definite work
> with coordinate responsibility for its execution is a
> fundamental of organization; a prerequisite to effective
> organization, to the maintenance of a vitally interested
> personnel cooperating to secure the greatest efficiency
> of the whole concern.[106]

Follett--

> A man should have just as much, no more and no less, respon-
> sibility as goes with his function or his task. He should
> have just as much, no more or no less, authority as goes
> with his responsibility.[107]

White--

> In choosing delegates it must be remembered that authority
> is being handed to them, as well as responsibility. No
> man should be held responsible for work unless he is given
> adequate authority to see that it gets done.[108]

---

[105]Fayol, <u>General and Industrial Management</u>, p. 21.

[106]Robinson, <u>Fundamentals of Business Organization</u>, p. 185.

[107]Follett, "The Meaning of Responsibility in Business Management," p. 319.

[108]Percival White, <u>Business Management</u>: An <u>Introduction to
Business</u> (New York: Henry Holt & Co., 1926), p. 115.

Hopf--

It is axiomatic that the exercise of any responsibility
carries with it, by implication at least, reasonable authority with respect to determination of practical questions
involved in carrying out such responsibility.[109]

In the year 1928, three of management's most prolific writers,

Alford, Urwick and Davis, were in the beginning stages of their rise

to prominence. In their respective writings, each took note of the

relationship existing between authority and responsibility.

Expanding upon his own earlier ideas, Alford advanced a

statement of the "law" of responsibility and authority. He maintained

this statement verbatim in each of his succeeding books.

Responsibility for the execution of work must be accompanied
by the authority to control and direct the means for doing
the work.[110]

Urwick also advanced a principle dealing with authority and

responsibility. Influenced by Taylor and Robinson, he formulated the

following statement:

The Principle of Correspondence--authority and responsibility
must be conterminous, coequal, and defined.[111]

---

[109]Harry A. Hopf, "Problems of Bank Organization," Bulletin of
the Taylor Society, XII (April, 1927), 362.

[110]Alford, "Laws of Manufacturing Management," p. 403. See also:
Alford, Laws of Management Applied to Manufacturing, p. 71; Alford,
ed., Cost and Production Handbook, p. 1331; Alford, Principles of Industrial Management for Engineers, p. 115. (Italics omitted.)

[111]Urwick, "Principles of Direction and Control," p. 178.

Urwick has since restated this principle to read:

The Principle of Correspondence--In every position in the
organization the responsibility and the authority should
correspond.[112]

Davis' first book shows evidence of his appreciation for the

relationship existing between authority and responsibility. He

remarked:

Responsibility and authority should be delegated with regard
to the kind and importance of the functions to be performed.
Responsibility can never be delegated satisfactorily unless
sufficient authority for its proper discharge is granted.[113]

He showed a continued appreciation for this relationship in

the succeeding editions of his first book[114] and also in his other

books.[115] In the 1951 work, The Fundamentals of Top Management, he

stated the following "principle of the coincidence of responsibility

and authority":

The delegation of responsibility should be accompanied by
a commensurate delegation of authority. Otherwise, it is
difficult to maintain accountability for the accomplishment
of assigned objectives.[116]

---

[112]Urwick, Notes on the Theory of Organization, p. 51; Urwick,
Organization in Business, p. 14. For a reconsideration of this principle, see: Urwick, Organization, pp. 93-94.

[113]Davis, The Principles of Factory Organization and Management,
p. 42.

[114]Davis, Industrial Organization and Management (2nd ed., 1940),
p. 71; 3rd ed., 1957, p. 77.

[115]For example, see: Davis, The Principles of Business Organization and Operation, p. 41.

[116]Davis, The Fundamentals of Top Management, p. 289.

Authored for the Alexander Hamilton Institute's "Modern
Business Course and Service," Business Organization by Cornell identified sixteen principles of management. Cornell, who differentiated
between principles of management and principles of organization,[117]
identified his fourteenth principle as the principle of responsibility
and authority. Like Alford's, Cornell's statement of this principle
stresses both control and performance as they relate to responsibility
and authority. He commented:

> The Principle of Responsibility and Authority--A person
> exercising authority should be held responsible for the
> carrying on of all activities within the scope of his author-
> ity. Conversely, a person should be held responsible for the
> carrying on of an activity only insofar as he has authority
> over that activity.[118]

Building upon the work of the earlier decade, the writers of
the 1930's widely recognized the applicability of the principle of
parity of authority and responsibility. Dennison, an industrialist
and a director of the International Management Institute, considered
the necessary combination of authority and responsibility a "bare
truism." He argued:

> To say that responsibility must go with authority is merely
> to state the general rule. . . . That authority must accom-
> pany responsibility is a bare truism, since no man can be
> held accountable for results he has no power to attain.[119]

---

[117]Cornell, Business Organization, p. 189, p. 205.

[118]Ibid., p. 213.

[119]Dennison, Organization Engineering, p. 155.

Recognition of the importance of parity of authority and
responsibility rapidly spread. Speaking at the Thirteenth International Cost Conference in Detroit, Wellington addressed himself to
the topic, "Basic Principles of Organization." In summarizing the
principles of "scientific organizing," he advanced a statement of
the principle of parity of authority and responsibility. He declared:

> Authority and responsibility must go hand in hand.
> No operating official should be forced to take the respon-
> sibility without having been granted the proper authority,
> and none should be allowed to exercise any authority incon-
> sistent with his responsibility.[120]

Symbolic of the widespread recognition and acceptance achieved
by the principle of parity of authority and responsibility, a past
president of the American Management Association, Michael C. Rorty,
included it among his "Ten Commandments of Good Organization." He
recognized that "responsibility should always be coupled with corresponding authority."[121]

Further indication of the widespread acceptance achieved by the
principle may be seen in the work of Balderston, Karabasz and Brecht.
In their treatment of the delegation of authority and responsibility,

---

[120]C. Oliver Wellington, "Basic Principles of Organization in
1932 Yearbook of the National Association of Cost Accountants (New
York: NACA, 1932), p. 6. See also: The presentation following
Wellington's address, Harry A. Hopf, "The Evolution of Organization,"
in 1932 Yearbook of the National Association of Cost Accountants,
pp. 68-102.

[121]Michael C. Rorty, Ten Commandments of Good Organization (New
York: American Management Association, 1934). Reprinted in The Encyclopedia of Management, ed. by Carl Heyel (New York: Reinhold Publishing Corp., 1963), p. 620. See also: W. R. Allstetter, "Comments
on the 'Ten Commandments'," Public Administration Review, III (Winter,
1943), 80.

they took equality of authority and responsibility as a given factor. They observed:

> Any given job has two aspects: the responsibility involved and the authority inherent in it. . . . It is always assumed that if a person is given a certain responsibility, he should have the authority necessary to discharge it.[122]

A similar view may be detected in the writing of Petersen and Plowman. They felt that authority implies responsibility. They held the belief that

> The terms "authority" and "responsibility" are usually linked. When one of the words is used the other is implied.[123]

Bethel, Atwater, Smith and Stackman shared the belief that authority should accompany responsibility. They made their feelings clear through the use of an amusing story:

> A famous professor of administration is credited with a definition of "hell" as <u>responsibility</u> <u>without</u> <u>authority</u>. . . . No man should be held responsible for work unless he has been given authority to prescribe how and when it shall be done and unless he is in a position to exercise control over the personnel that is doing it.[124]

---

[122]Balderston, Karabasz, and Brecht, <u>Management of an Enterprise</u>, pp. 396-97.

[123]Petersen and Plowman, <u>Business Organization and Management</u>, p. 53.

[124]Bethel, Atwater, Smith, and Stackman, <u>Industrial Organization and Management</u>, p. 132.

In his discussion of "Principles of Organization Structure,"
Brech expounded a principle of authority and responsibility. It reads:

> Authority and responsibility must be co-terminous and
> co-equal, i.e., responsibility for the fulfilment of given
> activities must be accompanied by the grant of the necessary
> formal authority to enable the appropriate instructions to
> lateral and subordinate personnel to be framed and
> enforced.[125]

In identifying ninety-six principles of organization, Brown
stated that "authority is coextensive with the definition of responsibility."[126] Two of his principles deal indirectly with the topic in
question. He stated:

> The inherent relationships of obligation and authority arise
> automatically from delegation of responsibility.[127]

> In each responsibility is inherent an equivalent authority.[128]

Moving into the 1950's, management thought continued to
recognize the principle of parity of authority and responsibility.
Newman wrote:

> Authority should equal responsibility--The idea that author-
> ity and responsibility should be coextensive is another
> of the most widely recognized principles of organization.[129]

---

[125]Brech, Management (1st ed., 1946), p. 58.

[126]Alvin M. Brown, Organization of Industry (New York: Prentice-
Hall, Inc., 1947), p. 39.

[127]Ibid., p. 37, p. 2. (Italics omitted.)

[128]Ibid., p. 39, p. 3. (Italics omitted.) See also: Brown,
Organization: A Formulation of Principle (New York: Hibbert Printing
Co., 1945), p. 256, p. 257.

[129]Newman, Administrative Action, p. 174.

Two additional authors of this era who also regarded authority
and responsibility as necessary companions were Glover and Niles.
Mirroring the thoughts of one another, they respectively commented:

> The responsibility for executing an order must be
> accompanied by the delegated authority to take action.
> Responsibility and control are intrinsic in authority.[130]

> Each assignment of responsibility requires corresponding
> delegation of authority.[131]

"Principles of Management" Textbooks

With the emergence of the first "principles of management"
textbooks in the early 1950's, the principle of parity of authority
and responsibility received further extensive recognition. Terry dealt
directly with the "coequality" of authority and responsibility. He
advanced the following principle:

> Principle of Authority and Responsibility--For sound
> organizational relationships the authority of a manager should
> be commensurate with his responsibility and, vice versa, his
> responsibility commensurate with his authority.[132]

Koontz and O'Donnell, in discussing the principle of parity of
authority and responsibility, commented:

> Since authority is the power of a manager to undertake
> assigned duties, and responsibility his obligation to use

---

[130]John G. Glover, Fundamentals of Professional Management (2nd
ed.; New York: Simmons-Boardman Publishing Corp., 1958), p. 200.

[131]Niles, The Essence of Management, p. 189.

[132]Terry, Principles of Management (2nd ed., 1956), p. 287; 5th
ed., 1968, p. 354. (Italics omitted.) For a similar but not identical
comment, see: 1st ed., 1953, p. 157.

authority to accomplish these tasks, it logically follows
that the authority and responsibility of a certain manager
should correspond.[133]

With the second edition of their book, Koontz and O'Donnell

introduced the following statement of the principle of parity of

authority and responsibility. It has remained unchanged through their

fourth edition.

> Principle of Parity of Authority and Responsibility: The
> responsibility exacted for actions taken under authority dele-
> gated cannot be greater than that implied by the authority
> delegated, nor should it be less.[134]

Following the lead of Terry and Koontz and O'Donnell, McFarland

also emphasized the principle of parity of authority and responsibility.

Commenting that "a state of inequality between responsibility and

delegated authority produces undesirable effects in an organization,"[135]

he proceeded to identify two principles correlating authority and

responsibility:

> Principle of Scope of Authority--The scope of authority dele-
> gated to a subordinate should be adequate for, but not more
> than adequate for, the successful performance of the respon-
> sibilities assigned, and the nature of the authority employed
> should be selected in relation to the nature of those respon-
> sibilities.[136]

---

[133]Koontz and O'Donnell, Principles of Management, p. 60; In a
modified form, 2nd ed., 1959, p. 95; 3rd ed., 1964, p. 65; 4th ed.,
1968, p. 76.

[134]Ibid., 2nd ed., 1959, p. 297; 3rd ed., 1964, p. 387; 4th ed.,
1968, p. 425.

[135]McFarland, Management, p. 221; 2nd ed., 1964, p. 307; 3rd ed.,
1970, p. 428.

[136]Ibid., 1st ed., 1958, p. 214.

Equating Authority and Responsibility--Authority and responsibility will tend to reach a state of equilibrium with one
another, that is, to become equal. When one exceeds the other,
forces will be set in motion tending to restore the balance.
Resistance to these forces will reduce effective performance
of the persons involved.[137]

Newman, Summer, and Warren broke with the tradition of unequiv-

ocally advocating the parity of authority and responsibility. In their

analysis they differentiated between "duties, authority, and obliga-

tion." They argued:

A common saying in popular management literature
declares that "authority and responsibility should always
be equal." The thought behind this statement is the convic-
tion that if we assign a man duties, we ought to furnish him
with enough authority--no more and no less--to carry them
out, and if we give him authority, we certainly expect from
him a corresponding obligation to use it wisely. Although
there are elements of truth in this contention, it is unfortunately an oversimplification.[138]

Newman, Summer, and Warren's concern with this concept largely

centered upon the word "equal." They explained their view by stating:

Duties are concerned with objectives and activities, authority with rights, and obligation with attitudes. These three
things are of different orders, and it is hard for an executive to find a common denominator for measuring equality among
them.[139]

In an effort to strive for what they believed to be more

accuracy, Newman, Summer, and Warren subsequently formulated the

---

[137]Ibid., p. 221; In a modified form, 2nd ed., 1964, p. 307.

[138]Newman and Summer, The Process of Management, p. 64; with
Warren, 2nd ed., 1967, p. 89.

[139]Ibid., 1st ed., 1961, pp. 64-65; 2nd ed., 1967, p. 89.

following modified guidelines:

1. To the boss, the man doing the delegating, "Duties, authority, and obligation depend on each other and you should
   therefore correlate them thoughtfully."

2. To the subordinate, the man receiving the delegation, "You
   are obligated to fulfill your duties to the maximum extent that
   is feasible in the light of your authority and the conditions
   under which you have to work."[140]

Haimann explicitly dealt with the parity of authority and

responsibility. Under the rubric, "Authority Should Equal Respon-

sibility," he wrote:

> One of the most widely recognized principles of manage-
> ment is the requirement that authority and responsibility
> should be coextensive. This means that the subordinate must
> have been delegated enough authority to undertake all the
> duties which have been assigned to him and for which he has
> accepted responsibility.[141]

Sounding much like McFarland, Haimann further added: "The

subordinate needs all the authority he should have, but he should not

have more than that. Inequality between delegated authority and

responsibility produces undesirable results."[142]

Longenecker also dealt with the relationship existing between

authority and responsibility. In discussing the topic, "Responsibility

of the Delegatee," he made the following comments:

> When authority is delegated, an obligation is thereby
> placed upon the subordinate. . . . Delegation of authority

---

[140]Ibid., 1st ed., 1961, p. 65; 2nd ed., 1967, p. 90.

[141]Haimann, Professional Management, p. 58.

[142]Ibid., p. 58. For a similar discussion, see: Haimann and
Scott, Management in the Modern Organization, pp. 203-05.

. . . carries the consequent imposition of responsibility on the part of the subordinate. One of the "principles" frequently voiced by writers on business organization is that responsibility and authority should be equal.[143]

Dale discussed the parity of authority and responsibility as a part of "classical" theory. He reported (without endorsement) the following statement as a "classical" interpretation of this principle:

Authority should be equal to responsibility; that is, when anyone is given responsibility for a task, he should be given enough authority to accomplish it successfully.[144]

Sisk, much like Longenecker, discussed the parity of authority and responsibility in connection with "effective delegation." Referring to it as a "fundamental" principle, he explained:

Principle of Parity of Authority and Responsibility--For effective delegation, the authority granted to a subordinate must be equal to the responsibility assigned to him.[145]

Except to reference the early comments of Fayol, Donnelly, Gibson and Ivancevich made no remarks regarding the relationship existing between authority and responsibility.[146] From merely reading their text, it is unclear whether or not this mention is an advocacy of Fayol's position.

---

[143]Longenecker, Principles of Management, pp. 230-31; 2nd ed., 1969, p. 262.

[144]Dale, Management, p. 234; In a modified form, 2nd ed., 1969, p. 189.

[145]Sisk, Principles of Management, p. 316. (Italics omitted.)

[146]Donnelly, Gibson, and Ivancevich, Fundamentals of Management, p. 42.

Albers did not discuss the principle of parity of authority and responsibility in his textbook.[147]

An Analysis of Meaning

As the preceding review of literature indicates, the first statement of the principle of parity of authority and responsibility made an early appearance in management literature and it has become one of the most widely agreed upon principles of management. Prompted by an initial statement by Taylor, its meaning has not changed in nearly seventy years. When compared with other principles, its consistency in meaning is truly remarkable.

Management pioneers such as Kimball, Jones, and Fayol recognized the importance of equal and inseparable authority and responsibility.

In the ten years following its recognition, the principle of parity of authority and responsibility became further entrenched in management thought.

During the nineteen-twenties, such notables as Robinson, Follett, Davis, Urwick, Alford, and Cornell recognized the parity of authority and responsibility as a fundamental principle of management. By the nineteen-thirties, it had become a standard and recognized management concept.

With the advent of the nineteen-thirties, Dennison declared the principle of parity of authority and responsibility to be a

---

[147]Albers, Organized Executive Action.

"truism." Rorty declared it a "Commandment of Good Organization."
Balderston, Karabasz and Brecht considered the parity of authority
and responsibility to be "assumed." Petersen and Plowman, as well as
Brech, wrote that authority and responsibility "implied" one another.

By the mid-nineteen-forties, authors such as Bethel et al.
and Brown were also endorsing the merits of parity of authority and
responsibility. This group helped lay the final framework for the
introduction of the "principles of management" textbooks of the nineteen-
fifties and sixties.

With only one exception[148] and with only two partially
differing voices, the authors reviewed for the most part concurred in
both their interpretations and in the importance which they attributed
to the principle of parity of authority and responsibility. Alford
and Cornell's dual emphasis upon control and performance as they
relate to the parity of authority and responsibility is clearly a
minority approach. Furthermore, it is believed that the qualifying
restatement of the concept of parity of authority and responsibility
by Newman, Summer, and Warren simply points up the fact that principles
are guidelines and are not meant to be rigid formats of operation. It
is in this respect that their viewpoint agrees with the majority of
others stated.

Whereas a consensus of meaning and significance exists regarding the principle, a glance at the material presented shows that

---

[148]Albers, Organized Executive Action.

different labels to identify the concept enjoy varying degrees of popularity. The phrase "principle of responsibility and authority" was favored by writers such as Alford, Cornell, Terry and Dale. Koontz and O'Donnell and Sisk preferred the label "principle of the parity of authority and responsibility." Urwick utilized the expression "principle of correspondence." Finally, Davis employed the locution "principle of coincidence."

While it appears that no label has gained a clear preference, for the purposes of semantic explicitness, a particular phraseology must be favored. Believing that the expression "principle of parity of authority and responsibility" is merely a clarifying expansion of the also popular wording "principle of authority and responsibility" and that the word "parity" is in effect simply a synonym for Urwick's "correspondence" and Davis' "coincidence," it will be favored.

Table 10 presents an approximate chronological collection of statements on the principle of parity of authority and responsibility.

Formulation of Definition

The formulation of a definition of the principle of parity of authority and responsibility is somewhat simplified by the consistency of meaning it has maintained throughout the development of management thought. While no two authors have expressed their explanations in identical wordings, their contents have been basically the same. The one predominant theme that has been continuously expressed from 1903 to date is that authority and responsibility should be: "corresponding,"

"inseparable," "equal," "coexistent," "conterminous," "coequal,"
"coincident," "commensurate," "equivalent," and "in parity."

Drawing upon this one consistent theme and upon the associated
knowledge of its advocates, the following definition for the principle
of parity of authority and responsibility is formulated.

Principle of the Parity of Authority and Responsibility

For effective organizational relationships, authority and
responsibility should be equal.

TABLE 10

A COLLECTION OF STATEMENTS
ON THE PRINCIPLE OF PARITY OF
AUTHORITY AND RESPONSIBILITY*

Author	Statement
Taylor	" . . . responsibility should invariably be accompanied by its corresponding measures of authority."
Ennis	"Authority and responsibility should be clearly defined and coordinated."
Kimball	"Authority and responsibility are inseparable and are essential to effective service."
E. D. Jones	"Authority and responsibility should be equal: they are two viewpoints from which to consider duty."
Fayol	"Authority is not to be conceived of apart from responsibility. . . . Responsibility is a corollary of authority, it is its natural consequence and essential counterpart, and wheresoever authority is exercised responsibility arises."
Robinson	" . . . authority and responsibility must be coexistent and conterminous. One without the other is useless."
Follett	"A man . . . should have just as much, no more or no less, authority as goes with his responsibility."
P. White	"No man should be held responsible for work unless he is given adequate authority to see that it gets done."
Hopf	"It is axiomatic that the exercise of any responsibility carries with it, by implication at least, reasonable authority with respect to determination of practical questions involved in carrying out such responsibility."

TABLE 10--Continued

Author	Statement
Alford	"Responsibility for the execution of work must be accompanied by the authority to control and direct the means for doing the work."
Urwick	"Authority and responsibility must be conterminous, coequal, and defined."
Davis	"The delegation of responsibility should be accompanied by a commensurate delegation of authority."
Cornell	"A person exercising authority should be held responsible for the carrying on of all activities within the scope of his authority. Conversely, a person should be held responsible for the carrying on of an activity only insofar as he has authority over that activity."
Dennison	"To say that responsibility must go with authority is merely to state the general rule. . . . That authority must accompany responsibility is a bare truism, since no man can be held accountable for results he has no power to attain."
Wellington	"Authority and responsibility must go hand in hand. No operating official should be forced to take the responsibility without having been granted the proper authority, and none should be allowed to exercise any authority inconsistent with his responsibility."
Rorty	"Responsibility should always be coupled with corresponding authority."
Balderston, Karabasz and Brecht	"It is always assumed that if a person is given a certain responsibility, he should have the authority necessary to discharge it."
Petersen and Plowman	"The terms 'authority' and 'responsibility' are usually linked. When one of the words is used the other is implied."
Bethel, Atwater, Smith and Stackman	"Hell" is "responsibility without authority."

TABLE 10--<u>Continued</u>

<u>Author</u>	<u>Statement</u>
Brech	"Authority and responsibility must be co-terminous and co-equal. . . ."
A. Brown	"In each responsibility is inherent an equivalent authority."
Newman	"The idea that authority and responsibility should be coextensive is another of the most widely recognized principles of organization."
Glover	"The responsibility for executing an order must be accompanied by the delegated authority to take action."
M. C. Niles	"Each assignment of responsibility requires corresponding delegation of authority."
Terry	"The establishment of authority and responsibility should be coequal."
Koontz and O'Donnell	" . . . authority and responsibility of a certain manager should correspond."
McFarland	"Authority and responsibility will tend to reach a state of equilibrium with one another, that is, to become equal."
Haimann	"One of the most widely recognized principles of management is the requirement that authority and responsibility should be coextensive."
Longenecker	"One of the 'principles' frequently voiced by writers on business organization is that responsibility and authority should be equal."
Dale	"Authority should be equal to responsibility; that is, when anyone is given responsibility for a task, he should be given enough authority to accomplish it successfully."
Sisk	" . . . the authority granted to a subordinate must be equal to the responsibility assigned to him."

*See comment at the end of Table 1, p. 70.

The Principle of Span of Management

Background

The concept of span of management is as ancient as the earliest written records of biblical times.[149] Since it has long been a controversial subject, it is perhaps the most discussed principle in classical, neo-classical or modern management theory literature. Throughout its development it has been referred to by various titles, viz., span of supervision, span of authority, span of control, etc.

Prussian General Carl von Clausewitz is generally credited with being the first writer to stress the importance of the span of management concept. Clausewitz set the maximum desirable span at the number ten. He expressed his thoughts by observing:

> Plainly . . . one person can only exercise direct command over a limited number.
>
> If there are more than ten parts, a difficulty arises in transmitting orders with the necessary rapidity and exactitude, for we must not forget that it is not the mere question of the order, else an Army might have as many Divisions as there are heads in a company, but that with orders, many directions and inquiries are connected which it is easier to arrange for six or eight Divisions than for twelve or fifteen.[150]

Military writers other than Clausewitz also discussed the span of management concept. Captain Arthur L. Wagner made note of it in

---

[149]See: Exodus 18:17-26; Deuteronomy 1:15.

[150]Carl von Clausewitz, On War, trans. by James J. Graham (3 vols New York: Barnes & Noble, Inc., 1968), III, 230. See also: pp. 231-32, pp. 235-36. Written circa 1830.

the following comment:

> There is a limit, quickly reached, to the size of the command
> that can be controlled directly by one man; and the proper
> direction of an army requires that it should be divided pri-
> marily into units small enough to be controlled by the voice,
> and influenced by the example of their leader.[151]

British General Ian S. M. Hamilton, writing about the concept,

advocated the use of spans of size three to six. He explained:

> The average human brain finds its effective scope in
> handling from three to six other brains.
> If a man divides the whole of his work into two branches
> and delegates his responsibility, freely and properly, to two
> experienced heads of branches he will not have enough to do.
> The occasions when they would refer to him would be too few to
> keep him fully occupied. If he delegates to three heads he will
> be kept fairly busy whilst six heads of branches will give most
> bosses a ten hours' day. . . .
> . . . .
> As to whether the groups are three, four, five, or six it is
> useful to bear in mind a by-law: the smaller the responsibility
> of the group member, the larger may be the number of the group-
> and vice versa. . . . The nearer we approach the supreme head
> of the whole organisation, the more we ought to work towards
> groups of three; the closer we get to the foot of the whole
> organisation . . . the more we work towards groups of six.[152]

Fayol was in partial agreement with the ideas of the above-

quoted militarists in his advocation of span of management. In a dis-

cussion of what well may have been the first presentation of the evolu-

tion of an enterprise through various stages of development, Fayol

suggested spans of management of fifteen for the lower levels of an

---

[151]Wagner, Organization and Tactics, p. 3.

[152]Ian S. M. Hamilton, The Soul and Body of an Army (New York:
George H. Doran Co., 1921), p. 229, p. 230.

organization and of four for the top levels.[153] However, with a

successive statement, he remarked:

> Faced with a great unit numbering hundreds or thousands of
> workers the problem seems insoluble at first sight. But the
> difficulty is made considerably easier by the particular insti-
> tution of the organization which arises from the existence of
> this very difficulty. Whatever his level of authority, one
> head only has direct command over a small number of subordi-
> nates, less than six normally. Only the . . . foreman or his
> equivalent . . . is in direct command of twenty or thirty men,
> when the work is simple.[154]

Writing a few years before Fayol, Mason had been similarly

aware of the numerous variables affecting an appropriate span of

management. Directing his remarks towards functional foremanship,

he commented:

> In distributing . . . duties among functional foremen . . .
> some will be able to superintend possibly fifty or sixty men,
> while others must limit their work to directing the opera-
> tions of fifteen or twenty. The foreman who sees only that
> machines are in good condition, the belts tightened, and the
> screws in place, need see each man only once or twice a day,
> and then for a few minutes. . . . Other functional directors
> would need to be with the men all the time, and to be ready
> to give each man a considerable portion of his time and atten-
> tion. Such an one would have only a few men in his charge. . . .[155]

A number of years after Fayol and Mason, Moreland (also

showing a military influence) linked span of management to the "urgency

---

[153]Fayol, General and Industrial Management, p. 55. For a study
that partially verifies Fayol's ideas, see: Robert D. Loken and
Winfield C. J. Thake, "How Many Managers Are There?," Current Economic
Comment, XIV (November, 1952), 18-27.

[154]Ibid., p. 98. See also: Fayol, "The Administrative Theory
in the State," p. 108.

[155]Mason, Business Principles and Organization, pp. 173-74.

of services to be rendered." He noted:

> It is a recognised principle that no individual authority
> should control more than a limited number of agencies, the
> number being defined roughly by the urgency of the services
> to be rendered. In military administration, where success
> may be essential to the national life, this limited number
> is very small indeed, usually less than four; and we have
> brigades of three regiments, corps of three divisions, and
> so on. The degree of urgency is normally less in civil
> administration and the limit for efficiency is consequently
> larger; but in countries where the business of the State is
> highly organized, it is usually less than ten.[156]

Speaking before the Boston Chapter of the Taylor Society in 1922,

industrialist Henry P. Kendall addressed himself to the subject of span

of management. He related the following incident and its point to his

audience:

> At a dinner the other evening I heard the president of the
> Western Electric Company [Charles G. DuBois] asked how many
> people should report directly to the president of a large
> industrial company. He said that eight or nine were report-
> ing to him at the present time, but that it was too many
> and he was reorganizing his function so that only four or
> five would report directly to himself; and I imagine that
> four or five is enough. Not that a chief executive should
> not have contact with others, but that is about as many
> general functions as should regularly and directly head up
> to him.[157]

---

[156]William H. Moreland, "The Science of Public Administration,"
Quarterly Review, CCXXXV (April, 1921), 418.

[157]Henry P. Kendall, "The Problem of the Chief Executive,"
Bulletin of the Taylor Society, VII (April, 1922), 40.

In 1925, Jones, acknowledging the remarks of Kendall and those in a subsequent article by Howard Coonley,[158] commented upon span of management. His remarks are reminiscent of earlier comments made by Mason and Fayol:

> The ratios between superior and subordinate may range from 1:5 to 1:25. Foremen may have from 10 to 25 men under them. . . . In higher executive positions, where each subordinate signifies a distinctive domain of activity to be supervised, the ratio of superior to subordinate will be less: perhaps, ideally, about 1:5.[159]

In the first textbook written on the subject of public administration,[160] White identified the principle of span of management as the "principle of economy of supervision." He wrote:

> Another principle comes into play in determining the number of departments and divisions, viz., the principle of economy of supervision. It is said that an administrative superior cannot effectively supervise the work of more than seven divisions or units.[161]

---

[158]Howard Coonley, "The Control of an Industry in the Business Cycle," Harvard Business Review, I (July, 1923), 386-87. Coonley, then President and later Chairman of the Board of the Walworth Manufacturing Company, Inc., reported his span of management to be six. See also: Coonley, "Some Fundamental Contributions of Scientific Management," Advanced Management Journal (January-March, 1941), 23.

[159]Jones, The Administration of Industrial Enterprises (2nd ed., 1925), p. 150.

[160]Julius E. Eitington, "Pioneers of Management," Advanced Management--Office Executive, II (January, 1963), 17-18; Eitington, "Personnel Management: Pioneers," in The Encyclopedia of Management, ed. by Heyel, p. 670.

[161]White, Introduction to the Study of Public Administration (1st ed., 1926), p. 68.

Reflecting the influence of earlier writers, White's 1939

revised edition of <u>Introduction</u> <u>to</u> <u>the</u> <u>Study</u> <u>of</u> <u>Public</u> <u>Administration</u>

did not carry the above-quoted comment. Instead, White remarked:

> The limits of coordination and supervision by one
> individual are suggested in the phrase, "span of control,"
> a derivative of the psychological term, span of attention.
> This phrase refers to the obvious fact there are limits to
> human capacity, and that when attention is spread too
> thinly over too many circumstances, unsatisfactory results
> occur.[162]

Dennison associated span of management with the concept of

leadership. In doing so, he warned against both unusually large and

small spans:

> If a man is really to lead men--to influence those immedi-
> ately under his direction--there will be some maximum
> number of them to whom he can give his fullest service. To
> spread himself out too thin over a large number is [a]
> notoriously poor management practice; and to have too small
> a number unnecessarily restricts his field of influence.
> The maximum varies slightly with the nature of the man and
> of his associates and of his job, but not so widely as
> often supposed; for anything more exacting than the direc-
> tion of simple or uniform mechanical work it seldom runs
> beyonds six to twelve people.[163]

Dutton also commented upon the relationship existing between

an executive's span of management and the amount and complexity of

work to be performed. He further commented upon the extreme variations

found in spans of management:

> The number of intermediates necessary between an executive
> and the rank and file will be determined by the demands of

---

[162]<u>Ibid</u>., Rev. ed., 1939, p. 47.

[163]Dennison, <u>Organization</u> <u>Engineering</u>, pp. 137-38.

supervision on the executives' time. The time required for
supervision, in turn, is more a function of amount and kind
of detail than number of men. Two or three subordinates may
keep the president busy. Often we see a relationship such
as chairman of the board--president, in which two men vir-
tually divide the work of a simple position, the chairman
confining his attention mainly to long-range policy matters
while the president handles the more immediate questions of
operation. Here one subordinate is enough.

On the other hand, one man may direct as many as two
or three hundred subordinates, where the work is a simple
flow process, in which exceptions and emergency situations
are rare. (Usually with this number of men, the foreman will
divide the group into smaller groups under gang bosses or
leading workmen, who can take the initiative in temporary
absence or preoccupation of the foreman.)[164]

In 1933, both Florence and Lt. Col. Eric G. Hart dealt with

the topic of span of management. Florence identified three managerial

principles "proper to the hierarchical system." His third principle

reads:

There is a limit to the number of subordinates that can be
directly commanded by one man.[165]

Hart recommended the limits of three and seven:

The "three and seven rule" is a very important one
in the matter of division. When one divides, it should, if
possible, be into not less than three nor more than seven
parts. If there be less than three there is a great tempta-
tion for the head to interfere and take personal control of
one or both the divisions under him. Also, where the divisions are equal in all respects, two is too small a number
to get any of the benefits of friendly competition. When
the number of divisions is more than seven, there are too

---

[164]Dutton, Principles of Organization, pp. 153-54.

[165]Florence, The Logic of Industrial Organisation, p. 121.

many to inspect and control adequately. It is not always possible to divide according to the "three and seven rule"-- geographical or other considerations may forbid; but, where possible, everything should be done to rescue it.[166]

Probably no other name is as closely associated with the span of management concept as that of V. A. Graicunas. In his famous essay, "Relationship in Organization," Graicunas related span of management to span of attention:

It has long been known empirically to students of organization that one of the surest sources of delay and confusion is to allow any superior to be directly responsible for the control of too many subordinates. . . .
. . . .
Generally speaking in any department of activity the number of separate items to which the human brain can pay attention at the same time is strictly limited. In very exceptional cases, for instance, an individual can memorize groups of figures of more than six digits when read out and can repeat them accurately after a brief interval. But in the vast majority of cases the "span of attention" is limited to six digits.[167]

During the same year that the Graicunas article originally appeared, Urwick repeated his colleague's reasoning as the basis for his own advocation of the principle of span of control:

The psychological conception of "span of attention" places strict limits on the number of separate factors which the human mind can grasp simultaneously.[168]

_____

[166]Eric G. Hart, "The Art and Science of Organization: I," The Human Factor (London), VII (October, 1933), 337-38. Serialized in two parts, October and November, 1933.

[167]V. A. Graicunas, "Relationship in Organization," Bulletin of the International Management Institute, VII (March, 1933), 39, 40.

[168]Urwick, "Organization As a Technical Problem," p. 54. See also: Urwick, Management of Tomorrow, p. 60; Urwick, "Executive Decentralization with Functional Coordination," Management Review, XXXIV (December, 1935), 356, 359.

Five years later, Urwick presented this statement in the form
of a principle. Speaking before the American Management Association,
he expressed the following view:

> No superior can supervise directly the work of more
> than five or, at the most, six subordinates whose work
> interlocks. . . .[169]

To appreciate the true intent of Urwick's statement, it should
be realized that he did not mean for this principle to be interpreted as
"a rigid rule to be applied woodenly in all situations."[170] He has
emphatically stressed the last part of his statement which reads:
" . . . whose work interlocks." It is a qualification that is often
misunderstood or overlooked.

The sharp opposition aroused by Urwick's statement of the
span of control principle is perhaps one of the more interesting
episodes in the annals of the field of management. Called upon numerous
times to defend his position, he has been designated the "doyen" of
classical theorists.[171]

---

[169]Urwick, Scientific Principles and Organization, p. 8. See
also: Urwick, The Elements of Administration, pp. 52-53; Urwick, Notes
on the Theory of Organization, p. 53; Urwick, The Pattern of Management
(Minneapolis, Minn.: University of Minnesota Press, 1956), pp. 59-60;
Urwick, Organization in Business, p. 14; Urwick, Organization, p. 95.

[170]Urwick, "The Manager's Span of Control," Harvard Business
Review, XXXIV (May-June, 1956), 41.

[171]V. Subramaniam, "The Classical Organization Theory and Its
Critics," Public Administration (London), XLIV (Winter, 1966), 436.

Urwick's statement of the principle of span of control was
attacked in 1946 by Simon.[172] Urwick first replied to his critic at
the May-June, 1948 London Lectures on Higher Management.[173] He particularly disapproved of Simon's rewording of each of the discussed concepts as laws rather than as principles.

A number of years later, Urwick again found it necessary to
defend his viewpoint. Suojanen denied the continued validity of the
principle of span of management due to the fact that developments in
modern social science negated its further usefulness. On this basis,
Suojanen declared:

> . . . the institutionalization of the organization and the
> development of primary relationships among the members of the
> executive group together provide such a high degree of
> control that the area of effective supervision of the chief
> executive is much wider than that predicted by the span of
> control principle.[174]

In response, Suojanen received an exceptionally sharp retort
from Urwick. In a well-documented critique, Urwick charged that
Suojanen not only distorted the materials used in his presentation but
attributed a non-existent maturity to the development of the social

---

[172]Herbert A. Simon, "The Proverbs of Administration," Public
Administration Review, VI (Winter, 1946), 53-67; Simon, Administrative
Behavior, p. 26.

[173]Urwick, "Principles of Management," 26. See also: Urwick, "The
Dynamics and the Mechanics of Administration," review of Administrative
Behavior by Herbert A. Simon in the A.M.A. Management Review, XXXVII
(May, 1948), 267-72.

[174]Waino W. Suojanen, "The Span of Control--Fact or Fable,"
Advanced Management Journal, XX (November, 1955), 13. See also:
Suojanen, "Leadership, Authority and the Span of Control," Advanced
Management Journal, XXII (September, 1957), 17-22.

sciences.[175] At this point, Simon, in answer to Urwick's charge
against Suojanen and partially in defense of himself, entered into the
discussion siding with Suojanen.[176] To date this question has yet to
be settled.

In a contribution contemporary to that of the Graicunas
article, Gulick directed himself to the question of span of management.
He identified numerous variables affecting the appropriate determination of a span of management (e.g., diversification of tasks, quality
of work performed and factors of geographical location) and subsequently
commented:

> Just as the hand of man can span only a limited number of
> notes on the piano, so the mind and will of man can span
> but a limited number of immediate managerial contacts. . . .
> The limit of control is partly a matter of the limits of
> time and of energy. As a result the executive of any

---

[175]Lyndall F. Urwick, "The Span of Control--Some Facts About the
Fables," Advanced Management Journal, XXI (November, 1956), 5-15. See
also: Urwick, "The Span of Control," Scottish Journal of Political
Economy, IV (June, 1957), 101-13. J. L. Meij and H. J. Kruisinga, both
of the Netherlands, entered into this exchange of views, see: Meij,
"Human Relations and Fundamental Principles of Management," in Human
Relations and Modern Management, ed. by Edward M. Hugh-Jones (Amsterdam:
North-Holland Publishing, 1958), pp. 1-17; Meij, "The Span of Control--
Fact and Fundamental Principle," Advanced Management Journal, XXII
(February, 1957), 14-16; Meij, "Some Fundamental Principles of a
General Theory of Management," Journal of Industrial Economics, IV
(October, 1955), 16-32; H. J. Kruisinga, "De spanwijdte van de leiding
als concrete norm, fabel of werkelijkheid?," ("The Span of Control, as
a Concrete Standard, Fable or Reality?") Maandblad voor Accountancy en
Bedrijfshuishoudkunde, XXXII, No. 7 (1957).

[176]Herbert A. Simon, "The Span of Control: A Reply," Advanced
Management Journal, XXII (April, 1957), 14, 29. Simon's response was
in regard not only to the Urwick paper presented in Advanced Management
Journal, but was also directed against a number of remarks Urwick made
in "The Manager's Span of Control," Harvard Business Review, XXXIV
(May-June, 1956), 39-47.

enterprise can personally direct only a few persons. He must
depend upon these to direct still others, and upon them in
turn to direct still others, until the last man in the organization is reached.[177]

Barnard directed himself to the question of the complexity of

interpersonal relationships.[178] Referring his readers to the work of

Graicunas, he discussed limitations upon group size. Barnard's

appreciation of the concept embodied in the span of management principle

is readily evident in the following comment:

> The complexity of the relationships in any group
> increases with great rapidity as the number of persons in
> the group increases. . . .
> . . . .
> A person has relationships not only with others indi-
> vidually and with groups, but groups related to groups. As
> the number of possible groups increases, the complexity of
> group relationship increases in greater ratio.

N.B.--Since this time Urwick has had a number of other occasions
to respond to his critics, see: Edward Rolla Park, "The Span of
Control: An Economist's View of the Facts and Fables," Advanced Man-
agement Journal, XXX (October, 1965), 47-51; response in: Urwick,
"Management and 'The American Dream'," Advanced Management Journal,
XXXI (April, 1966), 8-16. See: Subramaniam, "The Classical Organi-
zation Theory and Its Critics," 435-36; T. E. Stephenson, "The
Longevity of Classical Theory," Management International Review, VIII
(November-December, 1968), 77-83; response in: Urwick, "Why the
So-Called 'Classicists' Endure," Management International Review, XI
(January-February, 1971), 3-14. See also: Urwick, "Are the Classics
Really Out of Date?--A Plea for Semantic Sanity," S. A. M. Advanced
Management Journal, XXXIV (July, 1969), 4-12.

[177]Gulick, "Notes on the Theory of Organization," p. 7.

[178]Barnard, The Functions of the Executive, p. 107. See also:
Melvin T. Copeland, "The Job of an Executive," Harvard Business Review,
XVIII (Winter, 1940), 148-60; Barnard, "Comments on the Job of the
Executive," Harvard Business Review, XVIII (Spring, 1940), 295-308.

. . . the burden of coordination . . . will increase
in the proportion that the relationships increase; and the
ability of individuals and groups without leadership to
coordinate is . . . quickly outrun with increase in the
size of groups.[179]

Alford defined span of control as "the number of subordinates

who can be successfully directed by a superior." His statement of

this principle reads:

Principle of the Span of Control. The number of
subordinates reporting to a superior should preferably
be limited to no more than five or six.[180]

The nineteen-forties was a period of continued interest in the

development of the span of management principle. Petersen and Plowman

noted that "span of control refers to the maximum number of subordinates

which may be placed under the jurisdiction of one executive immediately

superior to them."[181] Davis and the 1949 Hoover Commission on the

Organization of the Executive Branch of the Government brought addi-

tional attention to the span of management concept.

Davis' analysis was a mathematical projection of different spans

of management associated with various theoretical organization

structures.[182] It was subsequently followed by an empirical study

---

[179]Ibid., p. 108, p. 109. See also: p. 106 and p. 289n for
statements in which Barnard advocates the "span of management" principle.

[180]Alford, Principles of Industrial Management for Engineers,
p. 115. See also: Alford and Bangs, eds., Production Handbook, p.
1386.

[181]Petersen and Plowman, Business Organization and Management, p.
98.

[182]Ralph C. Davis, The Influence of the Unit of Supervision and
the Span of Executive Control on the Economy of Organization Structure
(Columbus, Ohio: The Ohio State University, Bureau of Business
Research, Research Monograph No. 26, 1941), p. 1.

designed to test Davis' "law of functional growth" which states that
"'as a business grows, the various functions which must be performed
increase in their scope and complexity, as well as the amount of work
which must be performed, and the technical requirements for proper
performance.'"[183] A secondary outgrowth of this study was data that
generally upheld traditional beliefs concerning the span of management.[184]

The Federally sponsored Hoover Commission,[185] established to
analyze the organizational structure of the United States Executive
Branch, noted that "there are 65 departments, administrations,
agencies, boards, and commissions engaged in executive work all of

---

[183]Davis, The Principles of Business Organization and Operation,
p. 32.

[184]Alton W. Baker and Ralph C. Davis, Ratios of Staff to Line
Employees and Stages of Differentiation of Staff Functions (Columbus,
Ohio: The Ohio State University, Bureau of Business Research, Research
Monograph No. 72, 1954), p. 31. Baker and Davis found the average span
of operative supervision to be 16.7 and the average span of executive
supervision to be 6. For a later study of a similar nature, see:
Bruce E. De Spelder, Ratios of Staff to Line Personnel (Columbus, Ohio:
The Ohio State University, Bureau of Business Research, Research
Monograph No. 106, 1962), pp. 16-62.

[185]It should be noted that the Hoover Commission was preceded in
1937 by the President's Committee on Administrative Management. It
found that more than one-hundred agencies reported to the President,
see: U. S., The President's Committee on Administrative Management,
Report of the Committee With Studies of Administrative Management in
the Federal Government, Submitted to the President and to the Congress
in accordance with Public Law No. 739, 74th Congress, 2nd Session
[Louis Brownlow, chairman]. (Washington, D. C.: Government Printing
Office, 1937), p. 34.

of which . . . report directly to the President--if they report to anyone."[186] In its recommendations, the Commission favored a consolidation and a large reduction in the number of the units reporting to the President.

The writings of Balderston, Karabasz, Brecht and Riddle as well as those of Brech are also characterisric of this period. Recognizing the variability of an appropriate span, Balderston et al. noted:

> The effectiveness of an executive's supervision is related to his span of control. The span of control may be defined as the number of subordinates reporting to one superior. At the upper levels of authority, the activities are so numerous and complex that the ratio should not exceed four to one, or five to one. At the lower levels of supervision, when the work is more homogenous and the problems less perplexing, the ratio may be much larger, say ten to one, or even fifty to one in the case of the supervision of common laborers.[187]

Brech stated the span of management (control) concept in the form of a principle. It was the eighth of ten organizational principles which he identified. It stressed the idea of

---

[186]U. S., Commission on Organization of the Executive Branch of the Government, A Report to Congress by the Commission on Organization of the Executive Branch of the Government, [Herbert C. Hoover, chairman]. (Washington, D. C.: Government Printing Office, 1949), p. 35. Also published as The Hoover Commission Report on Organization of the Executive Branch of the Government (New York: McGraw-Hill Book Co., Inc., 1947), see: p. 25.

[187]Balderston, Karabasz, Brecht, and Robert J. Riddle, Management of an Enterprise (2nd ed., 1949), pp. 452-53.

"interrelatedness":

> When authority and responsibility are delegated, the span of control of the superior should be limited to five or six subordinates if their activities interlock, i.e., when authority and responsibility are delegated to subordinates in such a way that their activities are interrelated or interlock, no superior should be required to supervise or co-ordinate more than five or six such subordinates.[188]

Since this initial statement, Brech has restated his views on this concept in a more general manner:

> . . . the span of responsibility or supervision of a superior [should be] limited to a reasonable number of (executive or supervisory) subordinates, if their activities are interrelated.[189]

One of the more interesting studies relating organization structure to enterprise efficiency was conducted by Sears, Roebuck and Company and reported by one of its Vice-Presidents, James C. Worthy. Of special interest and relevance to this discussion is the following remark which is based upon the results of his final research:

> A number of highly successful organizations have not only paid little heed but have gone directly counter to one of the favorite tenets of modern management theory, the so-called "span of control," which holds that the number of subordinate executives or supervisors reporting to a single individual should be severely limited to enable that individual to exercise the detailed direction and control which is generally considered necessary. On the contrary,

---

[188]Brech, _Management_ (1st ed., 1946), pp. 58-59.

[189]Brech, "Management in Principle," (1963), p. 69.

these organizations often deliberately give each key executive so many subordinates that it is impossible for him to exercise too close supervision over their activities.[190]

The nineteen-fifties was a period of continued controversy concerning the span of management principle. Much material relating to it was written and numerous emperical studies were conducted to determine its validity.

Both Newman and Davis commented upon span of management. Having earlier acknowledged a variation in optimum spans at different levels of supervision, Davis offered guidelines to be followed.[191] He was of the opinion that:

> The range of the optimum unit of operative supervision extends probably from a minimum of 10 operatives to a maximum of 30 for most concerns.[192]

> The unit of executive supervision appears . . . to range from 3 to 8 or 9 subordinates.[193]

Newman also provided guidelines to aid in determining the optimum span of supervision (management) at different organization levels. With similar reasoning but advocating slightly different

---

[190]James C. Worthy, "Organizational Structure and Employee Morale," American Sociological Review, XV (April, 1950), 178. See also: Worthy, "Factors Influencing Employee Morale," Harvard Business Review, XXVIII (January, 1950), 65-67; Worthy, Big Business and Free Men (New York: Harper & Brothers, Inc., 1959), pp. 107-18.

[191]Davis, Industrial Organization and Management, p. 63.

[192]Davis, The Fundamentals of Top Management, p. 271.

[193]Ibid., p. 276.

figures, Newman wrote:

> Empirical studies suggest that executives in higher
> echelons should have a span of three to seven operating
> subordinates, whereas the optimum range for first-line
> supervisors of routine activities is usually from fifteen
> to twenty employees.[194]

Following Newman and Davis, Drucker modified the concept of
span of management and introduced what he referred to as "span of
managerial responsibility."[195] Drucker considered this "span" to be
much wider than the regular span of management and to have no fixed
size. He defined "span of managerial responsibility" as:

> . . . the number of people whom one superior can assist,
> teach and help to reach the objectives of their own jobs.[196]

The first of a series of empirical studies to deal specifically
with span of management was reported by Dale.[197] In all of the 141

---

[194]Newman, Administrative Action, p. 269.

[195]Peter F. Drucker, The Practice of Management (New York:
Harper & Row, Publishers, 1954), p. 139. Drucker credits Dr. H. H.
Race of the General Electric Company with coining the term "span of
managerial responsibility."

[196]Ibid., p. 139.

[197]Ernest Dale, "The Span of Control," Management News, XXIV
(July, 1951), 3-4. Dale, "Dymanics and Mechanics of Organization,"
in Organization Planning and Management Development, Personnel Series
No. 141 (New York: American Management Association, 1951), pp. 3-14;
Dale, Planning and Developing the Company Organization Structure (7th
imp.; New York: American Management Association, Research Report
No. 20, 1952), data drawn from Table One, p. 77 and Table Three, p.
80. In a more recent AMA sponsored survey, Dale found results that
were similar to those of his original study, see: Dale, Organization
(New York: American Management Association, 1967), pp. 94-96.

companies surveyed (both large and small), it was found that the number of subordinates reporting to the chief executives varied from one to twenty-four. The median for the large companies was between eight and nine; for the medium sized companies between six and seven.[198]

Since the original Dale study, numerous other attempts have been made to determine the degree to which companies actually apply the span of management principle. Healey, for example, polled the chief executives of 620 Ohio manufacturing plants which employed 100 or more employees. The following is one of the many conclusions that he reached in his study.

The span of control in practice tends to agree with the span advocated in theory.

In 93.7 per cent of the main plants and 84.2 per cent of the branch plants, the chief executive employs a span of less than 9 immediate subordinates. A span of 3 through 8 is used by 76.3 per cent of the main-plant leaders and 70.3 per cent of the branch managers. A group comprising 70 per cent of the main-plant executives and 60.6 per cent of the branch-plant managers limits the span to from 3 to 7 subordinates.[199]

---

[198]For an interesting interpretation of this data, see: "Bosses Break Rules on Span of Control," Business Week, August 18, 1951, pp. 102-03.

[199]James H. Healey, Executive Coordination and Control (Columbus, Ohio: The Ohio State University, Bureau of Business Research, Research Monograph No. 78, 1956), pp. 241-42. (Italics omitted.) This study is also reported in: Healey, "Coordination and Control of Executive Functions," Personnel, XXXIII (1956), 106-17.

Another study reported similar findings: "In each industry size group, the median number . . . of reporting subordinates was close to the recommended span of control. . . ."[200]

An extensive investigation into this area was directed by Woodward who studied the span of management at the highest and lowest levels of ninety-seven firms. Woodward found that the median number of persons responsible to the top executives of firms surveyed was six, while the median number of employees responsible to first-line supervisors was thirty.[201] These findings are partially similar to those reported by Baker and Davis four years earlier.

Haire also provided data concerning span of management. He found that in the firms studied, the average number of employees per first-line foremen was one to thirteen.[202]

A National Industrial Conference Board investigation, directed by Janger, found that the median span for the chief executives surveyed

---

[200]Thomas Kenny, "Why Top Management Control Needs Tightening," Dun's Review and Modern Industry, LXVIII (October, 1956), 65.

[201]Joan Woodward, Management and Technology, Problems in Progress in Industry No. 3 (London: Her Majesty's Stationary Office, 1958), p. 21; Woodward, Industrial Organization: Theory and Practice (London: Oxford University Press, 1965), p. 26, p. 69.

[202]Mason Haire, "Biological Models and Empirical Histories of the Growth of Organizations," in Modern Organization Theory: A Symposium of the Foundation for Research on Human Behavior, ed. by Haire (New York: John Wiley & Sons, Inc., 1959), p. 296.

was five with a range of one to twenty-four. At the lowest level of
the management hierarchy, the average span was found to be twenty with
a range of four to thirty-five.[203]

Entwisle and Walton, in their study of twenty colleges and
fourteen small companies, found a median span of management for college
presidents of five to seven and for company presidents of four to
seven.[204]

Moore analyzed the organization charts of sixty-two companies
presented in a study by Stieglitz[205] and concluded that most presidents
of the companies surveyed had from eight to eleven immediate subordinates.[206]

---

[203]Allen Janger, "Analyzing the Span of Control," _Management
Record_, XXII (July-August, 1960), 8.

[204]Doris R. Entwisle and John Walton, "Observations on the Span
of Control," _Administrative Science Quarterly_, V (March, 1961), 522-33.
For an interesting hypothetical analysis of the Entwisle and Walton
data, see: William H. Starbuck, "Organizational Growth and Development," in _Handbook of Organizations_, ed. by James C. March (Chicago:
Rand McNally & Co., 1965), pp. 500-01.

[205]Harold Stieglitz, _Corporate Organization Structures_, Industrial
Conference Studies in Personnel Policy No. 183 (New York: National
Industrial Conference Board, Inc., 1961), 8-9. For a comment on the
fervor created by the release of this study, see: "Storm Over Manage-
ment Doctrines," _Business Week_, January 6, 1962, pp. 72-74. This
survey has since been superceded by: Stieglitz and C. David Wilkerson,
Corporate Organization Structures, Studies in Personnel Policy No. 210
(New York: National Industrial Conference Board, 1968).

[206]Franklin G. Moore, _Management: Organization and Practice_
(New York: Harper & Row, Publishers, 1964), p. 364.

White found results remarkably similar to those of Dale's 1951 study in her survey of thirty-nine chief executives. Their median span of management was found to be eight, with a typical range from three to twelve.[207]

A more recent study on the span of management is that of Holden, Pederson and Germane who found that the span of management for fifteen industrial corporations ranged from one to fourteen with an average and median of ten.[208]

Perhaps the most recent study of the span of management is the one conducted by Viola.[209] He found that of 221 managers in the life insurance industry, seventy-one per cent had from one to nine subordinates reporting to them, with a mean of 6.75. In contrast to this, sixty per cent of this group's immediate superiors were reported as having spans of from one to nineteen subordinates.

---

[207]Karol K. White, _Understanding the Company Organization Chart_, Research Study No. 56 (New York: American Management Association, 1963), p. 56. For an additional interpretation of both the Stieglitz and White data, see: Gerald G. Fisch, "Stretching the Span of Management," _Harvard Business Review_, XLI (September-October, 1963), 74-85.

[208]Paul E. Holden, Carlton A. Pederson, and Gayton E. Germane, _Top Management_ (New York: McGraw-Hill Book Co., Inc., 1968), p. 61. It should be noted that this study is an up-dating of an earlier survey, see: Holden, Lounsbury S. Fish, and Hubert L. Smith, _Top-Management Organization and Control_ (Stanford University, Calif.: Stanford University Press, 1941).

[209]Richard H. Viola, "The Span of Management in the Life Insurance Industry: Some Research Findings," _Economic and Business Bulletin_, XXII (Winter, 1970), 18-25.

"Principles of Management" Textbooks

The empirical research about the span of management and the
market appearance of the first "principles of management" textbooks
were almost simultaneous. While aware of the numerous variables
involved in determining an appropriate span of control (management),
Terry advanced the following pertinent comment which is evidence of
a paradoxical confusion still existing today:

> Some experts consider four as the minimum and eight as the
> largest number desirable. However, the proper number varies
> with the particular circumstances, which includes such things
> as the type of work, the position, the ability of the execu-
> tive, faith in subordinates, and fear of possible rivals.[210]

Terry did not enunciate an explicit span of management principle,
however, he did formulate the following related concept:

> Principle of Increasing Organization Relationships As addi-
> tional persons are added to an organization structure, the
> number of organization relationships increase at a much
> greater rate than the number of persons added.[211]

By the fifth edition of his textbook, Terry had dropped the phrase
span of control in favor of span of authority.[212]

Koontz and O'Donnell devoted an entire chapter to the span of
management principle. In it, they coined the phrase span of management

---

[210]Terry, Principles of Management, p. 159.

[211]Ibid., p. 160; 2nd ed., 1956, p. 262; In a modified form,
5th ed., 1968, p. 312. (Italics omitted.)

[212]Ibid., 5th ed., 1968, p. 309.

in preference to the more traditional phrase span of control. They

explained the logic of their choice by writing:

> In much of the literature of management this princi-
> ple is referred to as the "span of control." Despite the
> general use of this term the authors prefer to use "span
> of management," since the span is one of management and not
> merely of control, here regarded as a basic function of
> management.[213]

In a manner similar to Terry's, Koontz and O'Donnell identified

numerous factors affecting the determination of an optimum span of

management. In explaining this principle, they commented:

> Span of Management Principle: There is a limit to the
> number of persons an individual can effectively manage, even
> though that limit is not finite for every case but will vary
> with the complexity of the relationships supervised and the
> ability of managers and subordinates.[214]

An orientation similar to that of his predecessors was taken

by "principles" author McFarland. Commenting that "a span of control

is the number of subordinate executives who report directly to a

higher executive," McFarland presented the previously discussed work

of Barnard and White.[215] In defining span of control, he explained:

> The principle of the span of control holds that: The larger
> the number reporting directly to an executive, the more
> difficult it tends to be for him to supervise and coordinate

---

[213]Koontz and O'Donnell, Principles of Management, p. 83n; 2nd
ed., 1959, p. 63n; 3rd ed., 1964, p. 216n; In a modified form, 4th ed.,
1968, p. 241n.

[214]Ibid., 2nd ed., 1959, p. 297; In a modified form, 3rd ed.,
1964, p. 386, pp. 424-25.

[215]McFarland, Management, p. 173; 2nd ed., 1964, p. 249; 3rd ed.,
1970, p. 350.

them effectively. The number of persons who can be effectively supervised is a function of the ability of the supervising executive and of the executive being supervised.[216]

Noting and favoring Koontz and O'Donnell's choice of the term span of management over that of span of control, Albers used it throughout his book. He defined span of management as simply "the number of subordinates under an executive," and asked the questions: "How many subordinates can be effectively managed by an executive? Is there an ideal number or a minimax solution to the problem?"[217] While not providing a firm answer to either question, he did review many of the studies performed in this area and also identified both "indigenous" and "exogenous" factors to be considered in the matter.

Newman and Summer preferred the term "span of supervision" to any other in use. Noting that there are certain limits to the number of subordinates that may be supervised by a superior, they formed their discussion upon a purely structural basis. Differentiating between a "tall" and a "flat" organization, they proceeded to discuss various factors affecting a manager's span of supervision. They concluded that each span should be "tailored" according to its corresponding position.[218]

---

[216]Ibid., 1st ed., 1958, pp. 173-74; In a modified form, 2nd ed., 1964, p. 249; 3rd ed., 1970, p. 350.

[217]Albers, Organized Executive Action, p. 70; 2nd ed., 1965, p. 83; 3rd ed., 1969, pp. 103-04.

[218]Newman and Summer, The Process of Management, p. 110; with Warren, 2nd ed., 1967, p. 135.

Haimann, and later Haimann and Scott, defined "span of management" as "the number of subordinates who can be effectively supervised and managed. . . ."[219] Haimann strongly stressed the point: "To repeat, the span of management is a function of many factors."[220] After reviewing the work of Graicunas, empirical studies in the area, and criticisms aimed at span of management, he concluded: "There is . . . no definite, fixed answer to the ideal number of subordinates a manager can effectively supervise."[221]

Reminiscent of Davis, Longenecker, in his discussion of span of control, noted: "It is possible to distinguish between the span of control of executives who have subordinate managers reporting to them and the span of control of supervisors who direct operative employees."[222] Limiting his discussion to the former, Longenecker simply defined span of control as "the number of immediate subordinates reporting to a given manager."[223] He summarized his presentation by

---

[219]Haimann, Professional Management, p. 139; In a modified form, with Scott, 2nd ed., 1970, p. 242.

[220]Haimann, Professional Management, p. 139.

[221]Ibid., p. 154.

[222]Longenecker, Principles of Management, p. 174; 2nd ed., 1969 p. 202.

[223]Ibid., p. 173; 2nd ed., 1969, p. 202.

writing:

> In considering the span of control, it appears that
> the determination of precise, quantitative limits that are
> generally applicable to many organizations is difficult,
> if not impossible.[224]

Making limited use of his previous research, Dale discussed

span of control (management) as a "classical" principle. Noting the

contributions of Hamilton, Graicunas, and Urwick, Dale reported

(without endorsement) the following statement as a "classical" inter-

pretation of the span of control:

> The Span of Control No superior should have more than
> six immediate subordinates whose work is interrelated.[225]

Sisk, after reviewing the works of Graicunas, Urwick, and Dale,

presented the span of management topic just as Koontz and O'Donnell

had done before him.[226]

More recently, Donnelly, Gibson and Ivancevich have followed

the approach utilized by Sisk. Writing that "the span-of-control

principle concerns the number of subordinates who directly report to a

supervisor; . . .", they also presented and critiqued the work of

Graicunas, Urwick and Davis.[227]

---

[224]Ibid., p. 183; 2nd ed., 1969, p. 212. (Italics omitted.)

[225]Dale, Management, p. 235; 2nd ed., 1969, p. 190.

[226]Sisk, Principles of Management, p. 269.

[227]Donnelly, Gibson, and Ivancevich, Fundamentals of Management,
p. 82. See also: pp. 216-19.

An Analysis of Meaning

As is indicated in the preceding review, the span of management principle is firmly entrenched in management theory. It, however,
has not gone unattacked by the newer behavioral approaches to management.

Attempts at proving or disproving the validity of span of
management have met with mixed results. They have only been reviewed
as part of this analysis to the extent that they might provide a more
common base for the formulation of the span of management concept into
a principle. This is a point that will be discussed shortly.

Referred to by Pfiffner and Sherwood as a "hoary artifact,"[228]
the span of management concept was first forwarded as a principle of
management by Urwick in 1938. It, however, was discussed much earlier
by such authors as Clausewitz, Wagner, Hamilton, Mason, Fayol, Moreland,
Kendall, Jones, White, Dennison, Dutton, Florence, Graicunas, and Hart.
Of the above group, the writings of Mason, Dutton and Florence are
surprisingly consistent with recent views on this topic. Each of these
authors seemed to recognize that a manager's appropriate span of management will vary depending upon the individuals and circumstances involved.

The most frequently quoted early reference in this area is
Graicunas' essay, "Relationship in Organization." It is largely
misunderstood that Graicunas recognized the impossibility of laying
"down hard and fast rules for the organization of relationships within
a factory" and that he intended his essay to be "essentially of a

---

[228]Pfiffner and Sherwood, Administrative Organization, p. 153.

speculative rather than a directly practical nature."[229] Nevertheless,
writers before and since have strived to standardize numerical guidelines in this area. Fayol recommended a span of four near the top of
an organization and from twenty to thirty at its lower levels. Kendall
recommended spans of from four to five; White advocated spans of seven;
Dennison endorsed spans of from six to twelve; Hart favored the limits
of three and seven; and Graicunas, Urwick, and Alford all favored spans
of six. Other writers, notably Jones; Balderston, Karabasz, Brecht,
and Riddle; and Davis, recommended differing spans for different levels
of an organization. Jones advocated spans of from one to five at the
top of an organization and from one to twenty-five at its lower levels.
Balderston et al. suggested spans of from one to four or five and from
one to fifty. Davis sanctioned spans of from ten to thirty for the
bottom of an organization and from three to nine at its top.

Of unquestionably good intention these early writers mainly
called upon their past experiences to form a basis for the logic of
their statements. As a result, these statements predominately took
the form of descriptive recommendations. It was not, however, until
specific empirical research in this area was available that dissenting
views began to gain favor over the less empirical intuitive statements.

The works of Dale; Healey; Haire; Janger; Entwisle and Walton;
White; Woodward; Viola; and Holden, Pederson, and Germane basically

---

[229]Graicunas, "Relationship in Organization," p. 39. Editor's
comment. See also: Arthur G. Bedeian, "Relationship in Organization:
A Clarification," Academy of Management Journal, XV (June, 1972),
238-39.

point out the variations present in actual practice. They do not,
however, unquestionably disprove the earlier classical pronouncements.
Confusion in this area is particularly complicated by: (1) the divergent interpretations of the same data by opposing groups; and (2) the
discrepant results obtained in different surveys. What seems to have
taken place is a more general recognition of the numerous variables
that make each individual situation a distinct and independent entity.
This general change in attitude became remarkably evident with the
introduction of the first "principles of management" textbooks. The
so-called neo-classical authors of these texts benefiting from the
indeterminateness of the latest work in the span of management area
began to modify the edicts of earlier authors. Instead of set numerical
guidelines being advanced, statements such as the following became
more the rule rather than the exception:

> Span of Management Principle: There is a limit to
> the number of persons an individual can effectively manage,
> even though that limit is not finite for every case but
> will vary with the complexity of the relationships super-
> vised and the ability of managers and subordinates.[230]

As this approach has become generally accepted, new approaches
of analyzing the span of management concept have been developed.
Organizations such as Lockheed Missiles & Space Company have developed
elaborate procedures to evaluate selected identifiable variables as a

---

[230]Koontz and O'Donnell, Principles of Management, 2nd ed., 1959,
p. 297; In a modified form, 3rd ed., 1964, p. 386, pp. 424-25.

basis for determining the optimum span of management in any desired
situation.[231]

Numerous recent mathematical treatments investigating span of
management have also been conducted. They indicate an increasing
awareness of the importance of the span of management. Blau and Scott
have developed an index "to measure the shape of the hierarchical
pyramid."[232] Hill has applied queueing theory to the determination of
the optimum span of management.[233] Both Beckmann and Thompson have
constructed numerous derivations to measure the cost of various spans
of management.[234] Melcher has advanced a formula to determine the

---

[231]See: Harold Stieglitz, "Optimizing Span of Control," Management Record, XXIV (September, 1962), 25-29; C. W. Barkdull, "Span-of-
Control--A Method of Evaluation," Michigan Business Review, XV (May,
1963), 25-32; Harold D. Koontz, "Making Theory Operational: The Span
of Management," The Journal of Management Studies, III (October, 1966),
229-43; Jon G. Udell, "An Empirical Test of Hypothesis Relating to
Span of Control," Administrative Science Quarterly, XII (December,
1967), 420-39.

[232]Peter M. Blau and W. Richard Scott, Formal Organizations (San
Francisco: Chandler Publishing Company, 1962), p. 168. See also:
Oliver E. Williamson, "Hierarchical Control and Optimum Firm Size,"
Journal of Political Economy, LXXV (April, 1967), 132-34.

[233]Lawrence S. Hill, "The Application of Queueing Theory to the
Span of Control," Academy of Management Journal, VI (March, 1963),
58-69. See also: Joel Zelnick, "Discussion: Queuing Theory Revisited,"
Journal of the Academy of Management, VI (June, 1963), 173; Hill,
"Discussion: Some Comments on 'Queuing Theory Revisited," Journal of
the Academy of Management, VI (September, 1963), 245-46; Hill, "Comment:
Queuing Theory Revisited Once Again," Journal of the Academy of Manage-
ment, VII (December, 1964), 317.

[234]Martin J. Beckmann, "Some Aspects of Returns to Scale in Business Administration," Quarterly Journal of Economics, LXXIV (August,
1960), 469; Robert E. Thompson, "Span of Control--Conceptions and
Misconceptions," Business Horizons, VII (Summer, 1964), 58. For a
similar discussion of this topic, see: Edward A. Nelson, "Economic
Size of Organizations," California Management Review, X (Spring, 1968),
61-72.

average span of management within an organization.[235] Emery has

adapted the original Graicunas formula to allow for "fragmentation and

coordination."[236] Finally, Scott has applied simulation modeling to

the determination of optimum spans of management.[237]

With the controversy over the span of management still exist-

ing,[238] efforts have recently been made to ally more closely classical

theory with modern organization theory. Parker has argued that the

main differences between the classical model and the Simon model are

in detail and terminology.[239] Pfiffner has accused social scientists

of having an "anti-management bias" and admonished them to overcome

---

[235]Arlyn Melcher, "Organizational Structure: A Framework for Analysis and Integration," in Academy of Management Proceedings (1965), ed. by Edwin B. Flippo (Bowling Green, Ohio, 1966), p. 149.

[236]James C. Emery, Organizational Planning and Control Systems: Theory and Technology (New York: Macmillan Company, 1969), pp. 10-11.

[237]Charles R. Scott, Jr., "Span of Control Optimization by Simulation Modeling," (Paper presented at the 32nd meeting of the Academy of Management, Minneapolis, Minn., August 15, 1972). (Mimeographed.)

[238]See: John A. Grant, "Span of Control: An Administrative Paradox," The Southern Journal of Business, IV (April, 1969), 19-32; Robert G. Wright, "An Approach to Find Realistic Spans of Management," Arizona Business Bulletin, XVII (November, 1970), 21-28; David D. Van Fleet, "An Approach to a History of Management Thought: The Span of Management," (Paper presented at the 32nd meeting of the Academy of Management, Minneapolis, Minn., August 14, 1972). (Mimeographed.)

[239]Robert S. Parker, "New Concepts of Administration--Its Meaning and Purpose," Public Administration Review (Sydney), XXI (December, 1961), 28.

it.[240] More recently, House and Miner partially combined management
theory with selected findings from the behavioral sciences in an
attempt to amalgamate their divergent viewpoints. After an extensive
review of the existing parallel literatures in the areas of span of
management and correlates of group size, they concluded that, to a
limited extent, both literatures closely support one another.[241]

Table 11 presents an approximate chronological collection of
statements on the principle of span of management.

Formulation of Definition

The formulation of a definition of the principle of span of
management is somewhat complicated by the realization that its development appears to have undergone two periods of growth. The first
period was marked by the presence of suggested numerical limitations,
and the second by general statements of variable application. As

---

[240]John M. Pfiffner, "Why Not Make Social Science Operational,"
Public Administrative Review, XXII (September, 1962), 109. Pfiffner's
contention has not gone unchallenged, see: Merrill J. Collett,
"Strategy Versus Tactics As the Object of Research in Public Adminis-
tration," Public Administration Review, XXII (September, 1962), 115-21;
Thomas L. Gardner, "First Things First," Public Administration Review,
XXII (September, 1962), 121-23; C. Mansel Keene, "Administration
Reality: Advances, Not Solutions," Public Administration Review, XXII
(September, 1962), 124-28.

[241]Robert J. House and John E. Miner, "Merging Management and
Behavioral Theory--The Interaction Between Span of Control and Group
Size," Administrative Science Quarterly, XIV (September, 1969), 462.
For three previous articles of a similar nature, see: Marshall W.
Meyer, "Expertness and the Span of Control," American Sociological
Review, XXXIII (December, 1968), 944-51; André L. Delbecq, "The World
Within the 'Span of Control'," Business Horizons, II (August, 1968),
47-56; Gerald D. Bell, "Determinants of Span of Control," American
Journal of Sociology, III (July, 1967), 100-09.

suggested by early authors, clearly there is a limit to the number of
employees a superior can effectively supervise. Just as clear, however,
is the fact that this limit will vary depending upon the individuals
and circumstances involved. This point seems to have been understood
by such early writers as Mason, Dutton, and Florence. Yet it was a
point unappreciated by others.

In regard to the preference of using the phrase "span of
management" over that of "span of control," the logic employed by
Koontz and O'Donnell in this matter seems to have gathered at least
partial approval by other writers. Following their logic, it will
also be forwarded here that a superior's span is one of much more than
simply control. Rather it is one of management in its entirety.

It is with these thoughts in mind that the proposed definition
will be stated in the form of a non-numerical generality and under the
title "span of management."

The Principle of Span of Management

There is a limit, dependent upon the circumstances and
individuals involved, to the number of subordinates that a
superior can effectively manage.

TABLE 11

A COLLECTION OF STATEMENTS
ON THE PRINCIPLE OF SPAN OF MANAGEMENT*

Author	Statement
Clausewitz	"Plainly . . . one person can only exercise direct command over a limited number. If there are more than ten parts, a difficulty arises in transmitting orders with the necessary rapidity and exactitude. . . ."
Wagner	"There is a limit, quickly reached, to the size of the command that can be controlled directly by one man. . . ."
Hamilton	"The average human brain finds its effective scope in handling from three to six other brains."
Mason	"In distributing . . . duties among functional foremen . . . some will be able to superintend possibly fifty or sixty men, while others must limit their work to directing the operations of fifteen or twenty."
Fayol	"Whatever his level of authority, one head only has direct command over a small number of subordinates, less than six normally. Only the . . . foreman or his equivalent . . . is in direct command of twenty or thirty men, when the work is simple."
Moreland	"It is a recognised principle that no individual authority should control more than a limited number of agencies . . . usually less than ten."
Kendall	"Four or five" is as many people as should report to a chief executive.
E. D. Jones	"The ratios between superior and subordinate may range from 1:5 to 1:25.

TABLE 11--<u>Continued</u>

<u>Author</u>	<u>Statement</u>
White	"It is said an administrative superior cannot effectively supervise the work of more than seven divisions or units."
Dennison	"If a man is really to lead men . . . there will be some maximum number of them to whom he can give his fullest service. . . . for anything more exacting than the direction of simple or uniform mechanical work it seldom runs beyond six to twelve people."
Dutton	"The number of intermediates necessary between an executive and the rank and file will be determined by the demands of supervision on the executives' time."
Hart	"When one divides, it should, if possible, be into not less than three nor more than seven parts."
Florence	"There is a limit to the number of subordinates that can be directly commanded by one man."
Graicunas	" . . . in the vast majority of cases the 'span of attention' is limited to six digits."
Urwick	"No superior can supervise directly the work of more than five or, at the most, six subordinates whose work interlocks."
Gulick	"Just as the hand of man can span only a limited number of notes on the piano, so the mind and will of man can span but a limited number of managerial contacts. . . ."
Alford	"The number of subordinates reporting to a superior should preferably be limited to no more than five or six at the executive level."
Balderston, Karabasz and Brecht	"At the upper levels of authority . . . the ratio should not exceed four to one, or five to one at the lower levels of supervision . . . the ratio may be much larger, say ten to one, or even fifty to one in the case of the supervision of common laborers."

TABLE 11--Continued

Author	Statement
Brech	" . . . the span of control of the superior should be limited to five or six subordinates if their activities interlock.
R. C. Davis	(a) The range of the optimum unit of operative supervision extends probably from a maximum of 10 operatives to a maximum of 30 for most concerns." (b) "The unit of executive supervision appears . . . to range from 3 to 8 or 9 subordinates.
Newman	"Empirical studies suggest that executives in higher echelons should have a span of three to seven operating subordinates, whereas the optimum range for first-line supervisors of routine activities is usually from fifteen to twenty employees."
Terry	The proper span of management "varies with the particular circumstances, which includes such things as the type of work, the position, the ability of the executive, faith in subordinates, and fear of possible rivals."
Koontz and O'Donnell	"There is a limit to the number of persons an individual can effectively manage, even though that limit is not finite for every case but will vary with the complexity of the relationships supervised and the ability of managers and subordinates."
McFarland	"The larger the number reporting directly to an executive, the more difficult it tends to be for him to supervise and coordinate them effectively. The number of persons who can be effectively supervised is a function of the ability of the supervising executive and of the executive being supervised."
Newman, Summer and Warren	" . . . we should tailor the span of supervision for each executive position."

TABLE 11--Continued

Author   Statement

Haimann and   "There is . . . no definite, fixed answer to
Scott   the ideal number of subordinates a manager can
                       effectively supervise."

Longenecker   "In considering the span of control, it appears
                       that the determination of precise, quantitative
                       limits that are generally applicable to many
                       organizations is difficult, if not impossi-
                       ble."

     *See comment at the end of Table 1, p. 70.

The Principle of Unity of Command

Background

Much like the other previously discussed principles of organization, the principle of unity of command made an early appearance in management literature. As far back as 1856, McCallum recognized the importance of unity of command considering it "indispensable to success." He observed:

> The enforcement of a rigid system of discipline in the government of works of great magnitude is indispensable to success. All subordinates should be accountable to, and be directed by their immediate superiors only; as obedience cannot be enforced where the foreman in immediate charge is interfered with by a superior officer giving orders directly to his subordinates.[242]

Wagner also recognized the importance of single subordination. He considered unity of command to be the foundation upon which all organization theory is based:

> The entire theory of organization rests upon the principle of individual responsibility and subordination, so that, no matter how small or how great the number of individuals gathered together, some one is responsible, to whom the others must be subordinate.[243]

Some years later, Church associated unity of command with the function of control. Bemoaning the lack of firmness in control

---

[242]McCallum, "Superintendent's Report," p. 104.

[243]Wagner, Organization and Tactics, p. 3.

standards, the disappointed Church remarked:

> . . . standardized practice in regard to Control is as yet
> not very definite. What standards exist are negative rather
> than positive. "No man can serve two masters" is one of
> these, or in other words, we must avoid the clashing of
> authority, and must establish clear lines of subordination
> throughout the plant.[244]

Even though the importance of unity of command was recognized

by earlier writers, Fayol is generally credited with its populariza-

tion. Being an ardent opponent of Taylor's "functional management,"[245]

Fayol considered unity of command to be important to the effective

operation of an organization.[246] He accordingly designated it a

principle of management and advised:

> For any action whatsoever, an employee should receive
> orders from one superior only. Such is the rule of unity
> of command . . . which to my way of thinking is at least
> equal to any other principle whatsoever.[247]

Fayol also enunciated a principle of unity of direction. He

held that the existence of unity of command was dependent upon the

maintenance of unity of direction and explained this second principle

---

[244]Church, The Science and Practice of Management, p. 121.

[245]Taylor, Shop Management, p. 99.

[246]Fayol, General and Industrial Management, pp. 69-70. For a
reply from a proponent of functional management to arguments of this
nature, see: Frank B. Gilbreth, Primer of Scientific Management (2nd
ed.; New York: D. Van Nostrand Co., 1914), p. 19.

[247]Ibid., p. 24.

thus:

> This principle is expressed as: one head and one
> plan for a group of. activities having the same objective.
> It is the condition essential to unity of action, co-
> ordination of strength and focusing of effort.[248]

The Business Training Corporation, unaware of Fayol's work,

identified unity of command as a "principle of good organization" and

provided it with the following lines of explanation:

> No person is made subordinate to two or more others,
> if it can be avoided. This is a frequent source of trou-
> ble, ill will and inefficiency, and an inexcusably foolish
> arrangement.[249]

By the early nineteen-twenties, the dispute between the advo-

cates of functional management and those of unity of command was

quickly waning. A supporter of the views of the latter group,

Lansburgh, believed that functionalization could be carried to an

undesirable extreme. It was with these feelings in mind that he

commented:

> The influence of those men who feel that a workman can
> properly serve only one boss has mainly prevailed. They
> are correct in the idea that there can be over-
> functionalization.[250]

In the early nineteen-thirties, even greater agreement was

reached concerning the validity of the principle of unity of command.

---

[248]Ibid., p. 25.

[249]Business Training Corporation, Vol. VI: Management, p. 20.

[250]Lansburgh, Industrial Management, p. 63.

It was advocated by such writers as Dutton, Florence, and Gulick.
The American Management Association even designated it a "commandment"
of good organization.

Dutton presented his discussion of unity of command under the
heading, "Undivided Responsibility." In part, it reads:

An individual must be solely responsible to one man
for the performance of a function. The violation of this
rule produces confusion as to the immediate course of action,
and uncertainty in the mind of the subordinate as to the one
to whom he shall look for orders in the future.[251]

In a similar yet more direct manner, Florence favored this
same type of relationship. He argued:

Commands should only be received by subordinates from one
immediate superior. There should, in short, be only one
chain or line of authority, and a unity of command.[252]

As a member of the Brownlow Committee, Gulick presented unity
of command as a necessary principle of management. Alluding to its
theological base ("A man cannot serve two masters"), he preceded to
reword this idea in the succeeding manner:

The principle [of unity of command] may be stated as follows:
A workman subject to orders from several superiors will be
confused, inefficient, and irresponsible; a workman subject
to orders from but one superior may be methodical, efficient,
and responsible.[253]

In 1934, Michael C. Rorty, President of the American Management
Association, issued his much quoted "Ten Commandments of Good

---

[251]Dutton, Principles of Organization, p. 148.

[252]Florence, The Logic of Industrial Organisation, p. 121.

[253]Gulick, "Notes on the Theory of Organization," p. 9. For the
Biblical background of this principle, see: Matthew 6:24; Luke 16:13.

Organization." The fourth of these commandments can easily be identi-

fied as the principle of unity of command. It reads:

> No executive or employee, occupying a single position
> in the organization, should be subject to definite orders
> from more than one source.[254]

Dimock wrote perhaps the first book to devote an entire chapter

to the subject of unity of command. Referring to unity of command as

"a central principle of managerial effectiveness," the chapter begins

with the following words:

> A central requirement of good management is the integra-
> tion of all parts of the enterprise under the executive
> direction of a single person. The reason for this is clear;
> in order to accomplish a given result, all elements of the
> program required in achieving its goals must be brought to-
> gether and coalesced.[255]

In a manner very similar in nature to Rorty's, Seckler-Hudson

presented a listing of twelve organization principles. The nineth

(unity of command) simply reads:

> Unity of command and purpose should permeate the organ-
> ization.[256]

Shortly after Seckler-Hudson, both Newman and Davis addressed

the topic of unity of command. Newman, sounding much like Gulick,

commented:

> A man cannot serve two masters well. One of the
> most widely recognized principles of organization is that

---

[254]Rorty, Ten Commandments of Good Organization, p. 620.

[255]Dimock, The Executive in Action, p. 206.

[256]Seckler-Hudson, "Principles of Organization and Management,"
p. 43. (Italics omitted.)

a member of an enterprise should normally have only one line supervisor; in other words, dual subordination should be avoided.[257]

In his presentation of the principle of unity of command, Davis referred his readers to the work of Fayol. Aware of the possible friction that might result from a violation of this principle, he particularly warned against line-staff conflict or what he termed "buck-passing."[258]

A good indication of the pervasive acceptance achieved by the principle of unity of command during this period is the inclusion of this concept by the Department of the Air Force in one of its training manuals. It explained unity of command as follows:

Unity of command means that the ultimate responsibility for and control of all actions directed toward the object of the organization are vested in one individual at each level of operations.[259]

More recently, another military body, the Industrial College of the Armed Forces, presented this topic in the following way:

In any event, nobody in the organization should have any doubt as to who is his "boss" and who are his subordinates--the so-called unity-of-command principle.[260]

---

[257]Newman, Administrative Action, p. 172. (Italics omitted.)

[258]Davis, The Fundamentals of Top Management, p. 432.

[259]U. S. Air Force, USAF Management Process (Air Force Manual 25-1, Department of the Air Force). (Washington, D. C.: Government Printing Office, 1954), p. 25.

[260]Fred R. Brown, "Organization and Management," in Management Concepts and Practice, ed. by Brown (Washington, D. C.: U. S. Industrial College of the Armed Forces, 1967), p. 23.

In advocating the unity of command, Niles remarked:

> The occupant of each position should know to whom
> he reports and who reports to him, and with whom--of
> higher, equal, or lower rank--he may or must consult.[261]

Allen slightly differentiated his explanation of this concept. Indicating an awareness of a subordinate's ability to report to several superiors on separate and distinct "responsibilities," he remarked:

> Each person can be accountable only to one superior
> for delegated responsibility and authority. If an individ-
> ual reports to two principals on the same responsibility,
> confusion and friction inevitably result. When this occurs
> the subordinate is never certain who will call him to
> account for a specific activity. . . .[262]

While Allen's explanation of the principle of unity of command was not original, it does show an evolving line of thought. Further evidence of this trend may be found in an article by Heydrick. Outlining what he believed to be the major principles of organization, Heydrick presented the unity of command principle in the following words:

> No employee should be accountable to more than one
> boss in the same key result area.[263]

In explanation of this statement, Heydrick elaborated:

> This basic principle of organization, sometimes called
> the "unity of command" principle, does not mean that an employee

---

[261]Niles, The Essence of Management, p. 186.

[262]Allen, Management and Organization, p. 122.

[263]Allen K. Heydrick, "Principles of Organization," Supervisory Management, XV (March, 1970), 5.

should never have more than one manager who gives him orders. Inevitably, there are jobs in which an employee must perform tasks for two or more managers. But such jobs should be kept to a minimum--and when they are necessary, the employees should perform different tasks for each manager to whom he reports.[264]

"Principles of Management" Textbooks

Terry approached the issue of unity of command in a manner dissimilar to that of his peers. Rather than unconditionally endorsing unity of command, he only warned against dual-subordination in situations involving a "particular operation." He also showed an understanding of the fact that a subordinate can "serve two masters," but only in response to separate issues. Terry's statement of this concept follows:

Principle of Unity of Order Giving For maximum effectiveness, orders concerning a particular operation should be received directly from one person only.[265]

Succeeding Terry, Koontz and O'Donnell formulated a principle of unity of command. Developed in each of the four editions of their textbook, the concept has been most recently stated in the following form:

Principle of Unity of Command. The more completely an individual has a reporting relationship to a single superior, the less the problem of conflict in instructions and the greater the feeling of personal responsibility for results.[266]

---

[264]Ibid., 5-6.

[265]Terry, Principles of Management, p. 293; 2nd ed., 1956, p. 432; 5th ed., 1968, p. 485. (Italics omitted.)

[266]Koontz and O'Donnell, Principles of Management (4th ed., 1968), pp. 74-75, p. 425, p. 632. For earlier statements of this principle, see: 1st ed., 1955, p. 295, p. 396; 2nd ed., 1959, p. 297, p. 445; 3rd ed., 1964, p. 387, p. 530.

In the first edition of his textbook, McFarland presented a
direct statement of the principle of unity of command. Centering his
definition of this concept around the idea of "final authority,"
he stated:

> The Unity of Command Principle Unity of effort, consistency
> of direction, and the effectiveness of coordination depend
> upon one executive as the locus of ultimate responsibility.
> To subject any person to the final authority of more than
> one superior tends to divide his loyalty and confuse his
> actions.[267]

In the second and third editions of his text, McFarland did
not refer to unity of command as a principle, but rather as a
"concept." He remarked:

> . . . this concept holds that ambiguity in a position
> of leadership or coordination leads to confusion, uncer-
> tainty, and error in the performance of subordinates.[268]

Following the lead of Terry, Koontz and O'Donnell, and
McFarland, Albers similarly discussed the topic of unity of command.
However, at no point in his discussion did he present an explicit
definition of this concept.

Authors Newman and Summer approached the question of unity of
command in terms of "dual subordination." While they did not explicitly formulate a principle of unity of command, they unquestionably
favored the contents such a statement would contain. Evidence of this

---

[267]McFarland, Management, p. 173.

[268]Ibid., 2nd ed., 1964, p. 400; In a modified form, 3rd ed.,
1970, p. 254.

is found in their following comment:

> An issue we face over and over in delegating is whether
> each man should have only one boss. On this point, formal
> organization theory is clear. A worker--operator or
> manager--may have relations with many people; he may even
> accept their advice on certain matters. But he needs one
> supervisor whose guidance can be regarded as final.[269]

The principle of unity of command was associated with the

delegation of authority by Haimann and Haimann and Scott. Referring

to this concept as "one of the most widely recognized principles of

management," they acknowledged instances of "shared authority" and

"functional authority" as its only exceptions. In the form of an

explanation, Haimann commented:

> . . . the delegation of authority flows from a single supe-
> rior to a single subordinate, and each subordinate reports
> to only one superior. This is what is known as the prin-
> ciple of unity of command. . . .[270]

Haimann and Scott modified the above quote to read:

> . . . the delegation of authority flows from a single
> superior to a single subordinate and each subordinate
> reports to only one superior. That is, he is accountable
> only to the superior from whom he receives his authority
> and to no one else. This is what is known as unity of
> command.[271]

Longenecker similarly approached the concept of unity of

command. He noted numerous disadvantages of multiple supervision and

possible outcomes associated with each. In the form of an explanation,

---

[269]Newman and Summer, The Process of Management, p. 66; with
Warren, 2nd ed., 1967, pp. 90-91.

[270]Haimann, Professional Management, p. 54.

[271]Haimann and Scott, Management in Modern Organization, p. 196.

he provided the following definition:

> Unity of Command The concept of unity of command holds
> that no individual should be subject to the direct command of
> more than one superior at any given time.[272]

Writing one year after Longenecker, Dale extensively dealt with

the principle of unity of command. First associating it with Fayol

and then later with "the classical theorists," he included it in his

"Glossary of Management Terms." The definition given is reprinted

below.

> Unity of Command Only one superior for each person.[273]

Sisk utilized the "no man can serve two masters" theme in his

discussion and noted:

> Principle of Unity of Command. Each subordinate should
> be accountable to one, and only one, superior.[274]

Much like Dale, Donnelly, Gibson and Ivancevich related their

discussion of the unity of command principle to the works of classical

theorists. They too presented their definition of unity of command in

their "Glossary of Terms." It reads:

> Unity of Command. A management principle which states
> that each subordinate should report to only one superior.[275]

---

[272]Longenecker, Principles of Management, p. 172; 2nd ed., 1969,
pp. 200-01.

[273]Dale, Management, p. 726; 2nd ed., 1969, p. 771.

[274]Sisk, Principles of Management, p. 318. (Italics omitted.)

[275]Donnelly, Gibson, and Ivancevich, Fundamentals of Management,
p. 422.

An Analysis of Meaning

     A clear understanding of the principle of unity of command has been present in the field of management since the beginning of this century. With the exception of the Taylorites during the first and second decades, there has been general agreement as to the desirability of unity of command. Varying authorities have differed in their presentation of this concept, however, these differences were generally not significant.

     Whereas early writers such as McCallum, Wagner and Church recognized the concept of unity of command, Fayol is generally credited with stating it in the form of a principle.

     Writing independently and unaware of the work of Fayol, the Business Training Corporation of New York City and such authorities as Diemer, Lansburgh, Dutton, Florence and the American Management Association each advocated use of the principle of unity of command.

     Later authors such as Gulick, Seckler-Hudson, Newman, Davis and Niles closely followed the statements of this early group. Unlike the development of the principle of span of management, the development of the unity of command principle was exceptionally free of debate. The statements of its supporters were in fact so similar that there is little to be gained by repeating any of them again. However, a slight trend of change may be seen in the writings of a few more current authors.

     Whereas the majority of "principles" authors followed the theme "each subordinate should have only one boss," others such as Terry, Allen and Heydrick expanded upon this view. Realizing the many possible situations where dual-subordination might be mandatory, they reflected this in their statements of the unity of command principle. This is not to indicate that the other authors quoted did not deal with this problem. A great majority of them did; however, they did not include this reasoning in their statements of definition.

Table 12 presents an approximate chronological collection of statements on the principle of unity of command.

Formulation of Definition

Like the principle of parity of authority and responsibility, the formulation of a definition of the principle of unity of command is somewhat simplified by the consistency of meaning it has maintained throughout the development of management thought. While no two authorities have advanced definitions of identical wording, their basic meanings have been the same. However, a small group of writers have slightly differentiated their explanations. For the purpose of clarification, it is believed to be best to follow the procedure of this latter group.

Thus, drawing upon the above comments and the one predominant explanatory theme that has been continuously advanced, the following definition for the principle of unity of command is forwarded.

Principle of Unity of Command

No subordinate should be held subject to the commands of more than one superior in regard to the same subject area.

TABLE 12

A COLLECTION OF STATEMENTS
ON THE PRINCIPLE OF UNITY OF COMMAND*

Author	Statement
McCallum	"All subordinates should be accountable to, and be directed by their immediate superiors only. . . ."
Wagner	"The entire theory of organization rests upon the principle of individual responsibility and subordination, so that, no matter how small or how great the number of individuals gathered together, some one is responsible, to whom the others must be subordinate."
Church	"'No man can serve two masters' . . . we must avoid the clashing of authority, and establish clear lines of subordination throughout the plant."
Fayol	"For any action whatsoever, an employee should receive orders from one superior only. Such is the rule of unity of command. . . ."
Business Training Corporation	"No person is made subordinate to two or more others if it can be avoided. This is a frequent source of trouble, ill will and inefficiency, and an inexcusably foolish arrangement."
Dutton	"An individual must be solely responsible to one man for the performance of a function. The violation of this rule produces confusion. . . ."
Florence	"Commands should only be received by subordinates from one immediate superior."
Gulick	"A workman subject to orders from several superiors will be confused, inefficient, and irresponsible; a workman subject to orders from but one may be methodical, efficient, and responsible."

TABLE 12--Continued

Author	Statement
Rorty	"No executive or employee, occupying a single position in the organization, should be subject to definite orders from more than one source."
Dimock	"A central requirement of good management is the integration of all parts of the enterprise under the executive direction of a single person."
Seckler-Hudson	"Unity of command and purpose should permeate the organization."
Newman	"One of the most widely recognized principles of organization is that a member of an enterprise should normally have only one line supervisor; in other words dual subordination should be avoided."
U. S. Air Force	"Unity of command means that the ultimate responsibility for and control of all actions directed toward the object of the organization are vested in one individual at each level of operations."
Allen	"Each person can be accountable only to one superior for delegated responsibility and authority. If an individual reports to two principals on the same responsibility, confusion and friction inevitably result."
F. Brown	"In any event, nobody in the organization should have any doubt as to who is his 'boss' and who are his subordinates--the so-called unity of command principle."
Heydrick	"No employee should be accountable to more than one boss in the same key result area."
Terry	"For maximum effectiveness, orders concerning a particular operation should be received directly from one person only."
Koontz and O'Donnell	"The more completely an individual has a reporting relationship to a single superior, the less the problem of conflict in instructions and the greater the feeling of personal responsibility for results."

TABLE 12--Continued

Author	Statement
McFarland	"To subject any person to the final authority of more than one superior tends to divide his loyalty and confuse his actions."
Newman, Summer and Warren	"A worker . . . may have relations with many people; he may even accept their advice on certain matters. But he needs one supervisor whose guidance can be regarded as final."
Haimann and Scott	" . . . the delegation of authority flows from a single superior to a single subordinate, and each subordinate reports to only one superior. That is, he is accountable only to the superior from whom he receives his authority and to no one else. This is what is known as the principle of unity of command. . . ."
Longenecker	"The concept of unity of command holds that no individual should be subject to the direct command of more than one superior at any given time."
Dale	Unity of command means "only one superior for each person."
Sisk	"Each subordinate should be accountable to one, and only one, superior."
Donnelly, Gibson and Ivancevich	Unity of command is "a management principle which states that each subordinate should report to only one superior."

*See comment at the end of Table 1, p. 70.

Summary

In analyzing the function of organizing, five of its more important and generally recognized principles were presented for discussion. The principles of unity of command and parity of authority and responsibility showed a surprising consistency of meaning. The scalar principle experienced a degree of confusion that largely centered around the use of the terms "chain of command" and "principle of authority." Of the principles analyzed, span of management and division of labor appeared to have engendered the greatest amount of terminological confusion. A clear expression of the principle of span of management was complicated by the realization that its development appears to have undergone two periods of growth. The first period was marked by the presence of suggested numerical limitations while the second was marked by general statements of variable application. Concerning the principle of division of labor, it was found necessary to make a distinction between it and the principle of specialization.

CHAPTER VI

THE FUNCTION OF CONTROLLING

Introduction

Planning, organizing and controlling are each vital functions in the management process. While management theory provides much information concerning planning and especially organizing, the function of controlling has only recently begun to be analyzed systematically.[1] This, however, is not meant to imply that concern for controlling does not have a long history. Copley states that control was the "central idea" of scientific management.[2] Taylor, the "Father of Scientific Management," considered control to be the "original object" of his experiments. In his Presidential Address before the American Society of Mechanical Engineers, he advocated:

> . . . taking the control of the machine shop out of the hands of the many workmen, and placing it completely in the hands of the management, thus superceding "rule of thumb" by scientific control.[3]

---

[1]Kenneth J. Arrow, "Control in Large Organizations," _Management Science_, X (April, 1964), 408; Arrow, "Research in Management Controls: A Critical Synthesis," in _Management Controls: New Directions in Basic Research_, ed. by Charles Bonini, Robert K. Jaedicke, and Harvey M. Wagner (New York: McGraw-Hill Book Co., Inc., 1964), p. 317.

[2]Frank B. Copley, _Frederick W. Taylor: Father of Scientific Management_ (2 vols.; New York: Harper & Brothers, 1923), I, 358.

[3]Frederick W. Taylor, "On the Art of Cutting Metals," Paper No. 1119 in _Transactions_ (American Society of Mechanical Engineers), XXVII (1906), 39.

Control has long been considered "to be one of the most neg-
lected and least understood areas of management activity."[4]   Its managerial role has often been mistakenly considered to be synonymous with
financial control.   In such a frame of reference, it has frequently
been regarded as the sole domain of the accountant or comptroller and,
in turn, equated with such techniques as budgets and financial ratios.

It is perhaps for this reason that "the word control has the
serious shortcoming of having different meanings in different contexts."[5]
This quality has been noted by such authors as Drucker, Luneski, and
Litterer.[6]   They each point out that management control may be viewed
in two parts.   One relates to the achievement of effective control over
subordinates through the direction of their activities.   The second
relates to the evaluation of the desired outcome of an activity and the
making of corrections when necessary.   This dichotomy has been summarized well by Reeves and Woodward:

> In the literature relating to organizational behaviour
> there is ambiguity in the use of the word control.   The confu-
> sion arises largely because to control can also mean to direct.

---

[4]Paul M. Dauten, Jr., Homer L. Gammill, and Stanley C. Robinson,
"Our Concepts of Controlling Need Re-Thinking," Journal of the Academy
of Management, I (December, 1958), 42.

[5]William T. Jerome, III, Executive Control--The Catalyst (New
York: John Wiley & Sons, Inc., 1961), p. 31.

[6]Drucker, The Practice of Management, p. 160; Drucker, "Con-
trols, Control and Management, in Management Controls, ed. by Bonini,
Jaedicke, and Wagner, p. 286; Chris Luneski, "Some Aspects of the
Meaning of Control," Accounting Review, XXXIX (July, 1964), 593;
Litterer, The Analysis of Organizations, p. 233.   See also: Fremont E.
Kast and James E. Rosenziweig, Organization and Management (New York:
McGraw-Hill Book Co., Inc., 1970), p. 467.

Precisely defined control refers solely to the task of ensuring that activities are producing the desired results. Control in this sense is limited to monitoring the outcome of activities, reviewing feedback information about this outcome, and if necessary taking corrective action.[7]

As a partial consequence of this confusion, control is considered to be "one of the thorniest problems of management today."[8] Although widely discussed, it seriously lacks a common area of understanding. It has "scarcely any generally accepted principles, and everyone in the field, therefore, works by intuition and folklore."[9] This lack of development has not gone unrecognized. Rowe has noted:

Although management control is widely discussed, little has been done to formulate a body of principles for use in business system design.[10]

Furthermore, Jerome has pointed out:

Principles and procedures and substantive content simply have not been rigorously developed in the area of executive control.[11]

------

[7]Tom K. Reeves and Joan Woodward, "The Study of Managerial Control," in Industrial Organization: Behaviour and Control, ed. by Woodward (London: Oxford University Press, 1970), p. 38.

[8]Alex W. Rathe, "Management Control in Business," in Management Control Systems, ed. by Donald G. Malcolm and Alan J. Rowe (New York: John Wiley & Sons, Inc., 1960), p. 30.

[9]Robert N. Anthony, Planning and Control Systems: A Framework for Analysis (Boston: Division of Research, Graduate School of Business Administration, Harvard University, 1965), p. vii. See also: Anthony, "Planning and Control Systems: A Framework for Analysis," Management Services, I (March-April, 1964), 18-24.

[10]Alan J. Rowe, "A Research Approach in Management Controls," in Management Control Systems, ed. by Malcolm and Rowe, p. 274.

[11]Jerome, Executive Control, p. 28.

More recently, Mockler has written:

> In spite of the fact that management control is one
> of the basic management functions, there is no comprehensive
> body of management control theory and principles to which
> executives can turn for guidance in performing their manage-
> ment control functions.[12]

In acknowledging the general lack of principles in the area of
control and the duality of meaning associated with the word control
itself, a variance of approach will be employed in developing the logic
of this chapter. Control will be taken to refer solely to the traditional "constant cyclic-type activity of plan-do-compare-correct" with
its "continuous, concomitant system of communication or flow of information."[13] In effect, this eliminates from consideration the works of
those authors who use the word control in their writings to mean "to
direct."[14]

Having set this restriction, an effort will be made to trace
the development of twentieth-century management control theory. In
addition, the evolution of the exception principle, the only generally
recognized principle of control, will be separately discussed.

---

[12]Robert J. Mockler, "Developing the Science of Management
Control," Financial Executive, XXXV (December, 1967), 80.

[13]Marvin Mundel, A Conceptual Framework for the Management
Sciences (New York: McGraw-Hill Book Co., Inc., 1967), p. 160.

[14]For an anthology of such writings, see: Arnold S. Tannenbaum,
Control in Organizations (New York: McGraw-Hill Book Co., Inc., 1968).

The Development of Twentieth-Century
Management Control Theory

Background

Emerson may perhaps be credited with the first meaningful contribution to the development of twentieth-century management control theory. In his book, The Twelve Principles of Efficiency, he heavily stressed the importance of control. His "Eighth Principle: Standards and Schedules" was an attempt to stress the use of time standards in achieving increased results from lessened effort. His "Sixth Principle: Reliable, Immediate and Adequate Records" and his "Eleventh Principle: Written Standard-Practice Instructions" were both clearly an attempt to achieve control through the comparison of present performance with past achievements. Emerson considered records to have two objectives: (1) "to increase the scope and number of warnings" and (2) "to annihilate time, to bring back the past, to look into the future. . . ."[15] Emerson's "Nineth Principle: Standardized Conditions" and "Tenth Principle: Standardized Operations" were an effort to obtain the uniformity necessary for control. While Emerson did not recognize control as an independent function of management, he did provide a framework for its further understanding.

Church also contributed to the development of management control theory. He identified five "organic functions of administration."[16]

---

[15]Emerson, The Twelve Principles of Efficiency, p. 206.

[16]Church, The Science and Practice of Management, p. 28.

The third of these functions was "control" and the fourth "comparison."
Control was considered to be "that function which coordinates all of
the other functions and in addition supervises their work." Church's
"comparison" function was markedly similar to Emerson's Sixth Principle
of "Records." It dealt with "that which concerns itself with the
setting up and comparison of standards"[17] and was based on "three
elements: (a) recognition of what facts are truly significant; (b)
accurate record and convenient presentation of these facts; (c) judicious action based on study of the facts."[18] As is evident, Church
may be largely credited with recognition of the main facets of the
control process.

The topic of control was also discussed by Diemer. Distinguishing between different types of control, he considered control to mean
"the methods by which the executive or managing heads of a business
carry out their authority to regulate its affairs in accordance with the
laws of the organization."[19] Later expanding upon this explanation,
Diemer commented:

> Control is that principle of management which demands
> that the management know what ought to be done and what is
> being done in all divisions and departments of the business.

---

[17]Ibid., p. 81.

[18]Ibid., p. 347. Church had previously discussed the comparison
function in an earlier article. See: Church and Alford, "The Principles of Management," 859.

[19]Diemer, Industrial Organization and Management, p. 2.

If what is being done differs from what ought to be done
control means knowing why it differs. Control means knowing
how to overcome the located defects, shortages or excessive
costs and actually remedying them.[20]

Fayol identified control as one of six functions of management.
He advocated its application on all things within the organization and
noted that control called for constant attention. To Fayol, control
meant "verifying whether everything occurs in conformity with the plan
adopted, the instructions issued and principles established."[21]

The first text devoted entirely to the subject of management
control may have been written by Lawson. Consisting of six lectures,
its purpose was "to set before those who are engaged in organization
work the true fundamental laws governing all direction and
control. . . ."[22] Lawson held that his work provided a base for
scientific management and that only after the laws of control were
interpreted could scientific management be correctly applied. His
presentation dealt mainly with the preparation of charts and records
and was truly a pioneer work in this area.

---

[20]Diemer, "The Principles Underlying Good Management," 282.

[21]Fayol, General and Industrial Management, p. 107. It should
be noted that some question exists concerning the accuracy of the translation of Fayol's work in this area, see: E. Sidney L. Goodwin,
"Control: A Brief Excursion on the Meaning of a Word," Michigan Business Review, XII (January, 1960), 13-17, 28; Lyndall F. Urwick, "The
Meaning of Control," Michigan Business Review, XII (November, 1960), 9-13.

[22]F. M. Lawson, Industrial Control (London: Sir Isaac Pitman
& Sons, Ltd., 1920), p. v.

The lack of the application of control theory in the United States during the early period of this century may be discerned from the 1921 national research study, Waste in Industry. Over one-third of its recommendations for the elimination of waste in industry involved one or more aspects of control. The study's first recommendation, "Improvement of Organization and Executive Control," is especially telling. It reads:

> Planning and control should be adopted as fundamentals of good management. For the most part they have not penetrated the mass of American industry.[23]

Control was related to planning by Lichtner who believed that "planned control" was "imperative" for successful operation. In defining what was meant by "Planned Control," he explained:

> Planning is the managerial function of working out the best combination of procedures through co-ordinating the requirements with the facilities for carrying out the work of the division. Control is the managerial function of putting these procedures into effect.[24]

Franklin extensively discussed the relationship between control and records. He presented records of assurance, information and control.[25] As two of the required specifications of records, Franklin named "Standards or Measuring Rules" and "Comparisons of Results and

---

[23]Committee on Elimination of Waste, Waste in Industry, p. 24.

[24]William O. Lichtner, Planned Control in Manufacturing (New York: Ronald Press Co., 1924), pp. 5-6.

[25]Benjamin A. Franklin, "Records As a Basis for Management," Management Engineering, III (September, 1922), 135.

Trends."[26]   Both specifications were clearly designed to aid in the

control and achievement of results expected.

Dutton presented control as a function of production and

subdivided it into planning, supervision, inspection and information.[27]

In 1925 and 1927, he expanded upon this reasoning by discussing control

as an element of production.[28]   In a later text, Dutton stressed the

importance of comparison, measurement and standardization.[29]

Control was identified by Robinson as the sixth of his "Eight

Fundamentals of Business Organization." He described control as

> . . . that fundamental which comprises the means of providing
> the manager and the executives of an organization with contin-
> uous, prompt, and accurate information concerning the efficiency
> of operation, what the business is doing, what it has done in
> the past, and what it can be expected to do in the future. A
> system of control collects the details of operation, segregates
> them, combines them, and classifies them into a form suitable
> for use.[30]

In addition, Robinson identified three principal elements of control:

(1) forecasting results, (2) recording of results, and (3) the placing

---

[26]Ibid., pp. 136-37.

[27]Henry P. Dutton, Factory Management (New York: Macmillan
Company, 1924), p. 7.

[28]Dutton, Business Organization and Management, pp. 24-25;
Dutton, The Control of Production, Vol. II: The Shaw Plant and Shop
Management Library (6 vols.; Chicago: A. W. Shaw Co., 1927), pp. 7-12.

[29]Dutton, Principles of Organization, p. 43, pp. 63-67, p. 93.

[30]Robinson, Fundamentals of Business Organization, p. 147.

of responsibility for expected results with provision for corrective action.[31]

White identified what he believed to be the elements of control. Referring to them as "subfunctions" of the "function of control," he closely related his discussion to planning. According to White, the person "who controls must direct, coordinate, maintain, and measure."[32]

Control was perhaps first recognized as a process by Follett.[33] She considered control to be a continuing activity[34] and "the aim of organization engineering."[35] Follett defined control "as power exercised as means toward a specific end; authority, as vested control."[36] In her later writings, she distinguished between "fact-control" and "correlated control" feeling that the understanding of each depended entirely upon the individual situation.[37]

---

[31]Ibid., pp. 107-08, pp. 137-39, p. 142, p. 147.

[32]White, Business Management, p. 113.

[33]Mary Parker Follett, "The Psychology of Control," in Psychological Foundations of Management, ed. by Henry C. Metcalf (Chicago: A. W. Shaw Co., 1927), p. 179.

[34]Follett, "Individualism in a Planned Society," p. 304. See also: Follett, "The Basis of Control in Business," The Journal of the National Institute of Industrial Psychology, III (January, 1927), 233-41.

[35]Mary Parker Follett, "The Psychology of Control," in Psychological Foundations of Management, ed. by Metcalf, p. 157.

[36]Mary Parker Follett, "Power," in Scientific Foundations of Business Administration, ed. by Metcalf, p. 175.

[37]Mary Parker Follett, "The Process of Control," in Papers on the Science of Administration, ed. by Gulick and Urwick, p. 161.

The first author to identify a set of principles of control may

have been Urwick. He presented control as being

> . . . concerned with the reaction of persons and materials
> to the decisions of direction, with the measurement of such
> reactions in terms of space, time, and quantity, and with
> methods of securing that the results of such reactions shall
> be in line with those contemplated by direction.[38]

The five principles of control Urwick listed were:

(a) The Principle of Responsibility
(b) The Principle of Evidence
(c) The Principle of Uniformity
(d) The Principle of Comparison
(e) The Principle of Utility[39]

By 1943, Urwick had dropped the first two of these principles and had

provided the following definitions for the remaining three:

> The Principle of Uniformity--All figures and reports
> used for purposes of control must be in terms of the organ-
> isation structure.

> The Principle of Comparison--All figures and reports
> used for purposes of control should be in terms of standards
> of performance required, and, of past performance.

> The Principle of Utility--Figures and reports used
> for purposes of control vary in value directly in proportion
> to the period separating them from the events which they
> reflect.[40]

Davis initially began to construct his philosophy of management

control in 1928. He defined control as "the instruction and guidance of

the organization and the direction and regulation of its activities."[41]

---

[38]Urwick, "Principles of Direction and Control," p. 163.

[39]Ibid., p. 179.

[40]Urwick, The Elements of Administration, p. 122. See also:
pp. 107-08.

[41]Davis, The Principles of Factory Organization and Management,
p. 82.

He expanded upon these ideas in 1934[42] and by 1940 had largely solidi-
fied his understanding of management control. It was at this time
that Davis identified planning, organizing, and controlling as the
three organic functions of management.[43] In line with this, he listed
eight control subfunctions: (1) routine planning; (2) scheduling;
(3) preparation; (4) dispatching; (5) direction; (6) supervision;
(7) comparison; and (8) corrective action.[44] In a later book, Davis
maintained this same framework of analysis with only minor variation.[45]

Expanding upon the ideas he had presented in an earlier book,[46]
Cornell formulated one of the first listings of the principles of
management. The eleventh of his sixteen principles was the principle
of control. Cornell stressed the importance of performance standards,
performance evaluation and corrective action. His principle of
control reads:

> Planning is of little value unless there is subsequent
> control to make certain that the plans are carried out.[47]

Rose approached control from the viewpoint of the Managing
Director. He divided control into three "viewpoints": Business,

---

[42]Davis, The Principles of Business Organization and Operation,
p. 67.

[43]Davis, Industrial Organization and Management, pp. 35-36.

[44]Ibid., p. 109.

[45]Davis, The Fundamentals of Top Management, p. 407, pp. 647-52.

[46]Cornell, Industrial Organization and Management, p. 28.

[47]Cornell, Business Organization, p. 212.

Trading, and Financial. Rose considered his ideas to be the logical

extension of the work of Fayol. He defined "higher control"

> . . . as a monthly survey of the functional activities of a
> commercial undertaking, carried out from the business, trading,
> and financial viewpoints, and based upon direct trend compari-
> son between the position at the moment and the position at the
> last financial year.[48]

Rose further discussed control in a second book and in a third attempted

to codify a number of his earlier writings. In the latter of these two

works, Rose re-entitled his four "aspects" of control the Business

position, the Operating position, the Profit and Loss position, and the

Financial position.[49]

Dent approached management control from the viewpoint of a

budget analyst. He defined budgetary control to mean "working to a

plan to secure the greatest measure of all-round efficiency and team-

work."[50] He felt that "budgetary control must be based upon the manage-

ment principles of planning of activities, delegation of responsibility

coupled with authority, definition of authority, and co-ordination of

effort."[51]

---

[48]Thomas G. Rose, _Higher Control_ (London: Sir Isaac Pitman &
Sons, Ltd., 1934), p. 67.

[49]Thomas G. Rose and Donald Farr, _Higher Management Control_ (New
York: McGraw-Hill Book Co., Inc., 1957), p. 12. See also: Rose,
Company Control (London: Gee & Company (Publishers), Ltd., 1952).

[50]Arthur G. H. Dent, _Management Planning and Control_ (London:
Gee & Company (Publishers), Ltd., 1935), p. 307. See also: Dent,
"Budgetary Control Study," _Industry Illustrated_ (London), II (May, 1934),
28-30, 36.

[51]_Ibid._

Glover and Maze attempted to explain the "instruments and methods" of control and endeavored to emphasize the following:

> . . . the necessity for setting standards and measuring actual accomplishment as a basis for control . . . to point out the methods for determining causes for variations between planned and actual accomplishment, and . . . [to indicate] the more important causes of such variations as well as their under-lying reasons.[52]

In accomplishing this task, they related managerial control to organization, manufacturing costs, and marketing and administrative costs.

One of the first empirical studies of corporate organization and control was performed by Holden, Fish, and Smith. It reported the top management practices of "thirty-one leading industrial corporations." As one of its conclusions, the study presented control as a prime responsibility of top management.[53] It further identified control as a process, embracing three elements: (1) Objective--to determine what is desired; (2) Procedure--to plan how and when a task is to be done, organization to determine who is responsible, and standards to determine what constitutes good performance; and (3) Appraisal--to determine how well a task was done.[54]

The nineteen-forties was an era of continued interest in management control. Dimock defined control as "the analysis of present performance, in the light of fixed goals and standards, in order to

---

[52]John G. Glover and Coleman L. Maze, Managerial Control (New York: Ronald Press Co., 1937), pp. v-vi.

[53]Holden, Fish, and Smith, Top-Management Organization and Control, p. 3.

[54]Ibid., p. 77.

determine the extent to which accomplishment measures up to executive

orders and expectations."[55] Rowland associated control with planning

by pointing out the relationship existing between the two.[56] Hopf

stressed the importance of speed in handling control information.[57]

Filipetti identified control as "the most important factor in organ-

ization."[58] Goetz approached the problem of management control from the

viewpoint of the accountant. He interpreted control to consist of

"securing conformity to plans."[59] McCaully discussed control for the

foreman and supervisor.[60] Both Thurston and Somervell related control

to organization and advocated the establishment of company control

---

[55]Dimock, The Executive in Action, p. 217.

[56]Floyd H. Rowland, Business Planning and Control (New York: Harper & Brothers, 1947), p. 3.

[57]Hopf, "Organization, Executive Capacity, and Progress," p. 40. See also: Hopf, "Evolution in Organization During the Past Decade," Advanced Management Journal, XII (September, 1947), 107.

[58]George Filipetti, Industrial Management in Transition (Homewood, Illinois: Richard D. Irwin, Inc., 1946), p. 260.

[59]Billy E. Goetz, Management Planning and Control (New York: McGraw-Hill Book Co., Inc., 1949), p. 3.

[60]Harry J. McCaully, Jr., Management Controls for Foremen and Supervisors (New York: Funk & Wagnalls Co., 1948). Two earlier texts by Erwin H. Schell and William B. Rice analyzed control for the business executive specifically, see: Schell, The Technique of Executive Control (New York: McGraw-Hill Book Co., Inc., 1924), and Rice, Control Charts in Factory Management (New York: John Wiley & Sons, Inc., 1947).

sections.[61] Trundle associated control with manufacturing, sales

accounting and industrial relations.[62] Wharton discussed control in

office operations.[63]

In 1948, Brech largely revised his initial framework of manage-

ment principles. He presented control as the "obverse" of planning

and advocated "standards of performance," "continuous comparison of

actual achievement or results against these predetermined standards,"

and a balancing of long-and-short-term consequences.[64] Brech has

recently defined control to mean:

> . . . checking current performance against objectives and
> targets in terms of predetermined standards contained in the
> plans, with a view to ensuring adequate progress and

---

[61]John B. Thurston, "A New Concept of Managerial Control," in
Company Development and Top Management Control, General Management
Series No. 134 (New York: American Management Association, 1945), pp.
9-23; Thurston, "The Control Unit: Newest Technique for Controlling
Decentralized Operations," Advanced Management Journal, XII (June,
1947), 74-87; Thurston, Coordinating and Controlling Operations, Sec.
I, bk. ii of Reading Course in Executive Technique, ed. by Carl Heyel
(41 Vols.; New York: Funk & Wagnalls Co., 1948), pp. 5-14; Frank A.
Lamperti and Thurston, Internal Auditing for Management (Englewood
Cliffs, N. J.: Prentice-Hall, Inc., 1953), chap. vii, "Control Unit,"
pp. 93-107; Brehon B. Somervell, "Organization Controls in Industry,"
in Organization Controls and Executive Compensation, General Management
Series No. 142 (New York: American Management Association, 1948), pp.
3-13.

[62]George T. Trundle, Managerial Control of Business (New York:
John Wiley & Sons, 1948). See also: Trundle, "Production Control,"
in Handbook of Business Administration, ed. by Donald, pp. 604-24.

[63]Kenneth J. Wharton, Administrative Control (London: Gee &
Co. (Publishers), Ltd., 1947). See also: Wharton, "Administrative
Organization and Control," The Accountant, August 16, 1947; August 23,
1947; August 30, 1947. Serialized in three parts.

[64]Brech, Management (2nd ed., 1948), p. 14.

satisfactory performance whether physical or financial; also
contributing to decision in continuing or changing the plans,
as well as "recording" the experience gained from the working of
these plans as a guide to possible future operations.[65]

Control was identified as a process of administration by

Newman. He defined control in the following manner:

> . . . seeing that operating results conform as nearly
> as possible to the plans. This involves the establishment
> of standards, motivation of people to achieve these stand-
> ards, comparison of actual results against the standard, and
> necessary corrective action when performance deviates from
> the plan.[66]

In line with this definition, Newman presented three essential steps

in the control process: (1) setting standards at strategic points,

(2) checking and reporting on performance, and (3) taking corrective

action.[67]

The nineteen-fifties witnessed the emergence of the first

"principles of management" textbooks. The content of these books was

basically developed from earlier management thought. Approaching con-

trol in a manner similar to earlier writers such as Fayol and Davis,

each of the "principles" books used in this analysis, with the exception

of Albers' text, presents control as a function of management.

A review of these texts shows a surprising similarity of

presentation. From Terry through Donnelly, Gibson and Ivancevich, a

consensus of standard topics of presentation is easily discerned.

Subjects generally discussed include an identification of the steps in

---

[65]Brech, _Organisation_ (2nd ed., 1965), pp. 13-14.

[66]Newman, _Administrative_ _Action_, p. 4.

[67]_Ibid._, p. 408.

the control process, the requirements of control, the determination of standards, means of measurement and types of control mechanisms. In relation to the last mentioned topic, budgetary control and the human response to controls are also generally presented. All, except for the Albers and Donnelly, Gibson and Ivancevich texts, take note of the exception principle. However, only three texts (Terry's, Koontz and O'Donnell's, and Sisk's) identify additional principles of control. Of these three texts, only Koontz and O'Donnell's provides a complete framework of management control principles.

The widespread absence of control principles in principles of management textbooks is indicative of the slow development in this area. While Terry and Sisk present a few selected principles of control, uncertainty in this area is verified by the fact that Sisk refers the reader to the work of Koontz for a more complete discussion of this topic.[68]

Showing the influence of Taylor, Goetz and Urwick, the background for Koontz's initial formulation of his principles of control framework may be traced to the first edition of his principles of management text.[69] Designed as a preliminary statement, Koontz revised this framework of presentation in the following year.[70] At that time, he identified fourteen principles of control. More recently he and

---

[68]Sisk, Principles of Management, p. 589n.

[69]Koontz, "A Preliminary Statement of Principles of Planning and Control," 45-60.

[70]Harold D. Koontz, "Management Control: A Suggested Formulation of Principles," California Management Review, I (Winter, 1959), 47-55.

O'Donnell have limited their framework to twelve control principles.
It should be remembered that Koontz was the first author since Urwick's
1928 formulation to attempt the presentation of a complete statement of
management control principles. Grouped into three general categories,
these are:

I. The Purpose and Nature of Control

    1. Principle of assurance of objective The task of control
is to assure accomplishment of objectives by detecting
potential or actual deviation from plans early enough
to permit effective corrective action.

    2. Principle of efficiency of controls The more control
approaches and techniques detect and illuminate the
causes of potential or actual deviations from plans with
the minimum of costs or other unsought consequences,
the more efficient these controls are.

    3. Principle of control responsibility The primary respon-
sibility for the exercise of control rests in the manager
charged with the execution of plans.

    4. Principle of direct control The higher the quality of
managers and their subordinates, the less will be the need
for indirect controls.

II. The Structure of Control

    5. Principle of reflection of plans The more controls are
designed to deal with and reflect the specific nature
and structure of plans, the more effectively they will
serve the interests of the enterprise and its managers.

    6. Principle of organizational suitability The more controls
are designed to reflect the place in the organization
structure where responsibility for action lies, the
more they will facilitate correction of deviation of
events from plans.

    7. Principle of individuality of controls Since it is the
task of controls to inform people who are expected to
act to avoid or correct deviations from plans, effective controls require that they be consistent with the
position, operational responsibility, competence, and
needs of the individual concerned.

III. The Process of Control

   8. Principle of standards Effective control requires
      objective, accurate, and suitable standards.

   9. Principle of critical-point control Effective control
      requires attention to those factors critical to apprais-
      ing performance against an individual plan.

   10. The exception principle The more a manager concentrates
      his control efforts on exceptions, the more efficient will
      be the results of this control.

   11. Principle of flexibility of controls If controls are to
      remain effective despite failure or unforeseen changes
      of plans, flexibility is required in the design of controls.

   12. Principle of action Control is justified only if indi-
      cated or experienced deviations from plans are corrected
      through appropriate planning, organizing, staffing and
      directing.[71]

To date, Koontz and O'Donnell's statement of the principle of

control is the clearest and most comprehensive formulation of its kind

in the area of management control. Its initial presentation has already

been referred to as a "classic of management literature."[72] In the few

years since its first appearance, the study of management control has

begun to emerge as an independent area of study. Authors such as

Jerome and Anthony have recently attempted to solidify the groundwork

upon which to construct a science of management control.

   Jerome initiated the development of a science of management

control by advancing the belief that control is "a subject area with its

---

[71]Koontz and O'Donnell, Principles of Management (4th ed., 1968),
pp. 731-35.

[72]Paul M. Dauten, Jr., ed., Current Issues and Emerging Concepts
in Management (Vol. I; Boston: Houghton-Mifflin Co., 1962), p. 116.
Editor's comment.

own distinctive concepts and precepts."[73] Anthony defined and discussed management control from a systems viewpoint and attempted to establish the proper role of control in a firm's operation.[74]

Research studies performed in the area of management control have recently been increasing in number. Paik has analyzed the control procedures of selected branch banks. Hekimian has reported the control operations of selected life insurance branch offices. Deming has studied the control system of a large electrical corporation. Villers has reported the planning and control practices of selected research and development organizations. Sord and Welsch have studied managerial control problems from the viewpoint of lower-level supervisors.[75]

---

[73]Jerome, Executive Control, p. 27.

[74]Robert N. Anthony, Planning and Control Systems: A Framework for Analysis (Boston: Division of Research, Graduate School of Business Administration, Harvard University, 1965).

[75]James S. Hekimian, Management Control in Life Insurance Branch Offices (Boston: Division of Research, Graduate School of Business Administration, Harvard University, 1965) with Appendix: "Management Controls in Branch Banks," by Chei-Min Paik (1963), pp. 169-83; Robert H. Deming, Characteristics of an Effective Management Control System in an Industrial Organization (Boston: Division of Research, Graduate School of Business Administration, Harvard University, 1968); Raymond Villers, Research and Development: Planning and Control (New York: Financial Executives Institute, 1964); Burnard H. Sord and Glenn A. Welsch, Managerial Planning and Control, Research Monograph No. 27 (Austin, Texas: Bureau of Business Research, University of Texas, 1964). For the reports of three earlier control studies, see: Robert N. Anthony, Management Controls in Industrial Research Organizations (Boston: Division of Research, Graduate School of Business Administration, Harvard University, 1952); Raymond J. Ziegler, "The Application of Managerial Controls in Selected Business Firms," (Unpublished Ph.D. dissertation, University of Florida, 1957); Sord and Welsch, Business Budgeting: A Survey of Management Planning and Control Practices (New York: Controllership Foundation, Inc., 1958).

Each of these studies provide realistic information concerning the actual operation of on-going control systems.

Six recent books, each dealing with various aspects of control, are also indicative of the growing widespread interest in management control theory. Deverell has shown the relationship between the planning and control process pointing out their interdependency. He has also presented a discussion of current control techniques.[76] Strong and Smith have dealt with current control techniques and attempted to show the essentiality of control.[77] Taking a different approach, Mundel has dealt mainly with the control concept and its application in the organic areas of production, sales, and finance.[78] Stokes has presented guidelines to aid in installing a "total control program." Viewing control from the vantage point of a top corporate executive, he has presented and discussed areas of critical control performance.[79] Asplund et al. have dealt with material and production management as special aspects of

---

[76]Cyril S. Deverell, Management Planning and Control (London: Gee & Co. (Publishers), Ltd., 1967).

[77]Earl P. Strong and Robert D. Smith, Management Control Models (New York: Holt, Rinehart and Winston, 1968).

[78]Marvin Mundel, A Conceptual Framework for the Management Sciences (New York: McGraw-Hill Book Co., Inc., 1967).

[79]Paul M. Stokes, A Total Systems Approach to Management Control (New York: American Management Association, 1968).

management control.[80] Mockler has identified and explored each of the
steps in the management control process.[81]

The combined contributions of the previously discussed authors
have provided a beginning for the development of a science of management control. Being years behind the maturity of planning and especially of organization theory, the study of management control theory
appears to be attempting a new level of sophistication. It is only
through continued interest and study in this area that such an
achievement will be attained.

Summary

As the preceding discussion indicates, twentieth century concern
for management control may be traced from the beginning of the "scientific management" revolution to present day management thought.
Introduced by the work of early writers such as Taylor, Emerson and
Church, the basics of what may today be identified as the control
process became well-known by the end of the first decade of this century.

While the importance of control was recognized by such authors
as Lawson, Franklin, Diemer, Dutton, Lichtner, Cornell, Robinson,
Williams, and White, a general lack of business control in the earlier
years is attested to by the conclusions of the Federated American

---

[80]Inegmar Asplund, ed., Management Control: A Survey of Production and Inventory Control Models in Theory and Practice (Lund, Sweden:
Studentlitteratur, 1969).

[81]Robert J. Mockler, The Management Control Process (New York:
Appleton-Century-Crofts, 1972).

Engineering Societies' study, <u>Waste</u> <u>in</u> <u>Industry</u>. It was not until 1927 that Follett identified control as a process and not until a year later that the first set of control principles was formulated.

Early texts, such as those by Rose, Dent, Glover and Maze, and Goetz, were predominantly oriented to accounting and finance. The 1941 Holden, Fish and Smith study was the first empirical attempt to explore corporate control. This interest has been revived recently by the works of Anthony, Paik, Hekimian, Deming, Villers, Sord and Welsch. It should also be noted that the interest in control has had a long record of international involvement. This is attested to by the works of Fayol, Lawson, Urwick, Rose, Dent, Brech, Deverell, and Asplund <u>et</u> <u>al</u>.

It has only been in recent years, since the advent of principles of management textbooks, that specific attempts have been made to lay a foundation for the development of a science of management control theory. The Koontz framework of management control principles has been followed by the work of Anthony, Jerome, Smith and Strong, Mundel, Stokes, and Mockler. Each has attempted to add to the area of knowledge generally referred to as "management control." Only with continued interest of this nature will the theory of control be able to advance. It is, unquestionably, an area of needed study.

The Exception Principle

Background

General disagreement and a lack of codification have basically characterized the development of the function of control. Yet, there is within the study of control a single area of noticeable agreement that does stand out. Reference is made to the principle of exception. Taylor is generally credited with enunciating the first business statement of this principle in an address made before the American Society of Mechanical Engineers.[82] In advocating its use, he explained:

> Under it [the exception principle] the manager should receive only condensed, summarized, and invariably comparative reports, covering, however, all of the elements entering into the management, and even these summaries should all be carefully gone over by an assistant before they reach the manager, and have all the exceptions to the past averages or standards pointed out, both the especially good and the especially bad exceptions, thus giving him in a few minutes a full view of progress which is being made, or the reverse, and leaving him free to consider the broader lines of policy and to study the character and fitness of the important men under him.[83]

To this he later added:

> The broad application of the exception principle is, of course, only possible with modern scientific management, in which everything is done in accordance with laws and rules; because if the workmen and the foremen are not working

---

[82]For a discussion of the Biblical background of this principle, see: Mooney and Reiley, The Principle of Organization, pp. 20-21. Reference is made to Exodus 18:25, 26; Deuteronomy 1:17.

[83]Taylor, "Shop Management," 1409; Taylor, Shop Management, pp. 126-27. See also: p. 109.

according to laws or rules, there is no standard, such as the
task, which draws a sharp line between failure and success.
If there are no rules, there can be no exceptions.[84]

Following Taylor's presentation, the significance of the
exception principle was readily acknowledged. Writers such as Sparling
and Robb included the exception concept in their writings. Sparling
associated this principle with increased efficiency and wrote:

> It should be the aim of the manager to organize his business
> so that it will "run itself." When a business is so organized,
> the manager is able to devote his time to larger affairs,
> leaving the details to be worked out by competent department
> managers. . . . In this way the application of correct princi-
> ples of organization is utilized, and a high degree of effi-
> ciency secured.[85]

This same idea was similarly presented by Robb. However, he
extended his analysis to make mention of certain associated limitations:

> The time that one can devote to a duty is limited, and
> his capacity is limited. It is no longer possible for the
> head of a great organization to know all the detail of an
> undertaking, or even to know of all the minor coordination.
> He can be directly responsible for but little of the actual
> action, but he must know when the action goes wrong. He must
> know the result toward which action is tending. He is respon-
> sible for the result. . . . He must be provided with informa-
> tion analyzed, sifted, and compiled, ready for the application
> of his judgment.[86]

The exception principle continued to gain acceptance. In the
year 1915 alone, such diverse writers as Smith, Porter, and Gowin each

---

[84]Taylor, quoted in Copley, Taylor, I, 302.

[85]Sparling, Introduction to Business Organization, p. 6.

[86]Russell Robb, "The Organization of Administration," Stone and
Webster Public Service Journal, IV (June, 1909), 406. Reprinted in
Robb, Lectures on Organization, p. 68.

commented upon this concept. Under the rubric "The Exception Principle

in Handling Reports," Smith appropriately remarked:

> Making a huge number of records and reports tends to produce
> a flood of stuff, which, if it is all read by the responsible
> parties, leaves them no time for anything else. As standards
> tend to be developed, the proper handling of record reports
> goes over to the exception principle. Shall the superinten-
> dent spend forty minutes examining a certain detailed report
> every day? If it is normal, no by no means. If it is abnormal
> in any respect, he should by all means focus attention on the
> abnormal spots, which could be pointed out to him by some
> assistant. Thus, instead of handling the mass, he handles
> exceptions, just as the doctor who does not see his patient
> everyday, but comes when the patient is disarranged.[87]

The exception principle was presented in a similar manner in

volume six of the Library of Factory Management. Chapter seven of this

volume entitled, "Executive Control" and contributed by Harry F. Porter,

contained a discussion of the exception principle under the heading:

"SIFTING SIGNIFICANT DETAILS FROM THOSE THAT LACK IMPORTANCE FOR THE

MANAGER." As part of his explanation, Porter observed:

> Another factor in maintaining a fresh perspective is
> to rid every case of non-essentials before it comes to a deci-
> sion. This executive when in his office cleans up an enor-
> mous mass of work in a short time; and his decisions, though
> usually given quickly, are almost never in error. He always
> has his facts boiled down in the simplest form.[88]

Like Smith and Porter, Gowin favored the exception principle.

Being interested in the activities of the executive, Gowin presented a

plan for the "subordination of material." This plan incorporated the

exception principle. In advocation of the plan, Gowin explained:

---

[87] J. Russell Smith, The Elements of Industrial Management
(Philadelphia: J. B. Lippincott Co., 1915), pp. 250-51.

[88] The Library of Factory Management, Vol. VI: Executive
Control (6 Vols.; Chicago: A. W. Shaw and Co., 1915), p. 130.

According to this general plan of subordinating material, the executive does not see every caller, but certain callers; does not talk with every one who calls up on the telephone, but a selected few; does not seek here and there for what he needs, but has it brought; does not pile his desk with undigested masses of figures, but studies boiled-down reports. Subordinates quarry at the base of the pyramid; he directs their efforts from the apex.[89]

Recognition of the exception principle may also be found in the works of other writers of this period. Jones considered the exception principle to be "a rule in scientific research" and a method by which to increase originality of thinking. He expressed these ideas, declaring:

A more difficult project is to increase the originality of one's thinking. In making efforts to escape into a world of more profitable ideas, it should be noticed that there is a rule of scientific research, that all exceptional cases, either condition of performance, whether above or below the average, should be given special attention. Such cases are special for the reason that the causes are unusual. The causes may be unusual in either promise or threat.[90]

Gilbreth, a strong advocate of the exception principle, contended that it improved the quality of an executive. He remarked:

The personal work of the executive should consist as much as possible of making decisions and as little as possible of making motions. General recognition of this fact has resulted in the common practice of assigning to the executive one or more secretaries, or clerks, to relieve him of certain parts of his work which involve mere motions and less important decisions than that part of the work retained by the executive. This procedure varies in degree according to the kind of work

---

[89]Gowin, The Executive and His Control of Man, p. 87.

[90]Jones, The Administration of Industrial Enterprises (2nd ed., 1925), p. 211. See also: Jones, The Business Administrator (New York: Engineering Magazine Co., 1914), pp. 69-72. Originally serialized in The Engineering Magazine, XLIV, XLVII-XLVIII (1912 and 1914).

done by the executive and how well he realizes the possi-
bilities of eliminating waste through the use of the "exception principle" in management.[91]

In a manner similar to Jones and Gilbreth's, both Thompson and
the Business Training Corporation provided positive support for the
exception principle. Thompson noted:

> In accordance with the theory that the ablest men are or
> should be the highest in the organization, the "exception"
> principle is used . . . by which all matters within the
> capacity of subordinate officials are finally determined by
> them and only such matters as are beyond their scope or
> authority are passed up the line, thus leaving the higher
> officials free to devote their time to the broadest and
> most important problems of administration.[92]

The Business Training Corporation advised:

> The only way in which the foreman can spread himself over the
> ground is by using the "exception principle."
>
> Successful men who have charge of large affairs do not
> spend much time on things that are going along in a routine
> way, but they spend a great deal of it on things that are
> not going as they should. This is the "exception principle,"
> which consists in finding the high spots and hitting them.[93]

The nineteen-twenties was a period of continued widespread
acceptance of the exception principle. Management's most well-known
authorities joined in its recognition. Lansburgh related the exception principle to "system." He believed that it aided in the

---

[91]Frank B. Gilbreth, "Graphical Control on the Exception Principle for Executives," Paper 1573a in _Transactions_ (American Society of
Mechanical Engineers), XXXVIII (1916), 1213.

[92]C. Bertrand Thompson, _The Theory and Practice of Scientific
Management_ (New York: Houghton-Mifflin Co., 1917), p. 48. See also:
p. 107.

[93]Business Training Corporation, Vol. II: _Handling Men_, p. 62.

development of the fundamentals of organization and explained its

operations in the following passage:

> System supplies the motive power for what has been
> termed the "exception principle" of management. When
> operating under this principle, instead of the head of
> an enterprise, a department, or even of only a few men,
> attempting to act personally on each case coming under
> his general jurisdiction, he acts on the exceptional matters
> only.[94]

Other writers declared the exception concept to be either a

"law" or a "principle." Acknowledging Taylor's influence in this area,

Alford presented the following statement:

> Law of Exceptions Managerial efficiency is greatly increased
> by concentrating managerial attention solely upon those exec-
> utive matters which are variations from routine, plan, or
> standard.[95]

Jones presented the exception principle under the title "Prin-

ciple of Executive Efficiency." Varying in title but not in content,

his statement was similar to those of previous writers:

> The Principle of Executive Efficiency The functions
> remaining to the personal care of any major executive should
> be so ordered and limited that only those matters which are
> exceptions to the routine under his control shall come to him
> for action. . . .[96]

The exception principle was related to the establishment of

standards by White. He sounded much like previous management

---

[94]Lansburgh, Industrial Management, p. 46.

[95]Alford, "Laws of Manufacturing Management," p. 404. See also:
Alford, Laws of Management Applied to Manufacturing, p. 74; Alford,
ed., Cost and Production Handbook, p. 1332; Alford, Principles of
Industrial Management for Engineers, p. 115; Alford and Bangs, eds.,
Production Handbook, p. 1386.

[96]Jones, Theories and Types of Organizations, p. 30.

contributors when he made the following comment:

> One advantage is that it [standards] permits the intro-
> duction of the so-called "exception principle," whereby
> everything is supposed to operate automatically, so to
> speak, until some emergency or exception arises which requires
> attention. In other words, if the system is carefully
> worked out, the executive does not have to bother with its
> operation at all, as long as no unforeseen event occurs.[97]

Cornell stated the exception principle in a manner similar to

Jones and Alford's. Stressing the "utilization of executive ability,"

he argued:

> Executive ability can be utilized fully only when the executive
> is relieved of all matters which can be reduced to a routine.
> Standards of performance must be setup, and all plans definitely
> laid. The executive can then devote his attention only to
> variations from the standard, to master planning and to those
> executive responsibilities that cannot be made matters of
> routine.[98]

Perhaps two of the most succinct yet clear statements of the

exception principle were made by Diemer and Dutton. Diemer advised:

> It is worth while for an executive to sift or "pan"
> his management information with a view to separating the
> gold dust of principles from the sand ore of procedure.[99]

Dutton likewise added:

> Only the new situation requires thought. The exception
> principle applies this truth.[100]

The exception principle was also discussed by Lord. Refer-

encing the work of Alford, Lord offered the following statement as a

---

[97]White, Business Management, p. 106.

[98]Cornell, Business Organization, p. 214.

[99]Diemer, "The Principles Underlying Good Management," 280.

[100]Dutton, Principles of Organization, p. 44. See also: Dutton,
Factory Management, p. 298.

"rule" of management by exception:

> Consistency of procedure must never interfere with an obvious exception to that procedure or to its system.[101]

Balderston, Karabasz and Brecht considered the exception principle to be "the capstone of well-developed management." In their analysis of this principle, they stressed the delegation of recurring matters as follows:

> The device by which most executives conserve their time is termed the "exception principle," which means merely the delegation to others of recurring matters. Once the executive sees that the recurrence will be frequent, he establishes a policy and routine as a guide to handling such situations and then delegates to subordinates the responsibility for dealing with them. He is thus able to concentrate his attention upon emergencies, special questions, and new problems.[102]

Davis commented upon the exception principle linking it to reporting and in particular performance reports:

> . . . they [performance reports] should conform to the so-called "exception principle." This means simply that only the significant exceptions to the standards of condition, procedure or performance should be called to the attention of the superior executive.[103]

Anderson and Schwenning associated the exception principle with "job synthesis." In a discussion concerning the content, the

---

[101]Chester Lord, "Management by Exception," Paper Man-53-4-49 in Transactions (American Society of Mechanical Engineers), LIII (1931), 50. (Italics omitted.) See also: Lord, "Visualized Management Control: A System Which Shows Up Exceptions and Slips," Management and Administration, VI (September, 1923), 319-22.

[102]Balderston, Karabasz, and Brecht, Management of an Enterprise, p. 413.

[103]Davis, The Principles of Business Organization and Operation, p. 75. See also: Davis, The Fundamentals of Top Management, p. 729.

specifications, and the analysis of jobs, they concluded:

> Jobs of all higher officers should not, and really cannot, be definitely standardized in terms of specific tasks, for these are by nature positions relieved of all work of a routine character in order to allow ample time for concentration upon exceptions to routine, emergencies, and matters of greater consequence.[104]

The nineteen-forties and nineteen-fifties also saw continued recognition of the exception principle. Petersen and Plowman defined the exception principle as follows: "Exceptional or unusual problems, when recognized as such by a subordinate executive, will not be decided by him but will be appealed or referred to his superiors."[105] In what may be considered an explanation of the operation of the exception principle, Trundle added: "The exception principle merely establishes and segregates the deviations from the normal and expected results, so that attention and remedial action can be focused on them."[106]

Urwick included the exception principle in his framework of elements of administration. Developing this framework in order to prove that a logical scheme of principles existed, he drew heavily upon the ideas of Taylor, Fayol, Mooney and Reiley. In his

---

[104]Anderson and Schwenning, The Science of Production Organization, p. 106.

[105]Petersen and Plowman, Business Organization and Management, p. 55.

[106]Trundle, Managerial Control of Business, p. 109.

identification of twenty-nine "principles of administration," Urwick

credited the genesis of the exception principle to Taylor.[107]

In stressing the exception principle, Newman advised concen-

tration on "unexpected or unusual results." However, he did warn

against complete reliance upon this procedure and favored the use of

an additional means of performance observation.[108]

Glover addressed the subject of the exception principle referr-

ing to it as the "Executive Law of Exceptions." He explained:

> Executives, as a general rule, cannot observe all performance,
> thus authority for control must be delegated to supervisors
> and the application of desirable instruments of control should
> be made effective by these supervisors. Thus control instru-
> ments must be developed so that they call attention to the
> supervisor when symptoms of variations appear, which if not
> checked immediately, may tend to defeat the control process.[109]

The first book devoted entirely to the exception principle

was authored by Bittel. In its opening chapter, the following defini-

tion of its subject is offered:

> Management by exception in its simplest form, is a
> system of identification and communication that signals the
> manager when his attention is needed; conversely, it remains
> silent when his attention is not required. The primary
> purpose of such a system is, of course, to simplify the

---

[107]Urwick, The Elements of Administration, p. 110, p. 123, p. 126; See also: Urwick, "Principles of Management," 46.

[108]Newman, Administrative Action, p. 420.

[109]Glover, Fundamentals of Professional Management (1st ed., 1954), p. 127.

management process--to permit a manager to find the problems
that need his action and to avoid dealing with those that are
better handled by subordinates.[110]

"Principles of Management" Textbooks

A review of the principles of management textbooks employed in
this analysis reveals that all but two include the exception principle
in their discussions. Terry presented a statement of this principle
in each of the five editions of his text. Having undergone only minor
variation in wording, his present statement reads:

Principle of Exception Controlling is expedited by
concentrating on the exceptions, or outstanding variations,
from the expected result or standard.[111]

The exception principle was also included in each edition of
Koontz and O'Donnell's principles of management textbook. It was not,
however, until Koontz presented an independent analysis of management
control that the present framework used in their textbook emerged.
Based on an earlier preliminary statement,[112] it offers the following

---

[110]Lester R. Bittel, Management by Exception (New York: McGraw-
Hill Book Co., Inc., 1964), p. 5. See also: Bittel, "Management by
Exception," in Handbook of Business Administration, ed. by Maynard, pp.
4-89. For two articles of a related nature, see: John W. Darr,
"Management by Exception As Applied to Monitoring and Reporting,"
APICS Quarterly Bulletin, III (October, 1962), 51-59; Charles G. Gibbons,
"Management by Exception," Advanced Management Journal, XXIX (January,
1964), 12-16.

[111]Terry, Principles of Management (5th ed., 1968), p. 555.
(Italics omitted.) For similar statements, see: 1st ed., 1953, p.
280; 2nd ed., 1956, p. 486.

[112]Koontz, "A Preliminary Statement of Principles of Planning
and Control," 45-60.

definition:

> The Exception Principle: Efficiency in control
> requires that attention of the manager be given primarily to
> significant exceptions.[113]

Koontz and O'Donnell have changed the wording of this statement

in more recent editions, but its content remains basically the same.[114]

McFarland did not provide an explicit statement of the excep-

tion principle. He did, however, discuss the principle in each of the

three editions of his book. Closely relating the exception principle

to the delegation of authority, he provided the following discussion:

> The delegated authority, in effect, sets limits within
> which the subordinate may act. When a situation calls for a
> decision or an action beyond these limits, the subordinate is
> usually instructed to refer the matter to the higher level
> for an authoritative decision. In much of the literature of
> management, this is called "the exceptions principle."[115]

Following McFarland's lead, Newman and Summer did not present a

direct definition of the exception principle. They did, however,

provide some indication as to the meaning they assigned to this princi-

ple when they referred to it throughout their discussion. At one

point they stated: "The so-called 'exception principle' simply refers

to an understanding an executive may have with his subordinates that so

long as operations are proceeding as planned, the subordinates should

---

[113]Koontz, "Management Control," 54.

[114]Koontz and O'Donnell, Principles of Management, p. 295; 2nd
ed., 1959, p. 706; 3rd ed., 1964, p. 624; 4th ed., 1968, p. 734.

[115]McFarland, Management (2nd ed., 1964), p. 305; 3rd ed., 1970,
p. 427. For a similar but not identical statement, see: 1st ed.,
1958, p. 221.

not bother him."[116] At a succeeding point they added: "An executive

may ask to be notified when deviations from standard exceed a certain

norm, thus applying the 'exception principle'. . . ."[117]

Haimann and Scott approached the exception principle in much

the same manner as did Terry. After acknowledging its original

expression by Taylor, they provided the following explanation: "As

applied to the control process, the [exception] principle states that

the manager should give detailed attention mainly to the unusual or

exceptional items because only they warrent [sic] executive

attention."[118]

Longenecker approached the exception principle by associating

it with "economy of control." Identifying it as a fundamental of

control, he utilized the phrase "management by exception" in his

discussion of this concept. Despite this variation, his presentation

closely paralleled those of previous writers. Longenecker explained:

> Economy of control effort utilizes the principle of
> management by exception. In using this approach, the manager
> devotes effort to unexpected or out-of-line performance.
> Some standard is assumed, and significant deviations from
> that standard constitute the exceptions. If performance

---

[116]Newman and Summer, The Process of Management, p. 406; 2nd ed.,
1967, with Warren, p. 501.

[117]Ibid., 1st ed., 1961, p. 624; 2nd ed., 1967, p. 741.

[118]Haimann and Scott, Management in the Modern Organization, p.
453. For a similar but not identical statement, see: Haimann,
Professional Management, p. 499.

conforms to anticipations, time spent in reviewing this fact
is largely wasted. Managing by exception permits the
manager to isolate nonstandard performance and to concentrate
upon it.[119]

Dale provided a clear statement of his definition of the

exception principle by including it in his "Glossary of Management

Terms." Its entry reads:

> Exception principle, management by A method of control under
> which only exceptional results, good or bad, are
> flagged for management attention.[120]

"Principles" author Sisk approached the exception principle

in a manner strongly reminiscent of Alford's.

> Principle of the Exception--The most efficient use of
> managerial time and energy is possible when control informa-
> tion stresses the exception and focuses attention upon those
> functions that need corrective action.[121]

Authors Albers and Donnelly, Gibson and Ivancevich did not

present a discussion of the exception principle in their respective

textbooks.[122]

An Analysis of Meaning

An appreciation and understanding of the exception principle

has been present since the beginning of twentieth century management

---

[119]Longenecker, Principles of Management, p. 471; 2nd ed., 1969,
pp. 558-59.

[120]Dale, Management, p. 719; 2nd ed., 1969, p. 760.

[121]Sisk, Principles of Management, p. 590.

[122]Albers, Organized Executive Action; Donnelly, Gibson and
Ivancevich, Fundamentals of Management.

thought. Originally enunciated by Taylor as a management principle,
it has been perhaps the least criticized of the "classical" principles
of management.

The exception principle has enjoyed continued recognition from
the time of its first formulation to its present-day usage. Early
writers such as Sparling, Robb, Smith, Porter, and Gowin each stressed
its importance. Jones considered the exception principle to be "a
rule in scientific research." Gilbreth contended that it improved the
quality of an executive. Thompson and the Business Training Corporation saw the exception principle as a way to increase the capacity of
the manager. With the exception of Thompson who stressed the proper
determination of the level of authority at which a decision should be
made, each of these early authors emphasized the need for managerial
concentration upon variations in performance.

During the nineteen-twenties, the exception principle was
associated with "system" by Lansburgh, related to standards by White,
designated a "law" by Alford, and designated a "principle" by Jones
and Cornell. Throughout this entire period, an outstanding feature of
the exception principle was its consistency of definition. This
phenomenon may perhaps be credited to the fact that it was originally
forwarded by such a well-known person as Taylor.

In the decades following its initial recognition, the exception
principle became a standard topic of discussion. Writers such as
Lord; Balderston, Karabasz, and Brecht; Davis; Petersen and Plowman;
Urwick; and Glover all included the exception principle in their
analyses. With the exclusion of Petersen and Plowman who offered an

explanation of the exception principle similar to Thompson's, a consistency of definition exists in the works of these authors.

With the introduction of the first principles of management texts in the early nineteen-fifties, there was a continuance of this consistency. However, its clarity was slightly interrupted. Whereas the majority of authors reviewed stressed the need for managerial concentration upon variations in performance, McFarland and Newman and Summer (like Thompson and Petersen and Plowman before them) emphasized the proper determination of the level of authority at which "exceptional" problems should be resolved. Consistency of meaning was re-established with the works of Haimann and Scott, Longenecker, Dale and Sisk.

In retrospect, the works of those authors who emphasized managerial concentration upon variations from standard have prevailed over the works of those authors who stressed the determination of the proper level of authority at which a decision should be made. The writings of this prevailing group may be divided into two categories: (1) those authors who interpreted the exception principle in a general manner to simply include deviations from standard and (2) those authors who restricted their interpretations to include only unusual or outstanding deviations from standard. This distinction is largely a matter of degree rather than one of content.

Table 13 presents a chronological collection of statements on the exception principle.

Formulation of Definition

In formulating a definition of the exception principle, the influence of Taylor must be given paramount consideration. In none of the other principles analyzed is one man so completely recognized as the originator of a concept. As a result, the meaning associated with the exception principle has tended to remain basically unchanged since its conception.

The majority of authors who have mentioned the exception principle in their writings have stressed two main themes: (1) the identification of exceptional variations (either good or bad) from standard, and (2) managerial concentration upon these variations. It is with these two themes in mind, and in consideration of Taylor's original explanation of this concept, that the following definition is offered.

The Exception Principle

Managerial concentration should be centered around the identification of exceptional variations from standard.

TABLE 13

A COLLECTION OF STATEMENTS
ON THE EXCEPTION PRINCIPLE*

Author	Statement
Taylor	Under the exception principle "the manager should receive only condensed, summarized, and invariably comparative reports," that "have all the exceptions to the past averages or standards pointed out, both the especially good and the especially bad exceptions. . . ."
Sparling	"It should be the aim of the manager to organize his business so that it will 'run itself.' When a business is so organized, the manager is able to devote his time to larger affairs, leaving the details to be worked out by competent department managers. . . ."
Robb	"The time that one can devote to a duty is limited, and his capacity is limited. It is no longer possible for the head of a great organization to know all the detail of an undertaking. . . . He must be provided with information analyzed, sifted, and compiled, ready for the application of his judgment."
E. D. Jones	"In making efforts to escape into a world of more profitable ideas, it should be noticed that there is a rule of scientific research, that all exceptional cases, either condition of performance, whether above or below the average, should be given special attention."
Thompson	The exception principle refers to a situation where "all matters within the capacity of subordinate officials are finally determined by them and only such matters as are beyond their scope or authority are passed up the line, thus leaving the higher officials free to devote their time to the broadest and most important problems of administration."

TABLE 13--<u>Continued</u>

Author	Statement
Business Train- ing Corporation	"Successful men who have charge of large affairs do not spend much time on things that are going along in a routine way, but they spend a great deal of it on things that are not going as they should."
Lansburgh	Under the exception principle, "instead of the head of an enterprise, a department, or even of only a few men, attempting to act personally on each case coming under his personal jurisdic- tion, he acts on the exceptional matters only."
Alford	"Managerial efficiency is greatly increased by concentrating managerial attention solely upon those executive matters which are variations from routine, plan, or standard."
T. R. Jones	"The functions remaining to the personal care of any major executive should be so ordered and limited that only those matters which are excep- tions to the routine under his control shall come to him for action. . . ."
P. White	Under the exception principle, "everything is supposed to operate automatically, so to speak, until some emergency or exception arises which requires attention. In other words, if the system is carefully worked out, the executive does not have to bother with its operation at all, as long as no unforeseen event occurs."
Cornell	"Executive ability can be utilized fully only when the executive is relieved of all matters which can be reduced to a routine. . . . The executive then can devote his attention only to variations from standard. . . ."
Diemer	"It is worth while for an executive to sift or 'pan' his management information with a view to separating the gold dust of principles from the sand and ore of procedure."
Dutton	"Only the new situation requires thought. The exception principle applies this truth."

TABLE 13--<u>Continued</u>

<u>Author</u>	<u>Statement</u>
Lord	"Consistency of procedure must never interfere with an obvious exception to that procedure or to its system."
Balderston, Karabasz and Brecht	"The device by which most executives conserve their time is termed the 'exception principle,' which means merely the delegation to others of recurring matters."
R. C. Davis	The exception principle means "that only the significant exceptions to the standards of condition, procedure, or performance should be called to the attention of the superior executive."
Petersen and Plowman	The exception principle means "that exceptional or unusual problems, when recognized as such by a subordinate executive, will not be decided by him but will be appealed or referred to his superiors."
Trundle	"The exception principle merely establishes and segregates the deviations from the normal and expected results, so that attention and remedial action can be focused on them."
Glover	" . . . . control instruments must be developed so that they call attention to the supervisor when symptoms of variation appear, which if not checked immediately, may tend to defeat the control process."
Bittel	"Management by exception in its simplest form, is a system of identification and communication that signals the manager when his attention is needed; conversely, it remains silent when his attention is not required."
Terry	"Controlling is expedited by concentrating on the exceptions, or outstanding variations, from the expected result or standard."
Koontz and O'Donnell	"Efficiency in control requires that attention of the manager be given primarily to significant exceptions."

TABLE 13--Continued

Author	Statement
McFarland	" . . . delegated authority . . . sets limits within which the subordinate may act. When a situation calls for a decision or an action beyond these limits, the subordinate is usually instructed to refer to the higher level for an authoritative decision. In much of the literature of management, this is called 'the exceptions principle.'"
Newman, Summer and Warren	"The so-called 'exception principle' simply refers to an understanding an executive may have with his subordinates that so long as operations are proceeding as planned, the subordinates should not bother him."
Haimann and Scott	"As applied to the control process, the exception principle states that the manager should give detailed attention mainly to the unusual or exceptional items because only they warrent [sic] executive attention."
Longenecker	"Management by exception permits the manager to isolate nonstandard performance and to concentrate upon it."
Dale	The exception principle is "a method of control under which only exceptional results, good or bad, are flagged for management attention."
Sisk	"The most efficient use of managerial time and energy is possible when control information stresses the exception and focuses attention upon those functions that need corrective action."

*See comment at the end of Table 1, p. 70.

CHAPTER VII

SUMMARY, RECOMMENDATIONS AND CONCLUSION

Summary

The extraordinary development of management theory throughout the present century has resulted in the creation of many new terms. It has also resulted in a shift of meaning for many old ones. This dissertation has been written in recognition of the terminological confusion which this has caused. Its purpose has been to undertake a thorough analysis of selected management concepts in an effort to: (1) clarify the meaning of these concepts by tracing their evolutionary development; (2) initiate a standardization of the fundamental terminology and definitions used in the field of management; (3) provide a beginning lexical source for additional future development and compilation of management terminology; and (4) contribute to the first and perhaps most vital step in the process of creating a valid and universally accepted general theory of management.

Following Chapter II (a brief note on the role of theory in management) and Chapter III (a historical review of the terminological conflict in management), the methodology employed throughout the main body of the dissertation has been one of analysis, clarification and recommendation. An exploratory study organized around the management functions of planning, organizing and controlling, the dissertation has analyzed the evolutionary development of thirteen management principles. An attempt has been made to clarify the terminology and definitions associated with each principle and a recommended definition for each has been formulated.

Designed to be a beginning effort, it is again mentioned that the definitions advanced for each principle are in no way meant to be inflexible to future managerial developments. Furthermore, any similarities in wording between the recommended definitions and previously existing definitions are largely a result of the inherent limitation of existing available symbols (words) to convey meaning. The author has constantly labored under a warning issued by the late Thomas G. Rose. Recognizing the terminological confusion developing within management, Rose called for a "standardization of terminology." He, however, cautioned:

> It is easy enough to demand definitions and excessively difficult to supply them. It will usually be found that the people who speak contemptuously of "loose definitions" and censor the author for lack of clarity, are unable to suggest something better.[1]

Hopefully, this dissertation and the succeeding action which it aspires to stimulate will prove to be efforts not covered by the above remark. Throughout the entire dissertation, an attempt has been made to draw upon the ideas and intents of management's early authors. The first phase of each section of the dissertation's main body involves

---

[1]Thomas G. Rose, "The Inexactitude of Terminology," Times Trade & Engineering (London), XXXVIII (August, 1937), 11. For an additional comment by Rose in this area, see: Rose, "Management or Administration?: In the Evolution of Management Principles There Must Be No Confusion of Terms," Industry (London), XVII (November, 1949), 532-34.

an evolutionary analysis of the terminology being studied. Following
this analysis, an attempt has been made to clarify the meaning of the
terms in question and to formulate for each a recommended definition.
Tables 14, 15, and 16 have been prepared to show the manner in which the
final definitions offered coincide with those proposed by earlier
writers. A significant degree of consistency may be observed. Combined, the tables include a chronological list of writings about each
of the principles selected for analysis. In each table, the definitions
proposed by the dissertation are compared with those offered in the
writings analyzed.

Table 14, which is devoted to the function of planning, reveals
that the evolution for each of planning's four main underlying princi-
ples--objective, balance, efficiency, and coordination--may be traced to
the first decade of this century. Three "newer" planning principles--
primacy of planning, commitment and flexibility--however, have a past
of less than two decades. In comparing the definitions offered by each
writer with those proposed by the dissertation, a strong trend of
consistency in regard to the principle of objective may be seen even
though it had to be distinguished from the principle of contribution to
objective. A similar but not as strong a trend is evident concerning
the principle of efficiency. Much of the discrepancy between its final
proposed definition and earlier definitions may be traced to confusion
which surrounds the use of the words "efficiency" and "effectiveness."
The variety of approaches used in explaining the principle of coordination accounts for the major dissimilarities between the dissertation's
proposed definition and many of its earlier definitions. The largest

area of disagreement between proposed and previously offered definitions involves the principle of balance. This may perhaps be explained
by the fact that balance is one of the more nebulous concepts analyzed.
In regard to the "newer" planning principles, in all cases the proposed
definitions closely parallel those of earlier writers.

Devoted to the function of organizing, Table 15 reveals a
strong consistency of meaning between each of the definitions proposed
and those of earlier writings. The distinction between the principle
of division of labor and the principle of specialization minimized
confusion in this area. The principle of parity of authority and
responsibility, the scalar principle and the principle of unity of
command each exhibit a strong consistency of meaning. This consistency
is further reflected in the dissertation's proposed definition of each
principle. The principle of span of management shows an early incon-
sistency of meaning; this may in part be explained by the popularity
of suggested numerical limitations in the definitions of that period.

Table 16, which is devoted to the exception principle, shows the
strongest trend of consistent meaning between earlier formulated definitions and that proposed in the dissertation. As previously mentioned,
this may be in part explained by the principle's close association with
its originator, Frederick W. Taylor.

In conclusion, an attempt has been made to assure a historical
consistency of meaning for all definitions proposed. In doing so, it
is felt that a more complete understanding of the meanings attached to
them by early management authors has resulted. It is further felt,

TABLE 14

PLANNING PRINCIPLES: A
COMPARISON OF DEFINITIONS*

List of Writings:

Author	Principles: Obj.	Unity of Obj.	Bal.	Effi- ciency	Coordi- nation	Primacy	Commit- ment	Flexi- bility
Taylor	X							
Church	X		O		X			
Emerson				O				
Robb	X			X				
Myers					X			
Kimball	X				X			
Murphy			O					
Fayol	X		O	X	O			
Knoeppel	X							
Feiss			O		X			
E. D. Jones			X		O			
Business Training Corporation			O					
Estes			O					
DeHaas				O				
Lansburgh	X			X				
Diemer	X	X						
Dutton	X	X	X					
Robinson	X	X	X					
Urwick					X			

TABLE 14--Continued

List of Writings:

Author		Principles:						
	Obj.	Unity of Obj.	Bal.	Effi-ciency	Coordi-nation	Primacy	Commit-ment	Flexi-bility
R. C. Davis			X		O			
Gulick				X	O			
Tead					X			
Balderston, Karabasz and Brecht					O			
Alford	X				X			
Gillespie	X							
Barnard					O			
White					X			
Petersen and Plowman					X			
H. Niles	X				X			
Dimock	X		O		O			
Spriegel			X					
Brech	X			O				
Simon				X				
Newman				X	O			
Glover				X		X	X	
Terry	X		X		X	X	X	X

TABLE 14--Continued

*In the first column of the table is an approximate chronological list of writings about selected principles of the function of planning, with the author of each writing given. In order to keep the table as simple as possible, titles are not given (a full reference is included for each writing, however, in the text of the dissertation). Each of the seven remaining columns represents a principle that has been previously discussed. For example, a book written by Taylor is listed first. On the right-hand side of the table is an "X" in the column headed "objective." This means that the explanation offered by Taylor is closely similar to that proposed by this dissertation. Following the entry citing the writings of Church, is an "O" in the column headed "Balance." This means that the explanation offered by Church is not closely similar to that proposed by this dissertation.

TABLE 15--Continued

List of Writings:

		Principles:				
Author	Division of Labor	Speciali- zation	Scalar	Authority and Re- sponsibility	Span of Mgmt.	Unity of Command
Dutton					X	X
Robinson			X	X		
P. White				X		
Williams			O		O	
L. White					O	
Black		X				
Follett				X		
Alford	X		X	X	O	
T. R. Jones	X					
Cornell		X	X	X		
Urwick		X	X	X	O	
Dennison				X	O	
Mooney & Reiley			X			
Wellington				X		
Florence			X		X	X
Hart					O	
Graicunas	O				O	
Balderston, Karabasz and Brecht				X	O	
R. C. Davis				X	O	
Rorty				X		
Gulick	O				X	X

TABLE 15--Continued

List of Writings:

Principles:

Author	Division of Labor	Speciali-zation	Scalar	Authority and Re-sponsibility	Span of Mgmt.	Unity of Command
A. Brown				X		
Spriegel			X			
Brech			X	X	O	
Newman				X	O	X
Tead			O			
Glover						
M. C. Niles				X		
U. S. A. F.				X		
Allen						O
F. Brown						X
Heydrick						X
Terry		O	X	X	X	X
Koontz and O'Donnell	X		X	X	X	X
McFarland		X	X	X	X	X
Albers	X	X				
Newman, Summer and Warren	X	X	X	O	X	X
Haimann and Scott		X	X		X	X
Dale				X		X
Longenecker				X	X	X

TABLE 16

CONTROLLING PRINCIPLES:
A COMPARISON OF DEFINITIONS*

List of Writings:	Principle:
Author	Exception
Taylor	X
Sparling	X
Robb	X
E. D. Jones	X
Thompson	O
Business Training Corporation	X
Lansburgh	X
Alford	X
T. R. Jones	X
P. White	X
Cornell	X
Diemer	X
Dutton	X
Lord	X
Balderston, Karabasz and Brecht	X
R. C. Davis	X
Peterson and Plowman	O
Trundle	X
Glover	X
Bittel	X
Terry	X
Koontz and O'Donnell	X
McFarland	O
Newman, Summer and Warren	O
Haimann and Scott	X
Longenecker	X
Dale	X
Sisk	X

*See comment at the end of Table 14, p.

that this in turn has led to a more accurate formulation of definitions
for the principles selected.

Recommendations

Based on the general proposition that the field of management
needs explicitly stated and generally accepted concepts, the definitions proposed in this dissertation may themselves be considered a
recommendation to alleviate the terminological confusion that exists
within the management field. It, however, seems quite unlikely that
such a task will be accomplished by one writer in a single effort. As
Brown has noted, "the writings on these subjects show too much individ-
uality to hope that their authors could be persuaded by any one other
man."[2]

In the form of an alternate recommendation, both Brown and
Urwick have separately suggested that a select group of management
scholars and practitioners be nominated to meet, study, and advance a
glossary of management terms.[3] Since it is recognized that the diverse
backgrounds of the wide-ranging membership of the management profession
presents an obvious handicap to an undertaking of this type, such a
nominated group ideally would consist of representatives from all areas
interested in the practice, study and advancement of management. More
specifically, this would involve representatives from four main groups,

---

[2]Alvin M. Brown, "What Do You Mean By That Remark?," Advanced
Management Journal, XVI (August, 1951), 8.

[3]Ibid.; Lyndall F. Urwick, "The Problem of Management Semantics," California Management Review, II (Spring, 1960), 82.

namely: business and industry managers, professional management society members, governmental managers, and management teachers.

As examples of organizations whose membership includes representatives of the four groups in question, the American Management Association, the Society for Advancement of Management, the Academy of Management[4] and the Council for International Progress in Management immediately come to mind. Among the many foreign associations, the British Institute of Management, the Australian Institute of Management, the Comité National de L'Organisation Française and the International Committee for Scientific Management also fit into this category.

Evidence of the feasibility of such a task is readily available from the fields of accounting and marketing. Both disciplines have long paid particular attention to the terminology and definitions they employ. Formed in 1920, the Committee on Terminology of the American Institute of Certified Public Accountants issued its first volume of definitions, Accounting Terminology, in 1931.[5] Its efforts have since

---

[4]It should be noted that in his 1966 Presidential Address before the Academy, Harold D. Koontz suggested that the Academy "promote understanding" through the compilation of a dictionary of management terms. Unfortunately, his suggestion has gone unheeded, see: Koontz, "Challenges for Intellectual Leadership in Management," in Academy of Management Proceedings (1963), ed. by Paul J. Gordon (Bowling Green, Ohio, 1964), p. 116.

[5]American Institute of Accountants, Special Committee on Terminology, chairman, Walter Mucklow, Preliminary Report of the Special Committee on Terminology, ed. by Alphyon P. Richardson (New York: Century Co., 1931).

resulted in the issuance of eight Accounting Research Bulletins and four Accounting Terminology Bulletins.[6]

The Committee on Definitions of the American Marketing Association was also formed in 1931. Under the chairmanship of Ralph S. Alexander, its work has been translated into fourteen languages.[7] Its most recent report, Marketing Definitions: A Glossary of Marketing Terms, was published in 1961.[8]

While neither the efforts of the Committee on Terminology of the American Institute of Certified Public Accountants or the Committee on Definitions of the American Marketing Association have met with complete success, they have both encouraged much discussion and debate. This achievement and the early acceptance of such a responsibility may in itself be considered a valued contribution.

The recognition and acceptance of a similar responsibility within the field of management would unquestionably do much to lead to a reduction in the terminological confusion that exists within it today. Before a general theory of management can be developed and the

---

[6]See: American Institute of Certified Public Accountants, Accounting Principles Board, Accounting Research and Terminology Bulletins (Final Edition; New York: AICPA, 1961), pp. 1-43.

[7]See: American Marketing Association, Committee on Definitions, chairman, Ralph S. Alexander, "Report of the Definitions Committee," Journal of Marketing, XIII (October, 1948), 202-17.

[8]American Marketing Association, Committee on Definitions, chairman, Ralph S. Alexander, Marketing Definitions: A Glossary of Marketing Terms (Chicago: American Marketing Association, 1960).

field of management can hope to achieve the status of a true science,

it must establish an accepted terminology. For this reason, it is

important that the best thinkers in the management profession be

encouraged to offer their views and constructive criticisms toward the

solution of this problem.

Over sixty years ago, Henry L. Moore wrote of a similar plight

in the field of economics. Today, his words accurately summarize the

present state of management terminology and its resulting effect upon

the advancement of management theory:

> Economic [read management] terms seem to pass in their
> historical development through a series of stages which, with-
> out pretension to rigidness, may be described as follows:
> first, no definition is given, but it is assumed that every
> one has a sufficiently clear idea of the subject to make a
> formal definition unnecessary; second, a definition is
> attempted and a number of exceptional forms are noted; third,
> with the further increase of data, the relative importance of
> the various forms changes, confusion in discussion is
> introduced, logomachy takes the place of constructive inves-
> tigation; fourth, a complete classification of the forms
> embraced under the original term is made, and problems are
> investigated with reference to these classes. The bewilder-
> ing vagueness of economic [read management] theory is largely
> due to the fact that the terms used are in all of these stages
> of development.[9]

---

[9]Henry L. Moore, "Paradoxes of Competition," _Quarterly Journal of Economics_, XX (February, 1906), 211. It should be noted that the field of economics has centered attention on the terminology and defi- nitions it employs for over 150 years, see: Thomas R. Malthus, _Defini- tions in Political Economy, preceded by an Inquiry into the Rules Which Ought to Guide Political Economists in the Definition and Use of Their Terms; with Remarks on the Deviations from These Rules in Their Writings_ (London: John Murray, 1827). For two efforts similar to that undertaken in this dissertation, see: Lindley M. Fraser, _Economic Thought and Language_ (London: A. & C. Black, Ltd., 1937); Fritz Machlup, _Essays on Economic Semantics_, ed. by Merton H. Miller (Englewood Cliffs, N. J., 1963).

The management profession has for too long ignored the basic necessity of developing and stating the meaning of the terminology it employs. It is imperative that the terms it uses and their associated definitions be made concise and unambiguous. If the management profession possesses the will and determination to take an affirmative stand in this area, it will succeed; if not, continued terminological confusion is almost a certainty.

Conclusion

A conclusion of this dissertation is that an attempt to initiate a discussion which will lead to the standardization of management terminology must be made. Groups such as the American Management Association, the Society for Advancement of Management and the Academy of Management must shoulder such a responsibility. Their willingness to do so could lead to the beginning of the cessation of the terminological confusion that has long plagued the field of management.

Areas not included in this dissertation also need to be investigated. Such research areas are: (1) other principles associated with the management functions of planning, organizing and controlling, (2) other accepted functions of management such as directing, and (3) other lesser agreed upon management functions such as staffing.

In undertaking to initiate alone such a task, the author fully recognizes that he has exposed himself to attack from all quarters of the management profession. This, however, is exactly the object sought and if achieved, would serve to meet the purposes of this dissertation.

ABSTRACT

Arthur George Bedeian, Doctor of Business Administration, 1973

Major: Management

Title of Dissertation: A Standardization of Selected Management
                        Concepts

Directed by: Dr. Giovanni B. Giglioni

Pages in Dissertation: 384   Words in Abstract: 480

ABSTRACT

Since "modern" management's beginning at the turn of this
century, there have been pleas from management practitioners and
academicians alike to solidify the underlying foundation upon which it
is based. However, until the field of management can boast of an all
inclusive and unified body of management theory, it will continue to
remain without such a needed and desired framework.

Confusion, controversy, and disagreement are traditionally
characteristic of a new and growing field of study. The field of
management is no exception. A large extent of the basic controversy
and confusion associated with management thought can be attributed to
disagreement over concepts and terminology. This absence of agreement
and the resulting lack of standardization associated with it are the
problems addressed by this dissertation. Its purpose has been to
undertake a thorough analysis of selected management concepts in an
effort to: (1) clarify the meaning of these concepts by tracing their
evolutionary development, (2) initiate a standardization of the

fundamental terminology and definitions used in the field of management, (3) provide a beginning lexical source for additional future development and compilation of management terminology, and (4) contribute to the first and perhaps most vital step in the process of creating a valid and universally accepted general theory of management.

Following Chapter II (a brief note on the role of theory in management) and Chapter III (a historical review of the terminological conflict in management), the methodology employed throughout the main body of the dissertation (Chapters IV-VI) is one of analysis, clarification and recommendation. An explanatory study organized around the management functions of planning, organizing and controlling, the dissertation analyzes the evolutionary development of thirteen management concepts, namely, the planning principles of objective, balance, efficiency, coordination, primacy, commitment and flexibility; the organizing principles of division of labor, scalar, parity of authority and responsibility, span of management and unity of command; and the exception principle of control. An attempt is made to clarify the terminology and definitions associated with each principle and a recommended definition for each is formulated.

Before a general theory of management can be developed and the field of management can hope to achieve the status of a true science, it must establish an accepted terminology. The management profession has for too long ignored the basic necessity of developing and stating the meaning of the terminology it employs. It is imperative that the terms it uses and their associated definitions be made concise and unambiguous.

A conclusion of this dissertation is that an attempt must be made to initiate a discussion which will lead to the standardization of management terminology. Groups such as the American Management Association, the Society for Advancement of Management and the Academy of Management must shoulder such a responsibility. Their willingness to do so could lead to the beginning of the cessation of the terminological confusion that has long plagued the field of management.

APPENDICES

APPENDIX I

SELECTED BIBLIOGRAPHY OF MANAGEMENT
DICTIONARIES AND GLOSSARIES

General

Allen, Louis A. Common Vocabulary of Professional Management. 3rd ed.
    Palo Alto, Calif.: Executive Press, 1968. 37 pages.

Benge, Eugene J. "Management Terms Needn't Be Gobbledygook." Factory,
    CXIX (March, 1961), 209-18.

Ettinger, Karl E. Management Glossary. Management Primer Series:
    "Principles and Practices of Productivity," Training Manual No.
    201, Technical Aids Branch, Office of Industrial Resources.
    Washington, D. C.: International Cooperation Administration,
    by the Council for International Progress in Management,
    1960. 35 pages.

Institute of Industrial Management (Melbourne). Definitions of Terms
    Used in Industrial Management. Melbourne: The Institute,
    Management Nomenclature Research Group, 1948. 27 pages.

Johannson, Hano, and Robertson, Andrew, comps. Management Glossary.
    Edited by E. F. L. Brech. Harlow, England: Longmans, Green
    & Co., Ltd., 1968. 146 pages.

Lindemann, Albert John, Lundgren, Earl F., and Kaas, H. K. von.
    Dictionary of Management Terms. Dubuque, Iowa: William C.
    Brown Book Co., 1966. 81 pages.

Personnel and Industrial Relations

Banki, Ivan S. The Dictionary of Administration & Supervision.
    Los Angeles, Calif.: Systems Research, 1971. 131 pages.

Becker, Esther R. Dictionary of Personnel and Industrial Relations.
    New York: Philosophical Library, 1958. 366 pages.

Benn, Alice E. The Management Dictionary. New York: Exposition Press,
    Inc., 1952. 381 pages.

APPENDIX I--<u>Continued</u>

Browne, Waldo R., comp. <u>What's What in the Labor Movement; A Dic-tionary of Labor Affairs and Labor Terminology</u>. New York: B. W. Huebsch, Inc., 1921. 577 pages.

Casselman, Paul H. <u>Labor Dictionary</u>. New York: Philosophical Library, 1949. 554 pages.

Doherty, Robert E., and De Marchi, Gerard A. <u>Industrial and Labor Relations Terms: A Glossary for Students</u>, Bulletin No. 44. 2nd ed. New York: Cornell University, School of Industrial and Labor Relations, 1971. 37 pages.

<u>Glossary of Personnel Management and Industrial Relations Terms</u>. John F. Mee, chairman. New York: Society for Advancement of Management, National Research Committee, 1959. 36 pages.

Hackett, James D. "Clearing Up the Uncertainty of Labor Terminology." <u>Management Engineering</u>, IV (May, 1923), 341-44.

Hopke, William E., ed. <u>Dictionary of Personnel and Guidance Terms</u>. Chicago: J. G. Ferguson, 1968. 464 pages.

<u>Labor Terminology</u>, Bulletin No. 25. Cambridge, Mass.: Bureau of Business Research, Publication of the Graduate School of Business Administration, VIII, No. 1, Harvard University, March, 1921. 108 pages.

Lee, John, ed. <u>Dictionary of Industrial Administration</u>. Vols. I and II. London: Sir Issac Pitman & Sons, Ltd., 1928-29. 1151 pages.

Ministry of Labour. <u>Glossary of Training Terms</u>. London: Her Majesty's Stationery Office, 1967. 51 pages.

<u>Personnel Terminology</u>, Special Report No. 10. James D. Hackett, chairman. New York: American Management Association, Commit-tee on Management Terminology, 1925. 32 pages.

Roberts, Harold S. <u>Dictionary of Labor-Management Relations.</u> Honolulu, Hawaii: University of Hawaii Industrial Relations Center, 1957-1963. (9 nos. in 1 vol., letters A-L covered)

Studensky, Paul. "Closed and Open Shop Terminology." <u>New Jersey</u> (N. J. Chamber of Commerce, Newark), VIII, No. 2 (1920), 21-23.

_____. <u>Roberts' Dictionary of Industrial Relations</u>. Rev. ed. Washington, D. C.: BNA Incorporated, 1971. 486 pages.

APPENDIX I--Continued

Telford, Fred. "Employment Terminology." Public Personnel Studies,
II (August, 1924), 152-66.

U. S. Navy. Naval Operations, Office of. Department of Navy Glossary
of Terms for Manpower Management and Personnel Administration.
Washington, D. C.: Government Printing Office, 1968. 133
pages.

Yoder, Dale, et al. Industrial Relations Glossary, Bulletin No. 6.
Minneapolis, Minn.: Industrial Relations Center, University
of Minnesota Press, 1948. 16 pages.

Production, Wage and Work Study

British Standard Glossary of Terms in Work Study. London: British
Standards Institution, 1959. 28 pages.

Glossary of Inventory Control Terms. General Memorandum No. 33.
Edited by Michel A. Carré. Cambridge, Mass.: Arthur D.
Little, Inc., 1963. 79 pages.

Glossary of Terms for Quality Control. London: European Organization
for Quality Control, Ministry of Aviation, 1965. 21 pages.

Glossary of Terms Used in Methods, Time Study and Wage Incentives.
James H. Eddy, chairman. New York: Society for Advancement
of Management, Research and Development Division, 1952. 32
pages.

U. S. Department of Labor, Bureau of Labor Statistics. Glossary of
Currently Used Wage Terms, Bulletin No. 983. Washington,
D. C.: Government Printing Office, 1950. 34 pages.

U. S. Department of Labor, Bureau of Labor Statistics. A Guide to
Labor Management Relations in the United States, Bulletin No.
1225. Washington, D. C.: Government Printing Office, 1958.
See: Chapter 4:01, "Glossary of Current Industrial Relations
Terms," pp. 1-30.

U. S. Department of Labor, Bureau of Labor Statistics. Glossary of
Current Industrial Relations and Wage Terms, by J. W. Bloch,
Bulletin No. 1438. Washington, D. C.: Government Printing
Office, 1965. 103 pages.

Wight, Oliver W., ed. Dictionary of Production and Inventory Control
Terms. 2nd ed. Detroit: American Production and Inventory
Control Society, Language and Technique Committee, 1966.
21 pages.

APPENDIX I--Continued

A Work Study Glossary. London: Institute of Economic Engineering,
    1953. 36 pages.

APPENDIX II

SELECTED BIBLIOGRAPHY OF GENERAL BUSINESS
DICTIONARIES AND GLOSSARIES

Alsager, Christen M. Dictionary of Business Terms. Chicago:
  Callaghan & Co., 1932. 429 pages.

Argenti, John, and Rope, Crispin. A New Glossary of Management
  Techniques. 2nd ed. London: Management Publications, Ltd.
  for the British Institute of Management, 1971. 32 pages.

Bosley, D. J. A Glossary of Commercial Terms. London: Blackie &
  Son, Ltd., 1964. 72 pages.

Clark, Donald T., and Gottfried, Bert A. Dictionary of Business and
  Finance. New York: Thomas Y. Crowell & Co., 1957. 409 pages.

Crowell's Dictionary of Business and Finance. Rev. ed. New York:
  Thomas Y. Crowell & Co., 1930. 601 pages.

Davids, Lewis E. Instant Business Dictionary. Mundelein, Illinois:
  Careers Institute, 1971. 320 pages.

Editorial Staff of Prentice-Hall, Inc. Encyclopedic Dictionary of
  Business. New York: Prentice-Hall, Inc., 1952. 704 pages.

Hamburger, Edward. A Business Vocabulary. Englewood Cliffs, N. J.:
  Prentice-Hall, Inc., 1966. 64 pages.

_____. A Business Dictionary. Englewood Cliffs, N. J.: Prentice-
  Hall, Inc., 1967. 198 pages.

Hicks, Charles B. The Technical Business Vocabulary of General Business Education, Microfilm AC-1, Publication No. 1580. Ann
  Arbor, Michigan: University Microfilm, 1949.

Jenkins, A. Ouseley's 1000 Business Terms and Phrases. London:
  J. H. Ouseley & Son, n. d. 117 pages.

Lazarus, Harold. American Business Dictionary. New York: Philosophical Library, 1957. 522 pages.

Marshall, Henry [pseud.]. Business Man's Dictionary and Guide to
  English. Garden City, N. Y.: Doubleday, Page & Co., 1920.
  652 pages.

_____, ed. The New Business Encyclopedia. Rev. ed. Garden City
  N. Y.: Doubleday & Co., Inc., 1963. See: "A Business
  Dictionary," pp. 469-509.

APPENDIX II--Continued

Nanassy, Louie C., and Selden, William H. Business Dictionary. New
    York: Prentice-Hall, Inc., 1960. 263 pages.

Nelson, L. F., ed. Pitman's Business Man's Guide: A Comprehensive
    Dictionary of Commercial Information. 14th ed. London:
    Sir Issac Pitman & Co., Ltd., 1967. 345 pages.

Perry, F. E. Business Terms, Phrases and Abbreviations. 13th ed.
    London: Sir Issac Pitman and Co., Ltd., 1966. 232 pages.

Pugh, Eric. A Dictionary of Acronyms and Abbreviations. 2nd ed.
    London: Clive Bingley, Ltd., 1970. 214 pages.

Pullan, A. G. P., and Alcock, D. W. The Commercial Dictionary. London:
    Sweet & Maxwell, Ltd., 1953. 316 pages.

Schwartz, Robert J. The Dictionary of Business and Industry. New
    York: Forkes & Sons, 1954. 561 pages.

Spiegel, J., comp. Standard Business Dictionary. Cincinnati, Ohio:
    Standard Publishing Company, 1923. 447 pages.

Standinford, Oliver, ed. Newnes Encyclopaedia of Business Management.
    London: Newnes Educational Publishing Co., Ltd., 1967. 637
    pages.

Treasury, The. Civil Service Department. Glossary of Management
    Techniques. London: Her Majesty's Stationery Office, 1967.
    26 pages.

Tver, David F. Dictionary of Business and Scientific Terms. 2nd ed.
    Houston, Texas: Gulf Publishing Co., 1968. 528 pages.

2,001 Business Terms and What They Mean. 2nd ed. New York: Alexander
    Hamilton Institute, 1963. 303 pages.

Williamson, David B., and McGinty, John J. A Definitionary of Busi-
    ness Terms. Eugene, Oregon: n. p., 1962. 51 pages.

Yorston, R. Keith. The Australian Commercial Dictionary. 2nd ed.
    Sydney: Law Book Co. of Australasia, 1950. 383 pages.

Zyrser, Alfred R., ed. The Random House Vest Pocket Dictionary of
    Business. New York: Random House, 1962. 238 pages.

APPENDIX III

GLOSSARY

BALANCE, Principle of--Managerial efficiency is increased through the relative development of the organizational units and functions of an enterprise in proportion to their importance.

COMMITMENT, Principle of--The planning period of a firm should extend through that future time in which all of its commitments will be fulfilled.

COORDINATION, Principle of--The successful attainment of enterprise goals is vitally dependent upon harmonious and interrelated organizational activity.

DIVISION OF LABOR, Principle of--The labor of an enterprise should be subdivided into separate tasks to allow specialization.

EFFICIENCY, Principle of--The goals of an enterprise should be attained efficiently, providing the best ratio of resources (human, financial, material or otherwise) expended to work achieved.

EXCEPTION, Principle of--Managerial concentration should be centered around the identification of exceptional variations from standard.

FLEXIBILITY, Principle of--The more flexible a plan, the more likely it will be able to respond to unforeseen events; however, the benefits of flexibility must be balanced against the resulting costs.

OBJECTIVE, Principle of--The clear statement of desired objectives is basic to the successful accomplishment of any undertaking.

PARITY OF AUTHORITY AND RESPONSIBILITY, Principle of--For effective organizational relationships, authority and responsibility should be equal.

PRIMACY OF PLANNING, Principle of--Planning is a prerequisite for the proper execution of each of the other managerial functions.

SCALAR, The Principle--Within every enterprise there should exist a clear line of tapering authority (a chain of command) from the top of the enterprise to its lowest level.

SPAN OF MANAGEMENT, Principle of--There is a limit, dependent upon the circumstances and individuals involved, to the number of subordinates that a superior can effectively manage.

APPENDIX III--<u>Continued</u>

SPECIALIZATION, Principle of--The restriction of the work of each person or group of persons to one or a limited number of tasks permits specialization of knowledge and skill.

UNITY OF COMMAND, Principle of--No subordinate should be held subject to the commands of more than one superior in regard to the same subject area.

UNITY OF OBJECTIVE, Principle of--The efforts of every organization and every part of every organization should contribute to the accomplishment of the organization's main objective.

I am far from meaning to present the foregoing definitions to the notice of the reader as in any degree complete, either in regard to extent, or correctness. In extent, they have been purposely limited, and in regard to correctness, I am too well aware of the difficulty of the subject to think I have succeeded in making my definitions embrace all I wish, and exclude all I wish.*

--Rev. Thomas Robert Malthus

---

*Malthus, <u>Definitions</u> <u>in</u> <u>Political</u> <u>Economy</u>, p. 260.

SELECTED BIBLIOGRAPHY

Albers, Henry H. _Organized Executive_ Action. New York: John Wiley
& Sons, Inc., 1961; 2nd ed., 1965, re-entitled _Principles of
Organization and Management_; 3rd ed., 1969, re-entitled
Principles of Management: A Modern Approach.

Alford, Leon P., ed. _Cost and Production Handbook_. New York: Ronald
Press Co., 1934.

_____. _Laws of Management Applied to Manufacturing_. New York:
Ronald Press Co., 1928.

_____. "Laws of Manufacturing Management," Paper No. 2014. _Trans-
actions_ (American Society Mechanical Engineers), XLVIII (1926),
393-438.

_____. _Principles of Industrial Management for Engineers_. New York:
Ronald Press Co., 1940.

_____, and Bangs, John R., eds. _Production Handbook_. New York:
Ronald Press Co., 1944.

Allcut, Edgar A. _Principles of Industrial Management_. Toronto: Sir
Isaac Pitman & Sons (Canada), Ltd., 1932.

Allen, Louis A. _Common Vocabulary of Professional Management_. 3rd ed.
Palo Alto, Calif.: Executive Press, 1968.

_____. _Management and Organization_. New York: McGraw-Hill Book
Co., 1958.

_____. _The Management Profession_. New York: McGraw-Hill Book Co.,
1964.

_____. "A Taxonomy of Management Work," Palo Alto, Calif.: Louis
Allen Associates, Inc., 1971. (Mimeographed.)

Allstetter, W. R. "Comments on the 'Ten Commandments'." _Public
Administration Review_, III (Winter, 1943), 80.

Alpert, Bernard and Dickson, Gary W. "Management Theory: Recent
Developments, Status and Potential." _University of Washington
Business Review_, XXVIII (Autumn, 1968), 5-17.

Alton, A. J. "Comparative Management Theory." _Management International
Review_, IX (January-February, 1969), 3-11.

The American Heritage Dictionary of the English Language. 1969.

American Institute of Accountants, Special Committee on Terminology, chairman, Walter Mucklow. Preliminary Report of the Special Committee on Terminology. Edited by Alphyon P. Richardson. New York: Century Company, 1931.

American Institute of Certified Public Accountants, Accounting Principles Board. Accounting Research and Terminology Bulletins. Final Edition. New York: AICPA, 1961.

American Marketing Association, Committee on Definitions, chairman, Ralph S. Alexander. Marketing Definitions: A Glossary of Marketing Terms. Chicago: American Marketing Association, 1960.

_____. "Report of the Definitions Committee." Journal of Marketing, XIII (October, 1948), 202-17.

Anderson, Edward H., and Schwenning, Gustav T. The Science of Production Organization. New York: John Wiley & Sons, Inc., 1938.

Anthony, Robert N. Management Controls in Industrial Research Organizations. Boston: Division of Research, Graduate School of Business Administration, Harvard University, 1952.

_____. "Planning and Control Systems: A Framework for Analysis." Management Services, I (March-April, 1964), 18-24.

Argyris, Chris. Organization of a Bank: A Study of the Nature of Organization and the Fusion Process, Studies in Organizational Behavior No. 1. New Haven, Conn.: Labor Management Center, Yale University, 1954.

[Arnold, William J.] Milestones of Management. 2 Vols. New York: Business Week, 1965-66.

Arrow, Kenneth J. "Control in Large Organizations." Management Science, X (April, 1964), 397-408.

_____. "Research in Management Controls: A Critical Synthesis." Management Controls: New Directions in Basic Research. Edited by Charles Bonini, Robert K. Jaedicke, and Harvey M. Wagner. New York: McGraw-Hill Book Co., Inc., 1964.

Asplund, Ingemar, ed. Management Control: A Survey of Production and Inventory Control Models in Theory and Practice. Lund, Sweden: Studentlitteratur, 1969.

Babbage, Charles. On the Economy of Machinery and Manufactures. Philadelphia: Carey & Lea, 1832.

Baker, Alton W., and Davis, Ralph C. Ratios of Staff to Line Employees
    and Stages of Differentiation of Staff Functions. Columbus:
    The Ohio State University, Bureau of Business Research, Research
    Monograph No. 72, 1954.

Balderston, C. Canby, Karabasz, Victor S., and Brecht, Robert P.
    Management of an Enterprise. New York: Prentice-Hall, Inc.,
    1935; 2nd ed., 1949, co-authored with Robert J. Riddle.

Bangs, John R., in collaboration with Charles D. Hart. Factory Manage-
    ment, Vol. VIII: Modern Business. New York: Alexander
    Hamilton Institute, 1930.

Banks, Warren E. "The Evolution of Management Thought: A Conceptual
    Scheme." Arkansas Business and Economic Review, II (May, 1969),
    7-13.

Barkdull, C. W. "Span-of-Control--A Method of Evaluation." Michigan
    Business Review, XV (May, 1963), 25-32.

Barnard, Chester I. The Functions of the Executive. Cambridge:
    Harvard University Press, 1938.

Beckmann, Martin J. "Some Aspects of Returns to Scale in Business
    Administration." Quarterly Journal of Economics, LXXIV
    (August, 1960), 464-71.

Bedeian, Arthur G. "Relationship in Organization: A Clarification."
    Academy of Management Journal, XV (June, 1972), 238-39.

Behling, Orlando. "Unification of Management Theory: A Pessimistic
    View." Business Perspectives, III (Summer, 1967), 4-9.

Bell, Daniel. Work and Its Discontents: The Cult of Efficiency in
    America. Boston: Beacon Press, 1956.

Bell, Gerald D. "Determinants of Span of Control." American Journal
    of Sociology, LXXIII (July, 1967), 100-09.

Benge, Eugene J. "Management Terms Needn't Be Gobbledygook." Factory,
    CXIX (March, 1961), 209-18.

Berelson, Bernard. Content Analysis in Communication Research. Glencoe,
    Ill.: Free Press, 1952.

Bethel, Lawrence L., Atwater, Franklin S., Smith, George H. E., and
    Stackman, Harvey A., Jr. Industrial Organization and Manage-
    ment. New York: McGraw-Hill Book Co., Inc., 1945.

Bittel, Lester R. Management by Exception. New York: McGraw-Hill
    Book Co., Inc., 1964.

_____. "Management by Exception." Handbook of Business Administration. Edited by Harold B. Maynard. New York: McGraw-Hill Book Co., Inc., 1967.

Black, John D. Introduction to Production Economics. New York: Henry Holt & Co., 1926.

Blau, Peter M., and Scott, W. Richard. Formal Organizations. San Francisco, Calif.: Chandler Publishing Company, 1962.

Boddewyn, Jean. "Management: The Trees, the Forest and the Landscape." Management International Review, VII, No. 2/3 (1967), 131-36.

"Bosses Break Rule on Span of Control." Business Week, August 18, 1951, pp. 102-03.

Brandeis, Louis D. Scientific Management and Railroads: Being Part of a Brief Submitted to the Interstate Commerce Commission. New York: Engineering Magazine, 1911.

Brech, Edward F. L. "Management in Principle." The Principles and Practices of Management. Edited by E. F. L. Brech. London: Longmans, Green and Co., Ltd., 1953.

_____. The Nature and Significance of Management. London: Sir Isaac Pitman & Sons, Ltd., 1946; 2nd ed., 1948, re-entitled Management: It's Nature and Significance; 3rd ed., 1953.

_____. Organisation: The Framework of Management. London: Longmans, Green and Co., Ltd., 1957; 2nd ed., 1965.

_____. "Organisation Structure--Summary and Review." British Management Review, VIII (July, 1949), 84-109.

_____. ed. The Principles and Practices of Management. London: Longmans, Green and Co., Ltd., 1953; 2nd ed., 1963.

_____. "The Principles of Management." British Management Review, VII, No. 1 (1948), 61-67.

_____. "Summary and Review." British Management Review, VII, No. 3 (1948), 87-102.

British Institute of Management. Glossary of Management Terms. London: BIM, 1954.

_____. Management Reading List: Glossaries of Management Terms. London: British Institute of Management, 1969. (Mimeographed.)

British Management Review, VII (May-June, 1948), 4-102.

Brodbeck, May, ed. Readings in the Philosophy of the Social Sciences. New York: Macmillan Co., 1968.

Brown, Alvin M. Organization: A Formulation of Principle. New York: Hibbert Printing Co., 1945.

_____. Organization of Industry. New York: Prentice-Hall, Inc., 1947.

_____. "What Do You Mean by That Remark?" Advanced Management Journal, XVI (August, 1951), 6-8.

Brown, David S. "POSDCORB Revisted and Revised." Personnel Administration, XXIX (May-June, 1966), 33-38.

Brown, Fred R. "Organization and Management." Management: Concepts and Practice. Edited by Fred R. Brown. Washington, D. C.: U. S. Industrial College of the Armed Forces, 1967.

Brown, Percy S. "Organization of the Manufacturing Division." Handbook of Business Administration. Edited by William J. A. Donald. New York: McGraw-Hill Book Co., Inc., for the American Management Association, 1931.

Brown, Wilfred B. D. Exploration in Management. New York: John Wiley & Sons, 1960.

_____. "Management Theory From Management Practice: The Concept of Contraction." Toward a Unified Theory of Management. Edited by Harold D. Koontz. New York: McGraw-Hill Book Co., Inc., 1964.

Business Training Corporation. Handling Men, Vol. II: Organization, Vol. III: Management, Vol. VI: Course in Modern Production Methods. 6 Vols. New York: Business Training Corporation, 1918.

Cameron, M. A. Principles of Management. London: George G. Harrap & Co., Ltd., 1948.

Carzo, Rocco, Jr. "Administrative Science and the Role of Value Judgments." Journal of the Academy of Management, III (December, 1900), 175-82.

Case, Fred E. "Letter to the Editor." Harvard Business Review, XL (November-December, 1962), 20, 30, 35, 186.

Chamber De Commerce De Paris, Institut D'Organisation Commerciale et Industrielle. Définitions de quelques termes usités dans l'Organisation Commerciale et Industrielle. Paris: n. p., 1934.

Child, John. British Management Thought, Studies in Management No. 5. London: George Allen and Unwin, Ltd., 1969.

Church, A. Hamilton. "Has 'Scientific Management' Science?" The American Machinist, XXXV (July 20, 1911), 108-12.

_____. "The Meaning of Commercial Organization." The Engineering Magazine, XX (December, 1900), 391-98.

_____. "The Meaning of Scientific Management." The Engineering Magazine, XLI (April, 1911), 97-101.

_____. "Practical Principles of Rational Management." The Engineering Magazine, Serialized in six parts, XLIV-XLV (January through June, 1913), 487-94, 673-80, 894-903; 24-33, 166-73, 405-11.

_____. The Science and Practice of Management. New York: Engineering Magazine Co., 1914.

_____, and Alford, Leon P. "The Principles of Management." American Machinist, XXXVI (May 30, 1912), 857-61.

Churchman, C. West. "Management Science--Fact or Theory?" Management Science, II (January, 1956), 185.

Clausewitz, Carl von. On War. Translated by James J. Graham. 3 Vols. New York: Barnes & Noble, Inc., 1968. Written circa 1830.

Collett, Merrill J. "Strategy Versus Tactics As the Object of Research in Public Administration." Public Administration Review, XXII (September, 1962), 115-21.

Committee on Elimination of Waste in Industry of the Federated American Engineering Societies, chairman, Herbert C. Hoover. Waste in Industry. New York: McGraw-Hill Book Co., Inc., 1921.

Cooke, Morris L. Academic and Industrial Efficiency, Bulletin No. 5 New York: Carnegie Foundation for the Advancement of Teaching, 1910.

_____. "On Mr. Schulze's Definitions." Bulletin of the Taylor Society, IV (October, 1919), 47-48.

Coonley, Howard. "The Control of an Industry in the Business Cycle." Harvard Business Review, I (July, 1923), 385-97.

_____. "Some Fundamental Contributions of Scientific Management." Advanced Management Journal, VI (January-March, 1941), 23-25.

Copley, Frank B. Frederick W. Taylor: Father of Scientific Management. 2 Vols. New York: Harper & Brothers, 1923.

Cornell, William B. Business Organization, Vol. III: Modern Business. New York: Alexander Hamilton Institute, 1930.

_____. Industrial Organization and Management. New York: Ronald Press Co., 1928.

Cyert, Richard M., and March, James G. A Behavioral Theory of the Firm. Englewood Cliffs, N. J.: Prentice-Hall, Inc., 1963.

Dale, Ernest. "Dynamics and Mechanics of Organization." Organization Planning and Management Development, Personnel Series No. 141. New York: American Management Association, 1951.

_____. Management: Theory and Practice. New York: McGraw-Hill Book Co., 1965; 2nd ed., 1969.

_____. Organization. New York: American Management Association, 1967.

_____. Planning and Developing the Company Organization Structure, Research Report No. 20. 7th imp. New York: American Management Association, 1952.

_____. "The Span of Control." Management News, XXIV (July 31, 1951), 3-4.

Dance, Frank E. X. "The 'Concept' of Communication." The Journal of Communication, XX (June, 1970), 201-10.

Darr, John W. "The Management-as-a-Process Concept: A Consideration." Industrial Management Review (M. I. T.) VI (Fall, 1964), 41-50.

Dauten, Paul M., Jr., ed. Current Issues and Emerging Concepts in Management. Vol. I. Boston: Houghton-Mifflin Company, 1962.

_____, Gammill, Homer L., and Robinson, Stanley C. "Our Concepts of Controlling Need Re-Thinking." Journal of the Academy of Management, I (December, 1958), 41-55.

Davis, Ralph C. The Fundamentals of Top Management. New York: Harper & Brothers, 1951.

_____. The Influence of the Unit of Supervision and the Span of Executive Control on the Economy of Organization Structure. Columbus: The Ohio State University, Bureau of Business Research, Research Monograph No. 26, 1941.

_____. The Principles of Business Organization and Operation. Columbus, Ohio: H. L. Hedrick, 1934; 4th ed., 1937.

_____. The Principles of Factory Organization and Management. New York: Harper & Brothers, 1928; 2nd ed., 1940, re-entitled Industrial Organization and Management; 3rd ed., 1957.

De Haas, J. Anton. Business Organization and Administration. New York: Gregg Publishing Co., 1920.

Delbecq, André L. "The World Within the 'Span of Control'." Business Horizons, II (August, 1968), 47-56.

De Leeuw, Adolph L. "The Final Measure of Industrial Efficiency." Management Engineering, I (September, 1921), 141-46.

Deming, Robert H. Characteristics of an Effective Management Control System in an Industrial Organization. Boston: Division of Research, Graduate School of Business Administration, Harvard University, 1968.

Dennison, Henry S. Organization Engineering. New York: McGraw-Hill Book Co., 1931.

Dent, Arthur G. H. "Budgetary Control Study." Industry Illustrated (London), II (May, 1934), 28-30, 36.

_____. Management Planning and Control. London: Gee & Co. (Publishers), Ltd., 1935.

Descartes, René. Discourse on Method. Translated by John Veitch. Chicago: Open Court Publishing Company, 1899, Written in 1637.

De Spelder, Bruce E. Ratios of Staff to Line Personnel. Columbus: The Ohio State University, Bureau of Business Research, Research Monograph No. 106, 1962.

Deverell, Cyril S. Management Planning and Control. London: Gee & Co. (Publishers), Ltd., 1967.

Diemer, Hugo. Factory Organization and Administration. Vol. II: Factory Management. 6 Vols. New York: McGraw-Hill Book Co., 1910; 2nd ed., 1914.

_____. Industrial Organization and Management. Chicago: La Salle Extension University, 1915.

_____. "The Principles Underlying Good Management." Industrial Management, LXVII (May, 1924), 280-83.

Dimock, Marshall E. The Executive in Action. New York: Harper & Brothers, 1945.

_____. A Philosophy of Administration. New York: Harper & Brothers, 1958.

Donnelly, James H., Jr., Gibson, James L., and Ivancevich, John M. Fundamentals of Management. Austin, Texas: Business Publications, Inc., 1971.

Douglas, Thomas W. "Management Theory and the Large Business Enterprise." Advanced Management Journal, XXXIII (July, 1968), 40-50.

Drucker, Peter F. "Controls, Control and Management." Management Controls: New Directions in Basic Research. Edited by Charles Bonini, Robert K. Jaedicke, and Harvey M. Wagner. New York: McGraw-Hill Book Co., Inc., 1964.

_____. The Practice of Management. New York: Harper & Row, Publishers, 1954.

Drury, Horace B. "Scientific Management: A History and Criticism." Studies in History, Economics and Public Law, Vol. 65, No. 2; Whole No. 157, pp. 271-545. 3rd ed. New York: Columbia University, 1922.

Duncan, John C. The Principles of Industrial Management. New York: D. Appleton & Co., 1911.

Duncan, W. Jack. "Fact and Value in Administrative Science: A Reconsideration of Management Theory and Practice." The Southern Journal of Business, VII (February, 1972), 1-10.

_____. "Methodological Orientation and Management Theory: An Analysis of Academic Opinion." Academy of Management Journal, XIII (September, 1970), 337-48.

Dutton, Henry P. Business Organization and Management. Chicago: A. W. Shaw Co., 1925.

_____. The Control of Production. Vol. II of The Shaw Plant and Shop Management Library. 6 Vols. Chicago: A. W. Shaw Co., 1927.

_____. Factory Management. New York: Macmillan Co., 1924.

_____. Principles of Organization as Applied to Business. New York: McGraw-Hill Book Co., Inc., 1931.

Dutton, John M., and Starbuck, William H. "On Managers and Theories." Management International Review, III (November-December, 1963), 25-35.

Eitington, Julius E. "Personnel Management: Pioneers." The Encyclopedia of Management. Edited by Carl Heyel. New York: Reinhold Publishing Corporation, 1963.

_____. "Pioneers of Management." Advanced Management--Office Executive, II (January, 1963), 16-19.

Emerson, Harrington. "Efficiency As a Basis for Operation and Wages." The Engineering Magazine, Serialized in nine parts, XXXV-XXXVI July, 1908 through April, 1909), 529-36, 661-72, 909-20; 33-42, 170-78, 337-46, 676-86, 815-32, 998-1002.

_____. Efficiency As a Basis for Operation and Wages. New York: Engineering Magazine Co., 1911.

_____. "Philosophy of Efficiency: An Outline of Its Elements." The Engineering Magazine, XLI (April, 1911), 23-26.

_____. "The Twelve Principles of Efficiency." The Engineering Magazine, Serialized in sixteen parts, XXXIX-XLI (June, 1910 through September, 1911), 321-30, 481-93, 679-91, 841-52; 77-82, 161-74, 413-26, 496-506, 761-68, 943-50; 27-32, 293-300, 441-47, 632-40, 810-18, 897-904.

_____. The Twelve Principles of Efficiency. New York: Engineering Magazine Co., 1913.

Emery, James C. Organizational Planning and Control Systems: Theory and Technology. New York: Macmillan Co., 1969.

Ennis, William D. Works Management. New York: McGraw-Hill Book Co., Inc., 1911.

Entwisle, Doris R., and Walton, John. "Observations on the Span of Control." Administrative Science Quarterly, V (March, 1961), 522-33.

Estes, Loring V. "Managing for Maximum Production." Industrial Management, Serialized in six parts, LVII-LVIII (March through August, 1919), 169-75, 284-88, 374-84, 439-43; 54-61, 134-38.

Ettinger, Karl E. Management Glossary. Management Primer Series: "Principles and Practices of Productivity," Training Manual No. 201, Technical Aids Branch, Office of Industrial Resources. Washington, D. C.: International Cooperation Administration, by the Council for International Progress in Management, 1960.

Ewing, David W. "Business Dictionaries." Harvard Business Review, XXX (September-October, 1955), 149-59.

Fayol, Henri. "Administration Industrielle et Générale." Bulletin de la Société de l' Industrie Minérale, X (5th Ser.), No. 3 (1916), 162 pages.

_____. Administration Industrielle et Générale. Paris: Dunod Press, 1947.

_____. "The Administrative Theory in the State." Translated by Sarah Greer. *Papers on the Science of Administration.* Edited by Luther H. Gulick and Lyndall F. Urwick. New York: Institute of Public Administration, Columbia University, 1937.

_____. *General and Industrial Management.* Translated by Constance Storrs. With a Foreword by Lyndall F. Urwick. London: Sir Isaac Pitman & Sons, Ltd., 1949.

_____. *Industrial and General Administration.* Translated by J. A. Coubrough. Geneva: International Management Institute, 1930.

Feiss, Richard A. "Centralization of Administrative Authority: Discussion: First Session." *Bulletin of the Taylor Society,* IV (April, 1919), 2-17.

Filley, Alan C. "Common Misconceptions in Business Management." *Business Horizons,* VII (Fall, 1964), 87-96.

_____, and House, Robert J. *Managerial Process and Organizational Behavior.* Glenview, Ill.: Scott, Foresman and Company, 1969.

Fisch, Gerald G. "Stretching the Span of Management." *Harvard Business Review,* XLI (September-October, 1963), 74-85.

Flippo, Edwin B. "Integrative Schemes in Management Theory." *Academy of Management Journal,* II (March, 1969), 91-98.

Florence, Philip Sargant. *The Logic of Industrial Organisation.* London: Kegan Paul, Trench, Trubner and Co., Ltd., 1933.

_____. "Management and the Size of Firms: A Reply." *The Economic Journal,* XLIV (December, 1934), 723-29.

Follett, Mary Parker. "The Basis of Control in Business." *The Journal of the National Institute of Industrial Psychology* (London), III (January, 1927), 233-41.

_____. "Business As an Integrative Unity." *Scientific Foundations of Business Administration.* Edited by Henry C. Metcalf. Baltimore: Williams and Wilkins Co., 1926.

_____. "Co-ordination." *Freedom and Co-ordination.* Edited by Lyndall F. Urwick. London: Management Publications Trust, Ltd., 1949.

_____. "The Illusion of Final Authority." *Bulletin of the Taylor Society,* II (December, 1926), 243-56.

_____. "Individualism in a Planned Society." Dynamic
Administration--The Collected Papers of Mary Parker Follett.
Edited by Henry C. Metcalf and Lyndall F. Urwick. New York:
Harper & Brothers, 1942.

_____. "The Meaning of Responsibility in Business Management."
Business Management As a Profession. Edited by Henry C.
Metcalf. Chicago: A. W. Shaw Co., 1927.

_____. "Power." Scientific Foundations of Business Administration.
Edited by Henry C. Metcalf. Baltimore: Williams and
Wilkins Co., 1926.

_____. "The Process of Control." Papers on the Science of Admin-
istration. Edited by Luther H. Gulick and Lyndall F. Urwick.
New York: Institute of Public Administration, Columbia University, 1937.

_____. "The Psychology of Control." Psychological Foundations of
Management. Edited by Henry C. Metcalf. Chicago: A. W.
Shaw Co., 1927.

Forrester, Jay W. "The Structure Underlying Management Processes."
Academy of Management Proceedings (1964). Edited by Edwin B.
Flippo. Bowling Green, Ohio, 1965.

Fox, R. M. "The Industrial Tower of Babel." The Labour Magazine, VII
(August, 1928), 163-65.

Franklin, Benjamin A. "Records As a Basis for Management." Management Engineering, III (September, 1922), 133-37.

Fraser, Lindley M. Economic Thought and Language. London: Adam and
Charles Black, Ltd., 1937.

Frederick, William C. "The Next Development in Management Science: A
General Theory." Journal of the Academy of Management, VI
(September, 1963), 212-19.

Galloway, Lee. Organization and Management, Vol. III: Modern Business.
Edited by Joseph F. Johnson. New York: Alexander Hamilton
Institute, 1909.

Gardner, Thomas L. "First Things First." Public Administration Review,
XXII (September, 1962), 121-23.

Gibbons, Charles C. "Management by Exception." Advanced Management
Journal, XXIX (January, 1964), 12-16.

Gilbreth, Frank B. "Graphical Control on the Exception Principle for Executives," Paper No. 1573a. Transactions (American Society Mechanical Engineers), XXXVIII (December, 1916), 1213-19.

_____. Primer of Scientific Management. 2nd ed. New York: D. Van Nostrand Co., 1914.

Gilbreth, Lillian M. "The Psychology of Management." Industrial Engineering and the Engineering Digest, Serialized in thirteen parts, XI-XIII (May, 1912 through May, 1913), 343-49, 429-38; 13-17, 65-68, 116-20, 155-58, 199-204, 248-53; 18-23, 66-70, 113-16, 161-66, 213-17.

_____. The Psychology of Management. New York: Sturgis & Walton Co., 1914.

Gillespie, James L. The Principles of Rational Industrial Management. London: Sir Isaac Pitman & Sons, Ltd., 1938.

Gillette, Halbert P., and Dana, Richard T. Cost Keeping and Management Engineering. New York: Myron C. Clark Publishing Co., 1909.

Glass, Norman P. "Administration and Administrative Management: A Critique of Henri Fayol's Administration Industrielle et Générale." Unpublished M. A. thesis, George Washington University, 1957.

Glover, John G. Fundamentals of Professional Management. New York: Republic Book Co., 1954; 2nd ed., Simmons-Boardman Publishing Corp., 1958.

_____, and Maze, Coleman L. Managerial Control. New York: Ronald Press Co., 1937.

Goetz, Billy E. Management, Planning and Control. New York: McGraw-Hill Book Co., Inc., 1949.

Going, Charles B. "The Efficiency Movement. An Outline." Transactions (Efficiency Society), I (1912), 11-20.

_____. Principles of Industrial Engineering. New York: McGraw-Hill Book Co., Inc., 1911.

Goodwin, E. Sidney L. "Control: A Brief Excursion on the Meaning of a Word." Michigan Business Review, XII (January, 1960), 13-17, 28.

Gordon, Paul J. "Transcend the Current Debate on Administrative Theory." Journal of the Academy of Management, VI (December, 1963), 290-302.

Gowin, Enoch B. The Executive and His Control of Men. New York:
    Macmillan Co., 1915.

Graicunas, V. A. "Relationship in Organization." Bulletin of the
    International Management Institute, VII (March, 1933), 39-42.

Grant, John A. "Span of Control: An Administrative Paradox." The
    Southern Journal of Business, IV (April, 1969), 19-32.

Green, Edward J., and Redmond, Gomer H. "Comments on a General Theory
    of Administration." Administrative Science Quarterly, II
    (September, 1957), 235-43.

Greenwood, Ronald. "Managerial Functions: A Classification of Major
    Contributions." Arkansas Business and Economic Review, II
    (May, 1969), 14-17.

Gulick, Luther H. "Management Is a Science." Academy of Management
    Journal, VIII (March, 1965), 7-13.

_____. "Notes on the Theory of Organization." Papers on the Science
    of Administration. Edited by Luther H. Gulick and Lyndall F.
    Urwick. New York: Institute of Public Administration, Columbia
    University, 1937.

_____. "Science, Values and Public Administration." Papers on the
    Science of Administration. Edited by Luther H. Gulick and
    Lyndall F. Urwick. New York: Institute of Public Administra-
    tion, Columbia University, 1937.

Haan, Hugo von. "International Aspects of the Terminology and Ideology
    of Management." International Labour Review, XXXVII (April,
    1938), 419-39.

Haber, Samuel. Efficiency and Uplift. Chicago: University of
    Chicago Press, 1964.

Haimann, Theo. Professional Management: Theory and Practice. Boston:
    Houghton Mifflin Co., 1962; 2nd ed., 1970, re-entitled Manage-
    ment in the Modern Organization and co-authored with William
    G. Scott.

Haire, Mason. "Biological Models and Empirical Histories of the Growth
    of Organizations." Modern Organization Theory: A Symposium
    of the Foundation for Research on Human Behavior. Edited by
    Mason Haire. New York: John Wiley & Sons, Inc., 1959.

Halff, John F. "Applying Scientific Method to the Study of Manage-
    ment." Journal of the Academy of Management, III (December,
    1960), 193-96.

Hamilton, Ian S. M. The Soul and Body of an Army. New York: George
H. Doran Company, 1921.

Hart, Eric G. "The Art and Science of Organization: I." The Human
Factor (London), VII (October, 1933), 333-40. Part II (November,
1933), 386-93.

Haynes, Warren W., and Massie, Joseph L. Management: Analysis,
Concepts and Cases. 2nd ed. Englewood Cliffs, N. J.: Prentice-
Hall Company, 1969.

Healey, James H. "Coordination and Control of Executive Functions."
Personnel, XXXIII (1956), 106-17.

_____. Executive Coordination and Control. Columbus: The Ohio
State University, Bureau of Business Research, Research
Monograph No. 78, 1956.

Hekimian, James S. "The Growing Split Between Management Theory and
Practice." Academy of Management Proceedings (1969). Edited
by William G. Scott and Preston P. Le Breton. Bowling Green,
Ohio, 1970.

_____. Management Control in Life Insurance Branch Offices. Boston:
Division of Research, Graduate School of Business Administration, Harvard University, 1965.

Heydrick, Allen K. "Principles of Organization." Supervisory Management, XV (March, 1970), 2-6.

Hill, Lawrence S. "The Application of Queueing Theory to the Span of
Control." Academy of Management Journal, VI (March, 1963),
58-69.

_____. "Comment: Queuing Theory Revisited Once Again." Journal
of the Academy of Management, VII (December, 1964), 317.

_____. "Discussion: Some Comments on 'Queuing Theory Revisited'."
Journal of the Academy of Management, VI (September, 1963),
245-46.

Hine, Charles D. "Modern Organization." The Engineering Magazine,
Serialized in seven parts, XLII-XLIII (January through July,
1912), 481-87, 720-22, 869-72; 44-48, 217-21, 348-52, 588-91.

_____. Modern Organization. New York: Engineering Magazine Co.,
1912.

Holden, Paul E., Fish, Lounsbury S., and Smith, Hubert L. Top-
Management Organization and Control. Stanford University,
Calif.: Stanford University Press, 1941.

_____, Pederson, Carlton, and Germane, Gayton E. Top Management. New York: McGraw-Hill Book Co., Inc., 1968.

Homans, George C. "A Conceptual Scheme for the Study of Social Organization." American Sociological Review, XII, No. 1 (1947), 13-26.

_____. The Human Group. New York: Harcourt, Brace & World, Inc., 1950.

Hopf, Harry A. "Evolution in Organization During the Past Decade." Advanced Management Journal, XII (September, 1947), 103-10.

_____. "The Evolution of Organization." 1932 Yearbook of the National Association of Cost Accountants. New York: NACA, 1932.

_____. "The Management Movement at the Cross-roads." n. p.: Privately printed, 1933.

_____. "Organization, Executive Capacity and Progress." Advanced Management Journal, XI (June, 1946), 34-47+.

_____. "Problems of Bank Organization." Bulletin of the Taylor Society, XII (April, 1927), 352-74.

House, Robert J., and Filley, Alan C. "Science, Theory, Philosophy, and the Practice of Management." Management International Review, VI (November-December, 1966), 97-107. Errata, VII, No. 4/5 (1967), 159.

_____. and Miner, John E. "Merging Management and Behavioral Theory-- The Interaction Between Span of Control and Group Size." Administrative Science Quarterly, XIV (September, 1969), 451-64.

Hyman, Stanley I. "Management--An Experimental Science?" Management International Review, X (November-December, 1970), 51-59.

Institute of Industrial Management (Melbourne). Definition of Terms Used in Industrial Management. Melbourne: The Institute, 1948.

International Committee for Scientific Management. C. I. O. S. Manual. Geneva: CIOS, 1949.

_____. List of Publications Concerning Management Terminology. Wiesbaden, Federal Republic of Germany: Betriebswirlschafticher Verlag Dr. Th. Gabler, 1963.

International Management Institute. Rapport intérimaire sur le terminologie de la rationalisation. Geneva: International Labour Office, 1930. (Mimeographed.)

Jaffe, William J. L. P. Alford and the Evolution of Modern Industrial Management. New York: New York University Press, 1957.

Janger, Allen. "Analyzing the Span of Control." Management Record, XXII (July-August, 1960), 7-10.

Jerome, William T., III. Executive Control--The Catalyst. New York: John Wiley & Sons, Inc., 1961.

Jevons, W. Stanley. Elementary Lessons in Logic. New ed. New York: Macmillan Company, 1882.

Johannson, Hano, and Robertson, Andrew, comps. Management Glossary. Edited by Edward F. L. Brech. Harlow, England: Longmans, Green and Co., Ltd., 1968.

Jones, C. R. "Management Takes Stock." Scope, VIII (July, 1949), 74-85.

Jones, Edward D. The Administration of Industrial Enterprises. New York: Longmans, Green and Co., Ltd., 1916; 2nd ed., 1925.

_____. The Business Administrator. New York: Engineering Magazine Co., 1914. Serialized in The Engineering Magazine, XLIV, XLVII-XLVIII (1912 and 1914).

Jones, Thomas R. Theories and Types of Organizations: Their History, Industrial and Economic Background and Trend, Production Executives Series No. 83. New York: American Management Association, 1929.

Junckerstorff, Kurt. "Management--an International Science." Management International Review, I (November-December, 1961), 148-52.

Kakar, Sudhir. Frederick Taylor: A Study in Personality and Innovation. Cambridge, Mass.: MIT Press, 1970.

Kaplan, Abraham. The Conduct of Inquiry. San Francisco: Chandler Publishing Co., 1964.

Kast, Fremont E., and Rosenzweig, James E. Organization and Management. New York: McGraw-Hill Book Co., 1970.

Keene, C. Mansel. "Administrative Reality: Advances, Not Solutions." Public Administration Review, XXII (September, 1962), 124-28.

Kendall, Henry P. "The Problem of the Chief Executive." Bulletin of the Taylor Society, VII (April, 1922), 39-46.

Kenny, Thomas. "Why Top Management Control Needs Tightening." Dun's Review and Modern Industry, LXVIII (October, 1956), 58-60, 65.

Kimball, Dexter S. "Economic Principles." Management's Handbook.
Edited by Leon P. Alford. New York: Ronald Press Co., 1924.

_____. Plant Management. Vol. IV: Modern Business. Edited by
Joseph F. Johnson. 24 Vols. New York: Alexander Hamilton
Institute, 1918.

_____. Principles of Industrial Organization. Vol. I: Factory
Management. 6 Vols. New York: McGraw-Hill Book Co., Inc.,
1913.

Knoeppel, Charles E. "Industrial Organization As It Affects Executives
and Workers," Paper No. 1672. Transactions (American Society
of Mechanical Engineers), XLI (1918), 909-24.

_____. "Laws of Industrial Organization." Industrial Management,
Serialized in four parts, LVIII-LVIX (October, 1919 through
January, 1920), 265-68, 381-83, 494-98; 43-46.

_____. Organization and Administration. Vol. VI: Factory Manage-
ment Course and Service. 12 Vols. New York: Industrial
Extension Institute, Inc., 1917.

Koontz, Harold D. "Challenges for Intellectual Leadership in Management." Academy of Management Proceedings (1963). Edited by
Paul J. Gordon. Bowling Green, Ohio, 1964, pp. 106-16.

_____. "Making Sense of Management Theory." Harvard Business
Review, XL (July-August, 1962), 24-48.

_____. "Making Theory Operational: The Span of Management." The
Journal of Management Studies, III (October, 1966), 229-43.

_____. "Management Control: A Suggested Formulation of Principles."
California Management Review, I (Winter, 1959), 47-55.

_____. "Management Theory and Research: Some Conclusions." Toward
a Unified Theory of Management. Edited by Harold D. Koontz.
New York: McGraw-Hill Book Co., Inc., 1964.

_____. "The Management Theory Jungle." Journal of the Academy of
Management, IV (December, 1961), 174-88.

_____. "A Preliminary Statement of Principles of Planning and
Control." Journal of the Academy of Management, I (April,
1958), 45-60.

_____. "The Rationale of Planning." Management: Organization and
Planning. Edited by Donald M. Bowman and Franklin M. Fillerup.
New York: McGraw-Hill Book Co., Inc., 1963.

_____, ed. Toward a Unified Theory of Management. New York: McGraw-Hill Book Co., Inc., 1964.

_____, and O'Donnell, Cyril J. Principles of Management: An Analysis of Managerial Functions. New York: McGraw-Hill Book Co., Inc., 1955; 2nd ed., 1959; 3rd ed., 1964; 4th ed., 1968.

Kriusina, H. J. "De spanwijdte van de leiding als concrete norm, fabel of werketijkheid?" Maandblad voor Accountancy en Bedrijfshurshoudkunde, XXXII, No. 7 (1957).

Lamperti, Frank A., and Thurston, John B. Internal Auditing for Management. Englewood Cliffs, N. J.: Prentice-Hall, Inc., 1953.

"Language of Scientific Management Spoken Here." New York Times, January 6, 1964, p. 55.

Lansburgh, Richard H. Industrial Management. New York: John Wiley & Sons, Inc., 1923; 2nd ed., 1928.

Laufer, Arthur C. "A Taxonomy of Management Theory: A Preliminary Framework." Academy of Management Journal, XI (December, 1968), 435-42.

Lawson, F. M. Industrial Control. London: Sir Isaac Pitman & Sons, Ltd., 1920.

Lee, John, ed. Dictionary of Industrial Administration. 2 Vols. London: Sir Isaac Pitman & Sons, Ltd., 1928-29.

Lewis, J. Slater. "The Mechanical and Commercial Limits of Specialization." The Engineering Magazine, XX (January, 1901), 709-16.

The Library of Factory Management, Vol. VI: Executive Control. Chicago: A. W. Shaw and Co., 1915.

Lichtner, William O. Planned Control in Manufacturing. New York: Ronald Press Co., 1924.

Lindemann, Albert J. Personal letter. July 29, 1971.

_____, Lundgren, Earl F., and Kaas, H. K. von. Dictionary of Management Terms. Dubuque, Iowa: William C. Brown Book Co., 1966.

Litchfield, Edward H. "Notes on a General Theory of Administration." Administrative Science Quarterly, I (June, 1956), 3-29.

Litterer, Joseph A. The Analysis of Organizations. New York: John Wiley & Sons, Inc., 1965.

Locke, John. An Essay Concerning Human Understanding. Abridged and Edited by Andrew S. Pringle-Pattison. Oxford, England: Clarendon Press, 1924. Written in 1690.

Loken, Robert D., and Thake, Winfield C. J. "How Many Managers Are There?" Current Economic Comment, XIV (November, 1952), 18-27.

Longenecker, Justin G. Principles of Management and Organizational Behavior. Columbus, Ohio: Charles E. Merrill Publishing Co., 1964; 2nd ed., 1969.

Lord, Chester B. "Management by Exception." Transactions (American Society of Mechanical Engineers), LIII (1931), 49-58.

_____. "Visualized Management Control: A System Which Shows Up Exceptions and Slips." Management and Administration, VI (September, 1923), 319-22.

Luneski, Chris. "Some Aspects of the Meaning of Control." Accounting Review, XXXIX (July, 1964), 591-97.

McCallum, Daniel C. "Superintendent's Report," March 25, 1856, in Annual Report of the New York and Erie Railroad Company for 1855 (New York, 1856). Partially reprinted in The Railroads: The Nation's First Big Business. Compiled and Edited by Alfred D. Chandler, Jr. New York: Harcourt, Brace & World, Inc., 1965.

McCaully, Harry J., Jr. Management Controls for Foremen and Supervisors. New York: Funk & Wagnalls Co., 1948.

McDonough, Adrian M. Information Economics and Management Systems. New York: McGraw-Hill Book Co., Inc., 1963.

McFarland, Dalton, ed. Current Issues and Emerging Concepts in Management. Vol. II. Boston: Houghton Mifflin Company, 1966.

_____. Management: Principles and Practices. New York: Macmillan Company, 1958; 2nd ed., 1964; 3rd ed., 1970.

_____. "Theory As an Angle of Vision in Management Research." Academy of Management Proceedings (1965). Edited by Edwin B. Flippo. Bowling Green, Ohio, 1966, pp. 3-11.

McGregor, Douglas. The Human Side of Enterprise. New York: McGraw-Hill Book Co., Inc., 1960.

Machlup, Fritz. Essays on Economic Semantics. Edited by Merton H. Miller. Englewood Cliffs, N. J.: Prentice-Hall, Inc., 1963.

Malthus, Thomas R. Definitions in Political Economy. London: John
    Murray, 1827.

"Management in Conference." The Manager, XXII (November, 1954), 695-723.

"Management Pattern: Some Trophies From the 'Jungle'." Business Week,
    February 16, 1963, p. 140.

March, James G., and Simon, Herbert A., with the collaboration of Harold
    Guetzkow. Organizations. New York: John Wiley & Sons, 1958.

Marx, Melvin H. "The General Nature of Theory Construction." Theories
    in Contemporary Psychology. Edited by Melvin H. Marx. New
    York: Macmillan Company, 1963.

Mason, Frank R. Business Principles and Organization. Chicago: Cree
    Publishing Co., 1909.

Mee, John F. "A History of Twentieth Century Management Thought."
    Unpublished Ph.D. dissertation, The Ohio State University, 1959.

_____. "Management Movement." International Handbook of Management.
    Edited by Karl E. Ettinger. New York: McGraw-Hill Book Co.,
    Inc., 1965.

_____. Management Thought in a Dynamic Economy. New York: New
    York University Press, 1963.

Meij, Jacob L. "Human Relations and Fundamental Principles of Manage-
    ment." Human Relations and Modern Management. Edited by
    Edward M. Hugh-Jones (Amsterdam: North-Holland Publishing Com-
    pany, 1958.

_____. "Some Fundamental Principles of a General Theory of Manage-
    ment." Journal of Industrial Economics, IV (October, 1955),
    16-32.

_____. "The Span of Control--Fact and Fundamental Principle."
    Advanced Management Journal, XXII (February, 1957), 14-16.

Melcher, Arlyn. "Organizational Structure: A Framework for Analysis
    and Integration." Academy of Management Proceedings (1965).
    Edited by Edwin B. Flippo. Bowling Green, Ohio, 1966, pp. 130-49.

Meyer, Marshall W. "Expertness and the Span of Control." American
    Sociological Review, XXXIII (December, 1968), 944-51.

Meyers, G. J. "The Science of Management." Journal of the American
    Society of Naval Engineers, XXIII (November, 1911), 994-1015.

Millman, R. William. "Some Unsettled Questions in Organization Theory." Academy of Management Journal, VII (September, 1964), 189-95.

Mockler, Robert J. "Developing the Science of Management Control." Financial Executive, XXXV (December, 1967), 80-93.

_____. The Management Control Process. New York: Appleton-Century-Crofts, 1972.

Mooney, James D. "Organizing the Small Plant." Small Plant Management. Edited by Edward H. Hempel. New York: McGraw-Hill Book Co., Inc., for the Small Plant Committee, Management Division, American Society of Mechanical Engineers, 1950.

_____. "The Principles of Organization." Papers on the Science of Administration. Edited by Luther H. Gulick and Lyndall F. Urwick. New York: Institute of Public Administration, Columbia University, 1937.

_____, and Reiley, Alan C. Onward Industry! New York: Harper & Brothers, 1931; 2nd ed., 1939, re-entitled The Principles of Organization.

Moore, Franklin G. Management: Organization and Practice. New York: Harper & Row, 1964.

Moore, Henry L. "Paradoxes of Competition." Quarterly Journal of Economics, XX (February, 1906), 211-30.

Moreland, W. H. "The Science of Public Administration." Quarterly Review, CCXXXV (April, 1921), 413-29.

Mosson, Thomas M. "Management Theory and the Limits of Common-Sense." Management International Review, IV (January-February, 1964), 25-37.

Mundel, Marvin. A Conceptual Framework for the Management Sciences. New York: McGraw-Hill Book Co., Inc., 1967.

Murphy, Carroll D. "The Hardest Question in Business." Business Management. Vol. I: The Library of Business Practice. Chicago: A. W. Shaw Co., 1914.

Nelson, Edward A. "Economic Size of Organizations." California Management Review, X (Spring, 1968), 61-72.

Neuschel, Richard F. "Management's Need for Theory and Research." Toward a Unified Theory of Management. Edited by Harold D. Koontz. New York: McGraw-Hill Book Co., Inc., 1964.

Newman, William H. Administrative Action. New York: Prentice-Hall, Inc., 1951.

_____, and Summer, Charles E. The Process of Management. Englewood Cliffs, N. J.: Prentice-Hall, Inc., 1961; 2nd ed., 1967, co-authored with E. Kirby Warren.

Niles, Henry E. "Formal and Informal Organization in the Office." NOMA Forum, XV (December, 1939), 23-32.

_____. "Principles or Factors in Organization." Personnel, XIX (November, 1942), 570-78.

Niles, Mary C. The Essence of Management. New York: Harper & Brothers, 1958.

Northcott, Clarence H., Wardropper, J. W., Sheldon, Oliver, and Urwick, Lyndall F. Factory Organisation. London: Sir Isaac Pitman & Sons, Ltd., 1928.

Odiorne, George S. "The Management Theory Jungle and the Existential Manager." Academy of Management Journal, IX (June, 1966), 109-16.

O'Donnell, Cyril J. "Planning Objectives." California Management Review, V (Winter, 1963), 3-10.

"Organization Defined." American Management Review, XIV (October, 1925), 306-08.

Park, Rolla Edward. "The Span of Control: An Economist's View of the Facts and Fables." Advanced Management Journal, XXX (October, 1965), 47-51.

Parker, Robert S. "New Concepts of Administration--Its Meaning and Purpose." Public Administration (Sydney), XXI (December, 1961), 21-32.

Parsons, Talcott. "The Present Position and Prospects of Systematic Theory in Sociology." Twentieth Century Sociology. Edited by George D. Gurvitch and Wilbert E. Moore. New York: Philosophical Library, Inc., 1945.

Petersen, Elmore, and Plowman, E. Grosvenor. Business Organization and Management. Chicago: Richard D. Irwin, Inc., 1941.

Pethia, Robert F. "Some Content Analytic Findings on Values in Normative Administrative Theory." Academy of Management Proceedings (1969). Edited by William G. Scott and Preston P. Le Breton. Bowling Green, Ohio, 1970, pp. 145-53.

_____. "Values in Positive and Normative Administrative Theory: A Conceptual Framework and a Logical Analysis." Proceedings of the 10th Annual Academy of Management Conference, Midwest Division (1967). Edited by Alan C. Filley. Carbondale, Ill.: Business Research Bureau, Southern Illinois University, 1967, pp. 1-19.

Pfiffner, John M. "Why Not Make Social Science Operational." Public Administration Review, XXII (September, 1962), 109-14.

_____, and Sherwood, Frank C. Administrative Organization. Englewood Cliffs, N. J.: Prentice-Hall, Inc., 1960.

Poincare, J. Henri. Science and Hypothesis. Translated by George G. Halsted. New York: Science Press, 1905.

Porter, Holbrook F. J. "Historical Sketch of the Organization of the Efficiency Society." Transactions (Efficiency Society), I (1912), 20-28.

Prasad, S. Benjamin. "Management Theory and the Limits of Common-Sense: Comment." Management International Review, IV (November-December, 1964), 209-13.

Quine, Willard V. "Truth by Convention." Philosophical Essays for Alfred North Whitehead. Compiled by Otis H. Lee. New York: Longmans, Green and Company, 1936.

Rathe, Alex W. "Management Controls in Business." Management Control Systems. Edited by Donald G. Malcolm and Alan J. Rowe. New York: John Wiley & Sons, Inc., 1960.

Redfield, William C. "Scientific Spirit in Management." American Machinist, XXXVI (April 18, 1912), 612-15.

Reeves, Tom K., and Woodward, Joan. "The Study of Managerial Control." Industrial Organization: Behaviour and Control. Edited by Joan Woodward. London: Oxford University Press, 1970.

Reichskuratorium für Wirtschaftlichkeit. Wirtschaft, Wirtschaftlichkeit, Ständische Wirtschaftsordnung, Veroffentlichungen No. 99. Berlin: RKW, 1933.

Rigby, Paul H. Conceptual Foundations of Business Research. New York: John Wiley & Sons, 1965.

Robb, Russell. Lectures on Organization. Boston: Privately printed, 1910.

_____. "The Limits of Organization." Stone and Webster Public Service Journal, IV (May, 1909), 301-13.

_____. "Organization As Affected by Purpose and Conditions." Stone and Webster Public Service Journal, IV (April, 1909), 220-33.

_____. "The Organization of Administration." Stone and Webster Public Service Journal, IV (June, 1909), 394-406.

Robinson, Marshall A. "The Science of Organizations: A Pediatric Note." Management International Review, VI (July-August, 1966), 3-5.

Robinson, Webster R. Fundamentals of Business Organization. New York: McGraw-Hill Book Co., Inc., 1925.

Rodgers, Winston. Standard Terminology. Conference Series No. 7. London: British Institute of Management, July, 1949.

Roethlisberger, Fritz J., and Dickson, William J., with the assistance and collaboration of Harold A. Wright. Management and the Worker. Cambridge: Harvard University Press, 1939.

Rorty, Michael C. Ten Commandments of Good Organization. New York: American Management Association, 1934. Reprinted in The Encyclopedia of Management. Edited by Carl Heyel. New York: Reinhold Publishing Corporation, 1963.

Rose, Thomas G. Company Control. London: Gee & Co. (Publishers), Ltd., 1952.

_____. Higher Control. London: Sir Isaac Pitman & Sons, Ltd., 1934.

_____. "The Inexactitude of Terminology." Times Trade & Engineering (London), XXXVIII (August, 1937), 11.

_____. "Management or Administration?: In the Evolution of Management Principles There Must Be No Confusion of Terms." Industry (London), XVII (November, 1949), 532-34.

_____, and Farr, Donald. Higher Management Control. New York: McGraw-Hill Book Co., Inc., 1957.

Rowe, Alan J. "A Research Approach in Management Controls." Management Control Systems. Edited by Donald G. Malcolm, and Alan J. Rowe. New York: John Wiley & Sons, Inc., 1960.

Rowland, Floyd H. Business Planning and Control. New York: Harper & Brothers Publishers, 1947.

Schell, Edwin H. The Technique of Executive Control. New York: McGraw-Hill Book Co., Inc., 1924.

Scheuplein, Harald. "Towards the Unification of Management Theory." Management International Review, IIX (November-December, 1968), 95-96.

Schöllhammer, Hans. "The Comparative Management Theory Jungle." Academy of Management Journal, XII (March, 1969), 81-97.

Schulze, J. William. "Some Definitions." Bulletin of the Taylor Society, IV (August, 1919), 3-4.

Scott, Charles R., Jr. "Span of Control Optimization by Simulation Modeling." Paper presented at the 32nd meeting of the Academy of Management, Minneapolis, Minn., August 15, 1972. (Mimeographed.)

Scott, William G. Organization Theory: A Behavioral Analysis for Management. Homewood, Illinois: Richard D. Irwin, Inc., 1967.

Sears, Marian V. "Management." Planning and Control Systems: A Framework for Analysis. By Robert N. Anthony. Boston: Division of Research, Graduate School of Business Administration, Harvard University, 1965.

Seckler-Hudson, Catheryn. "Principles of Organization and Management." Processes of Organization and Management. Edited by Catheryn Seckler-Hudson. Washington, D. C.: Public Affairs Press, 1948.

Selltiz, Claire, Jahoda, Marie, Deutsch, Morton, and Cook, Stuart W. Research Methods in Social Relations. Rev. One-volume ed. New York: Holt, Rinehart and Winston, Inc., 1959.

Shay, Philip W. "The Emerging Discipline of Management." Handbook of Business Administration. Edited by Harold B. Maynard. New York: McGraw-Hill Book Co., Inc., 1967.

Sheldon, Oliver. The Philosophy of Management. London: Sir Isaac Pitman & Sons, Ltd., 1923.

Shull, Fremont A., Jr. "The Nature and Contribution of Administrative Models." Academy of Management Journal, V (August, 1962), 124-38.

Simon, Herbert A. Administrative Behavior. Foreword by Chester I. Barnard. New York: Macmillan Co., 1947.

_____. "The Proverbs of Administration." Public Administration Review, VI (Winter, 1946), 53-67.

_____. "The Span of Control: A Reply." Advanced Management Journal, XXII (April, 1957), 14, 29.

Sisk, Henry L. Principles of Management: A Systems Approach to the
    Management Process. Cincinnati: South-Western Publishing Co.,
    1969.

Slichter, Sumner H. "Efficiency." Encyclopaedia of the Social
    Sciences, 1st ed., Vol. V.

Smith, Adam. An Inquiry into the Nature and Causes of the Wealth of
    Nations. 2 Vols. London: A. Strahan and T. Cadell, 1776.

_____. Lectures on Justice, Police, Revenue and Arms. Reported by
    a student in 1763, edited with an Introduction and notes by
    Edwin Cannan. Oxford, England: Clarendon Press, 1896.

Smith, J. Russell. The Elements of Industrial Management. Philadelphia:
    J. B. Lippincott Co., 1915.

Somervell, Brehon B. "Organization Controls in Industry." Organization
    Controls and Executive Compensation, General Management Series
    No. 142. New York: American Management Association, 1948.

Sord, Burnard H., and Welsch, Glenn A. Business Budgeting: A Survey
    of Management Planning and Control Practices. New York:
    Controllership Foundation, Inc., 1958.

_____. Managerial Planning and Control, Research Monograph No. 27.
    Austin, Texas: Bureau of Business Research, University of
    Texas, 1964.

Sparling, Samuel E. Introduction to Business Organization. New York:
    Macmillan Co., 1906.

Special Libraries Association, Special Committee, chairman, Alma C.
    Mitchill. Business and Trade Dictionaries: A Classified Guide
    to the Sources of Business Terminology and Definitions. New
    York: The Association, 1934.

Spriegel, William R. Principles of Business Organization. Englewood
    Cliffs, N. J.: Prentice-Hall, Inc., 1946; 2nd ed., 1952,
    re-entitled Principles of Business Organization and Operation.

_____. Principles of Industrial Organization and Control, Education
    and Training Unit 363. Chicago: Harvester Central School,
    International Harvester Company, n. d. (circa 1947).

Starbuck, William H. "Organizational Growth and Development." Hand-
    book of Organizations. Edited by James G. March. Chicago:
    Rand McNally & Company, 1965.

Stene, Edwin O. "An Approach to a Science of Administration." The
    American Political Science Review, XXXIV (December, 1940),
    1124-37.

Stephenson, T. E. "The Longevity of Classical Theory." Management International Review, VIII (November-December, 1968), 77-83.

Stieglitz, Harold. Corporate Organization Structures, Studies in Personnel Policy No. 183. New York: National Industrial Conference Board, Inc., 1961.

_____. "Optimizing Span of Control." Management Record, XXIV (September, 1962), 25-29.

_____, and Wilkerson, C. David. Corporate Organization Structures, Studies in Personnel Policy No. 210. New York: National Industrial Conference Board, 1968.

Stokes, Paul M. A Total Systems Approach to Management Control. New York: American Management Association, 1968.

"Storm Over Management Doctrines." Business Week, January 6, 1962, pp. 72-74.

Strong, Earl P., and Smith, Robert D. Management Control Models. New York: Holt, Rinehart and Winston, 1968.

Subramaniam, V. "The Classical Organization Theory and Its Critics." Public Administration (London), XLIV (Winter, 1966), 435-46.

Suojanen, Waino W. "Comments: The Tactics of Jungle Warfare: Clarification." Academy of Management Journal, VII (September, 1964), 229-30.

_____. The Dynamics of Management. New York: Holt, Rinehart and Winston, Inc., 1966.

_____. "Leadership, Authority, and the Span of Control." Advanced Management Journal, XXII (September, 1957), 17-22.

_____. "Management Theory: Functional and Evolutionary." Journal of the Academy of Management, VI (March, 1963), 7-17.

_____. "Notes on General Theory of Management." Advanced Management Journal, XXII (February, 1957), 17-20.

_____. "The Span of Control--Fact or Fable." Advanced Management Journal, XX (November, 1955), 5-13.

Tannenbaum, Arnold S. Control in Organizations. New York: McGraw-Hill Book Co., Inc., 1968.

Tannenbaum, Robert. "Observations on Large Group and Syndicate Discussions." Toward a Unified Theory of Management. Edited by Harold D. Koontz. New York: McGraw-Hill Book Co., Inc., 1964.

Taylor, Frederick W. "The Gospel of Efficiency: The Principles of
     Scientific Management." The American Magazine, Serialized in
     three parts, LXXI (March through May, 1911), 564-69, 785-93,
     101-13.

_____. "The Gospel of Efficiency: The Principles of Scientific
     Management." World's Work (London), Serialized in three parts,
     XVII-XVIII (May through July, 1911), 614-23; 91-99, 168-82.

_____. "On the Art of Cutting Metals," Paper No. 1119. Transactions
     (American Society of Mechanical Engineers), XXVII (1906),
     31-350.

_____. "The Principles and Methods of Scientific Management."
     Journal of Accountancy, Published in two parts, XII (June and
     July, 1911), 117-24, 181-88.

_____. The Principles of Scientific Management. New York: Harper
     & Brothers, 1911.

_____. "The Principles of Scientific Management." Applied Science
     (Toronto), VII (N. S.) (January, 1913), 76-80.

_____. "The Principles of Scientific Management." Bulletin of the
     Taylor Society, II (December, 1916), 14-23.

_____. "Scientific Management." New England Railroad Club Proceed-
     ings, October 10, 1911. Boston, Massachusetts, 1912, pp. 138-87.

_____. "Shop Management," Paper No. 1003. Transactions (American
     Society of Mechanical Engineers), XXIV (1903), 1337-1480.

_____. Shop Management. New York: Harper & Brothers, 1911.

Tead, Ordway. Administration: Its Purpose and Performance. New York:
     Harper & Brothers, 1959.

_____. The Art of Administration. New York: McGraw-Hill Book
     Co., Inc., 1951.

_____. The Art of Leadership. New York: Whittlesay House, McGraw-
     Hill Book Co., Inc., 1935.

_____. The Problem of Terminology in Management Research, Institute
     of Management Series No. 5. New York: American Management
     Association, 1928.

"The Terminology of Rationalisation and Scientific Management."
     International Labour Review, XXXVI (August, 1937), 250-54.

Terry, George R. Principles of Management. Homewood, Illinois: Richard D. Irwin, 1953; Rev. 1956, 1960, 1964, 1968.

Thompson, Clarence B. The Theory and Practice of Scientific Management. New York: Houghton-Mifflin Co., 1917.

Thompson, James D. "On Building an Administrative Science." Administrative Science Quarterly, I (June, 1956), 102-11.

Thompson, Robert E. "Span of Control--Conceptions and Misconceptions." Business Horizons, VII (Summer, 1964), 49-58.

Thurston, John B. "The Control Unit: Newest Techniques for Controlling Decentralized Operations." Advanced Management Journal, XII (June, 1947), 74-87.

_____. Coordinating and Controlling Operations. Sec. I, Bk. ii of Reading Course in Executive Technique. Edited by Carl Heyel. 41 Vols. New York: Funk & Wagnalls Company, 1948.

_____. "A New Concept of Managerial Control." Company Development and Top Management Control, General Management Series No. 134. New York: American Management Association, 1945.

Towne, Henry R. "The Engineer As Economist," Paper No. 207. Transactions (American Society of Mechanical Engineers), VII (1886), 428-32.

Trundle, George T. Managerial Control of Business. New York: John Wiley & Sons, 1948.

_____. "Production Control." Handbook of Business Administration. Edited by William J. A. Donald. New York: McGraw-Hill Book Co., Inc., for the American Management Association, 1931.

Udell, Jon G. "An Empirical Test of Hypothesis Relating to Span of Control." Administrative Science Quarterly, XII (December, 1967), 420-39.

U. S. Air Force. USAF Management Process, Air Force Manual 25-1, Department of the Air Force. Washington, D. C.: Government Printing Office, 1954.

U. S. Commission on Organization of the Executive Branch of the Government. General Management of the Executive Branch, A Report to Congress by the Commission on Organization of the Executive Branch of the Government, [chairman, Herbert C. Hoover]. Washington, D. C.: Government Printing Office, 1949.

U. S. Commission on Organization of the Executive Branch of the Govern-
    ment, [chairman, Herbert C. Hoover]. The Hoover Commission
    Report on Organization of the Executive Branch of the Govern-
    ment. New York: McGraw-Hill Book Co., Inc., 1949.

U. S. Congress. House. The Taylor and Other Systems of Shop Manage-
    ment. Hearings Before Special Committee of the House of
    Representatives to Investigate the Taylor and Other Systems of
    Shop Management Under the Authority of H. Res. 90 [William B.
    Wilson, chairman]. Washington, D. C.: Government Printing
    Office, 1912.

U. S. Congress. Senate. Evidence Taken by the Interstate Commerce
    Commission in the Matter of Proposed Advances in Freight Rates
    by Carriers (August to December, 1910). S. Doc. 725 (Ser. Set
    5908), 61st Cong., 3rd sess., 1910-11.

U. S. Congress. Senate. Final Report and Testimony Submitted to
    Congress by the Commission on Industrial Relations. [Frank P.
    Walsh, chairman]. S. Doc. 415 (Ser. Set 6929), 64th Cong.,
    1st sess., 1914.

U. S. The President's Committee on Administrative Management. Report of
    the Committee with Studies of Administrative Management in the
    Federal Government, Submitted to the President and to the
    Congress in accordance with Public Law No. 739, 74th Congress,
    2nd Session, [chairman, Louis Brownlow]. Washington, D. C.:
    Government Printing Office, 1937.

Urwick, Lyndall F. "Are the Classics Really Out of Date?--A Plea for
    Semantic Sanity." S. A. M. Advanced Management Journal, XXXIV
    (July, 1969), 4-12.

_____. "Comment: Leadership and Language." Academy of Management
    Journal, VIII (June, 1965), 146-49.

_____. "Communications from Readers." Review of Towards a Unified
    Theory of Management. Edited by Harold D. Koontz. California
    Management Review, VIII (Fall, 1965), 93-96.

_____. "The Dynamics and the Mechanics of Administration." Review
    of Administrative Behavior, by Herbert A. Simon. A. M. A.
    Management Review, XXXVII (May, 1948), 267-72.

_____. The Elements of Administration. New York: Harper & Row
    Publishers, Inc., 1943.

_____. "Executive Decentralization with Functional Coordination."
    Management Review, XXIV (December, 1935), 355-68.

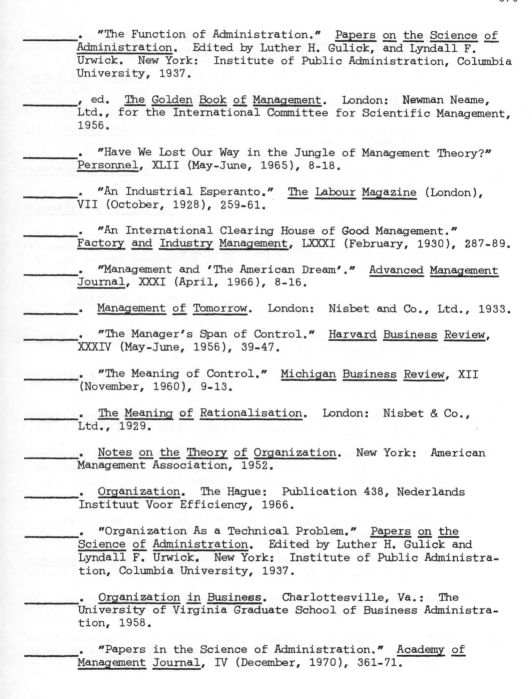

_____. "The Function of Administration." Papers on the Science of Administration. Edited by Luther H. Gulick, and Lyndall F. Urwick. New York: Institute of Public Administration, Columbia University, 1937.

_____, ed. The Golden Book of Management. London: Newman Neame, Ltd., for the International Committee for Scientific Management, 1956.

_____. "Have We Lost Our Way in the Jungle of Management Theory?" Personnel, XLII (May-June, 1965), 8-18.

_____. "An Industrial Esperanto." The Labour Magazine (London), VII (October, 1928), 259-61.

_____. "An International Clearing House of Good Management." Factory and Industry Management, LXXXI (February, 1930), 287-89.

_____. "Management and 'The American Dream'." Advanced Management Journal, XXXI (April, 1966), 8-16.

_____. Management of Tomorrow. London: Nisbet and Co., Ltd., 1933.

_____. "The Manager's Span of Control." Harvard Business Review, XXXIV (May-June, 1956), 39-47.

_____. "The Meaning of Control." Michigan Business Review, XII (November, 1960), 9-13.

_____. The Meaning of Rationalisation. London: Nisbet & Co., Ltd., 1929.

_____. Notes on the Theory of Organization. New York: American Management Association, 1952.

_____. Organization. The Hague: Publication 438, Nederlands Instituut Voor Efficiency, 1966.

_____. "Organization As a Technical Problem." Papers on the Science of Administration. Edited by Luther H. Gulick and Lyndall F. Urwick. New York: Institute of Public Administration, Columbia University, 1937.

_____. Organization in Business. Charlottesville, Va.: The University of Virginia Graduate School of Business Administration, 1958.

_____. "Papers in the Science of Administration." Academy of Management Journal, IV (December, 1970), 361-71.

_____. The Pattern of Management. Minneapolis: School of Business Administration, University of Minnesota, 1956.

_____. "Principles of Direction and Control." Dictionary of Industrial Administration. Edited by John Lee. London: Sir Isaac Pitman & Sons, Ltd., Vol. I, 1928; Vol. II, 1929.

_____. "Principles of Management." British Management Review, VII, No. 3 (1948), 15-48.

_____. "The Problem of Management Semantics." California Management Review, II (Spring, 1960), 77-83.

_____. "Scientific Management in Europe." Encyclopaedia Britannica. 14th ed. Vol. XIV.

_____. Scientific Principles and Organization. New York: American Management Association, Institute of Management Series No. 19, 1938.

_____. "The Span of Control." Scottish Journal of Political Economy, IV (June, 1957), 101-13.

_____. "The Span of Control--Some Facts About the Fables." Advanced Management Journal, XXI (November, 1956), 5-15.

_____. "The Tactics of Jungle Warfare." Journal of the Academy of Management, VI (December, 1963), 316-29.

_____. "Why the So-Called 'Classicists' Endure." Management International Review, XI (January-February, 1971), 3-14.

Van Fleet, David D. "An Approach to a History of Management Thought: The Span of Management." Paper presented at the 32nd meeting of the Academy of Management, Minneapolis, Minn., August 14, 1972. (Mimeographed.)

Veblen, Thorstein. The Theory of Business Enterprise. New York: Charles Scribner's & Sons, 1904.

Veld, J. In't. "Towards a General Theory of Administration." Management International Review, II (January-February, 1962), 37-44.

Villers, Raymond. Research and Development: Planning and Control. New York: Financial Executives Institute, 1964.

Viola, Richard H. "The Span of Management in the Life Insurance Industry: Some Research Findings." Economic and Business Bulletin, XXII (Winter, 1970), 18-25.

Wagner, Arthur L. Organization and Tactics. New York: B. Westmann Co., 1895.

Weber, Max. The Theory of Social and Economic Organizations. Translated by Alexander M. Henderson and Talcott Parsons. New York: Free Press of Glencoe, 1947.

Wellington, C. Oliver. "Basic Principles of Organization." 1932 Yearbook of the National Association of Cost Accountants. New York: NACA, 1932.

Wharton, Kenneth J. Administrative Control. London: Gee and Company (Publishers), Ltd., 1947.

_____. "Administrative Organization and Control." The Accountant (London), August 16, 1947, pp. 99-101; August 23, 1947, pp. 117-19; August 30, 1947, pp. 131-33.

Wheeler, Bayard O. "Renaissance in Business Theory." University of Washington Business Review, XXIV (February, 1965), 43-52.

White, Karol K. Understanding the Company Organization Chart, Research Study No. 56. New York: American Management Association, 1963.

White, Leonard D. Introduction to the Study of Public Administration. New York: Macmillan Co., 1926; 2nd ed., 1939.

_____. "The Meaning of Principles in Public Administration." The Frontiers of Public Administration. Studies in Public Administration, Vol. VI. Edited by John M. Gaus, Leonard D. White, and Marshall E. Dimock. Chicago: University of Chicago Press, 1936.

White, Percival. Business Management: An Introduction to Business. New York: Henry Holt and Company, 1926.

Williams, D. Ervin. "The Management Process From a Functional Perspective POCD? POMC? POIM? POAA?" Atlanta Economic Review, XXI (April, 1971), 26-27.

Williams, Henry H. "The Art of Organizing." Factory and Industrial Management, LXXIX (May, 1930), 1081-82.

Williams, William L. "Undergrowth in the Management Theory Jungle." Business Horizons, XII (February, 1969), 56-58.

Williamson, Oliver E. "Hierarchical Control and Optimum Firm Size." Journal of Political Economy, LXXV (April, 1967), 123-38.

Willower, Donald J. "Concept Development and Research." Educational Research: New Perspectives. Edited by Jack A. Culbertson and Stephen P. Hencley. Danville, Ill.: Interstate Printers & Publishers, Inc., 1963.

Wolf, William G., ed. Management: Readings Toward a General Theory. Belmont, Calif.: Wadsworth Publishing Company, Inc., 1964.

_____. "Toward the Development of a General Theory of Management." Comparative Administrative Theory. Edited by Preston P. Le Breton. Seattle: University of Washington Press, 1968.

Woodward, Joan. Industrial Organization: Theory and Practice. London: Oxford University Press, 1965.

_____. Management and Technology, Problems in Progress in Industry No. 3. London: Her Majesty's Stationery Office, 1958.

Woolf, Donald A. "The Management Theory Jungle Revisited." Advanced Management Journal, XXX (October, 1965), 6-15.

The World Economic Conference. Final Report. Document C. E. I. 44 (1). Geneva: League of Nations, 1927.

Worthy, James C. Big Business and Free Men. New York: Harper & Row, Inc., 1959.

_____. "Factors Influencing Employee Morale." Harvard Business Review, XXVIII (January, 1950), 61-73.

_____. "Organizational Structure and Employee Morale." American Sociological Review, XV (April, 1950), 169-79.

Wright, Robert G. "An Approach to Find Realistic Spans of Management." Arizona Business Bulletin, XVII (November, 1970), 21-28.

Zelnick, Joel. "Discussion: Queuing Theory Revisited." Journal of the Academy of Management, VI (June, 1963), 173.

Ziegler, Raymond J. "The Application of Managerial Controls in Selected Business Firms." Unpublished Ph.D. dissertation, University of Florida, 1957.

For Product Safety Concerns and Information please contact our EU
representative GPSR@taylorandfrancis.com Taylor & Francis Verlag GmbH,
Kaufingerstraße 24, 80331 München, Germany

Printed and bound by CPI Group (UK) Ltd, Croydon, CR0 4YY
08/05/2025
01864408-0005